Free and User Supported Software for the IBM PC

For my grandparents
Emilio Amor, Remedios Rojo de Amor,
Manuel López and María Couceiro de López.
With all my love and admiration
for the poignant lessons of quiet heroism,
honor, strength and love taught by their example.

—Victor D. López

For my fourth grade teacher, Ms. Betts,
whose concern, love, and dedication,
changed the lives of so many children.

—Kenneth J. Ansley

Free and User Supported Software for the IBM PC

A Resource Guide for Libraries and Individuals

by

Victor D. López

and

Kenneth J. Ansley

McFarland & Company, Inc., Publishers

Jefferson, North Carolina, and London

British Library Cataloguing-in-Publication data are available

Library of Congress Cataloguing-in-Publication Data

López, Victor, 1958–
Free and user supported software for the IBM PC : a resource guide for libraries and individuals / Victor López and Kenneth J. Ansley.
p. cm.
[Includes index.]
Includes bibliographical references.
ISBN 0-89950-499-X (sewn softcover : 50# alk. paper) ∞
1. Libraries—Special collections—Computer programs. 2. IBM Personal Computer—Programming. 3. Acquisition of computer programs. 4. Computer programs—Evaluation. I. Ansley, Kenneth J., 1958– . II. Title.
Z692.C65L67 1990
025.3′44—dc20 89-43656
CIP

Manufactured in the United States of America

McFarland & Company, Inc., Publishers
Box 611, Jefferson, North Carolina 28640

Table of Contents

Introduction

The proliferation of personal computers in the latter part of the 1980s and early 90s has made it all but necessary for the average person to become computer literate. Computers are found at work, in school and in the home in growing numbers. The trend for the foreseeable future is clearly for greater computerization. As of this writing, an IBM-compatible computer with 640 kilobytes of RAM, two floppy disk drives, serial and parallel ports, monochrome graphics, a modem for telecommunications and a dot-matrix printer can be purchased for under $1,000, with many starter systems (e.g., a single drive, and no printer or modem) available for less than $500. Today, nearly everyone can afford to own a computer. Nevertheless, while computer "hardware" has steadily been decreasing in price throughout the last decade, computer "software"—the programs needed to make any computer work—have not decreased in price at a similar rate. Thus, in 1989 chances are that the average computer buyer spent much more in software than in the computer system itself. For example, even if one shops around and finds the least expensive suppliers of software in the country, a copy of a leading word processing program such as Word Perfect 5.0, or WordStar Professional 5.5 will cost between $250 and $400, with the list price hovering at the $500 mark. The same is true for a leading spreadsheet such as Lotus 1-2-3, Release 3.0 or Super Calc 5 or a database program such as dBase 4. By the same token, one can easily spend $50 or more on a single computer game. Thus, a computer bought for well under $1,000 can easily end up costing thousands of dollars when the software needed to run it is added to the initial purchase price. To make matters worse, programs must often be purchased "sight unseen," with the purchaser relying on the software manufacturer's reputation or published reviews of the programs; most retailers of software simply do not have every program available for shoppers to "try before they buy." Neither retailers nor software manufacturers generally permit returns on software packages unless they are defective. Hence, if you find that the leading spreadsheet program you bought on your accountant's recommendation, hoping it would help you balance your checkbook, does not fit your needs (it is too difficult to learn, requires more memory or drives than your computer has, or is otherwise not suited for your intended use), you cannot return it for credit or a refund. In this way, that highly-rated, excellent program may, for you, become a $495 paper weight.

Help is available for the unwary buyer. There are thousands of software titles that can be obtained for use or for review either free of charge or for a modest copying fee of a few dollars per disk. These include word processors, spreadsheets, databases, communication programs, games, personal finance programs and thousands more. Many of these rival their expensive commercial siblings, and some exceed them. All represent a tremendous value.

Public Domain and Shareware Defined

Software, to put it simply, is a collection of instructions that tells a computer what to do. Whether you wish to balance your checkbook, write a letter to Mom or test your reflexes in a fast-paced arcade game, you need to tell the computer how to go about accomplishing each of those tasks. You can do this in one of two ways: program the computer yourself, a process which requires both substantial expertise and time, or buy a program from someone else. Most computer users lack the time, skill or interest to go the first route. For them, the only viable option is to buy the programs they wish to use. These programs are readily available from various sources, including computer stores and mail-order retailers. The only problem is that they are not necessarily inexpensive, as previously discussed. Yet, a computer without software is useless. This was something painfully discovered by the computing pioneers of the Dark Ages (circa 1970s). What many of these early computer hobbyists, or "hackers," did was to write applications programs for their own use which they then made available to their friends and fellow computerists, generally without asking for anything in return. These programmers simply wished to share with others the fruits of their labor.

As computers proliferated, particularly in the late 1970s and early 1980s with the onslaught of affordable computer systems from Atari, Coelco, Tandy, Texas Instruments, Commodore and IBM, the number of people writing programs for their machines steadily grew. Many of these programmers believed in the old "hacker" or "hobbyist" tradition of sharing their work, and thus released their programs into the public domain for anyone to copy and use without cost. They signed a release stating that the programs may freely be distributed so long as no fee was charged (other than a modest copying fee, usually of not more than $10 per disk), and the programs were not modified in any way. There are thousands of such programs today in the public domain; these are distributed by many sources and are of varying degrees of quality ranging from exceptional to literally useless. One need only pick up any computer magazine or periodical today to see a wide array of companies and public individuals offering "free software" for a modest copying fee, usually $2.00 to $10.00 per disk.

Shareware, on the other hand, is not in the public domain. Programs distributed under the shareware concept are released by people who retain all rights to them and who *want* and *expect* to be paid for their work in developing the programs. Under the shareware concept, anyone may freely copy and distribute copies of the programs under the same conditions applicable to public domain software. But the programs are generally made available only on a *trial basis:* if you like a shareware program and intend to use it, you are expected to send the author a contribution or a stated registration fee. As a practical matter, not every user of shareware products sends the author the suggested registration fee, but enough to do so as to provide the author with varying degrees of income from his program. It's unfortunate that most people don't register the programs they use, since registration fees are usually quite modest, even for the best programs, and registration brings with it many additional benefits, such as enhanced versions of some programs, bound manuals, future upgrades and the like. In any event, the benefit to the user in trying out shareware offerings is quite clear: a wide variety of software can be tried and evaluated prior to making a substantial investment in it, and programs which he finds useful can be registered at a very low cost.

The variety of available shareware and public domain programs is quite impressive, if not mind-boggling. And, just as with public domain, quality varies widely. With the many thousands of programs available for the IBM PC and compatible computers in the public domain and as shareware, one problem is in deciding what to try. A tempting approach is to try as many programs as possible; after all, it only costs a few dollars per disk. But even at the modest fee charged for these programs, it's quite possible to spend several hundred (or thousand) dollars acquiring programs which sound promising, and then spend countless hours sifting through them to find the ones suited to one's needs. For a person who loves to work with computers and enjoys the "thrill of discovery," this is a viable approach; such is the case for this book's coauthors. But for the average computer user, this can be an expensive, time consuming and even infuriating experience. In this book we have distilled what we believe to be a cross section of the finest available public domain and shareware programs, spending hours and, in some cases, months, using each program, and then writing a hands-on review. Our purpose is not to present a tutorial on how to use each program, but rather an overview of each program's features, utility and "feel." Towards that end, we have individually rated each program and highlighted its main features. We have also included actual "screen dumps" to show how each program will look on your computer screens. The latter are unretouched and were produced with an inexpensive dot matrix printer. They are intended to give the reader an idea of what the programs look like; any less than perfect results are strictly the fault of our rather mundane equipment. Nevertheless, we feel that these rough graphic images will give you, our reader, a better understanding of how these programs work, and are offered in the belief that a picture (even if somewhat fuzzy) is still worth a thousand words.

Finally, we'd like to stress that this is by no means a definitive text on public domain or shareware software (although we have written it because we knew of no other like it). There are hundreds of additional noteworthy programs which could have been included, and more of them continually appear. We hope to be able to update this book in the future to include programs which we have not had the opportunity to personally review, future updates to some of the old favorites reviewed herein and, of course, cover the new programs sure to emerge in the future. In these pages you will simply find most of our favorites, which we trust will also become yours.

Victor D. López, Esq.

Kenneth J. Ansley

1: Word Processing Programs and Writers' Tools

Introduction

Of all the applications programs available for personal computers, the most popular is word processing. Writers were one of the first groups of professionals to embrace the personal computer as a productivity tool. In the late 1970s, before the dawn of the IBM Personal Computer, sturdy and relatively inexpensive (just over $3,000) machines by Kaypro, Osborne and several other manufacturers began to gain wide acceptance. These machines ran on the CP/M operating system, a precursor to the MS/DOS and PC/DOS operating systems running today on most IBM and compatible computers. These machines, while quite limited by today's standards, were capable of running some rather complex word processing, spreadsheet and database programs. Among these, Micro Pro's WordStar, one of the first full-featured word processing programs, became an almost instant best-seller. Micro Pro was one of the first to offer cut-rate prices to computer manufacturers who bundled their software with their machines—a brilliant marketing strategy which offered consumers powerful business software at the lowest possible cost; many manufacturers, such as Kaypro and Osborne offered these programs to consumers without additional cost as a sales incentive. And when writers discovered the flexibility which a word processing program afforded them, they were instantly won over, rushing joyously into the new computer age.

The early word processing programs were rather crude by today's standards. They contained no graphics capability, and they were by no means user friendly; a myriad of multiple key commands had to be memorized in order to execute dozens of necessary functions (pull-down menus were not available; the early word processing programs were seemingly meant to be used more by computer programmers than the average person). Nevertheless, the freedom from the more tedious aspects of writing such as constant retyping of entire documents even when minor revisions were necessary, led writers to embrace these wonderful programs—and the machines which ran them—with undaunted enthusiasm.

For someone who has done any significant amount of writing on a typewriter, or, heaven forbid, longhand with pen and paper, the freedom which even a simple word processor offers is awesome. Spelling or typographical errors can be corrected with ease, and text can be inserted, deleted, copied or moved around within a single or multiple documents. Anyone who has ever typed a term paper of any significant length can appreciate the time and effort required to add a single line of text, let alone a paragraph or series of paragraphs, to the finished document. If an alteration is required on page three of a ten-page paper, pages three through ten must be retyped—no small matter for writers with deadlines, or college students with other pressing assignments. But with a word processor, text can be added, deleted, or changed around within any document without having to retype anything else. A ten-page paper can be printed effortlessly in minutes, with a word processor, whereas it can take an unskilled typist many hours to reproduce.

In addition to allowing for quick revisions and updates of existing documents, a word processing program can greatly enhance the quality of the writing itself. Writing with a word processor rather than a typewriter, one need not be overly concerned about typographical errors, misspellings or corrections in general; a writer can concentrate on the writing itself without having to continually interrupt the writing process to make needed corrections. With a word processor, corrections can be made after the fact, once a first draft is completed. The writing process is thus much smoother, and the output generally superior.

In addition to facilitating the writing process, word processors have various capabilities for document enhancement which are simply outside the range of even the best electronic typewriters. These include the capability of printing in a wide variety of font styles and type sizes, checking the spelling of a document with large, sophisticated spelling checkers, hyphenating words automatically at the end of a line, wrapping test from one line to the next without needing to strike a carriage return and reformatting text automatically to fit within different margin settings.

The list of available features is both lengthy and impressive. It is even possible to consult an on-line thesaurus or dictionary while working within a document; there are several stand-alone commercial thesauri and dictionaries which can work within any word processor. Some professional word processing software packages such as Word Perfect 5.0, WordStar 5.0, Microsoft Word and others include these features as an integral part of the software package; but keep in mind that their average list price is in the $500 range. A stand-alone thesaurus can be purchased for well under $100.

The word processing packages available in the public domain (may be used free of charge by anyone) or distributed as shareware (copies may be obtained free of charge, but registration at a modest cost is expected if you like and use the programs) are wide ranging in both their available features and in their general quality. Some of these programs are meant for inexperienced users and are quite easy to learn and use, although they may not contain all of the features of the leading commercial programs. Others rival their more expensive commercial siblings in their powerful features and flexibility. As with all applications software falling within the categories of public domain or shareware, there is something for nearly anyone's specific needs, regardless of how complex or modest they might be.

It should be noted here that while most computer users don't need the most powerful word processor available, the needs of many such users do change; and it is always nice to have a word processor with sufficient power and flexibility to adapt to one's evolving requirements—especially since learning a word processor, or any applications program, for that matter, requires a substantial investment in time, and people tend to become "attached" to the programs they use regularly.

A user who wishes to acquire a simple word processor for letter writing may find a $30 package purchased at the local hobby store meets his needs quite nicely; but when his needs change and he outgrows the entry-level program it will have to be replaced by a more powerful one, and the time learning to use it will have been wasted. This problem is easily avoided by selecting a program which is more powerful than one needs at present—a program which has enough features not just for today, but for the foreseeable future as well.

This chapter will introduce you to some of the best public domain and shareware word processing programs and related writers' tools. We will look at a variety of word processing packages, as well as programs which allow you to check your writing style, create an outline of your thoughts to better organize them, and generally assist you with the writing process. Whether you are an old hand at word processing or a beginner considering buying your first word processing program, you should find many of the following programs well suited to your needs, and a marvelous bargain as well.

PC-Write™ Version 2.7

PC-Write is one of the best and most powerful shareware programs available, as well as one of the most successful shareware programs ever released. PC-Write is powerful enough so as to have been favorably compared in major computer publications with leading professional word processing packages, such as WordStar, Word Perfect, Microsoft Word, Multi Mate and others. In its price range of under $100 (registration fee),

```
File to load or create (Esc:cancel F8:dir): "work.doc"

PC-Write (R). Version 2.70. Released on 01-Oct-86. Registration #000000
(C) Copyright 1983-1986 by Bob Wallace, Quicksoft. All Rights Reserved.
Shareware: Please help distribute PC-Write by sharing unmodified copies
of the diskettes in the U.S. and Canada.  Please don't copy the manual.
Please don't share copies elsewhere, to support our foreign publishers.
=> If you are using PC-Write, please buy a manual or a registered copy. <=

Compliments of:  Jesse Armentrout - Fido Northwest - 513-662-5884

A registered copy provides you all the following benefits for only $89:
>  Printed hardbound copy of the full PC-Write manual and Quick Guide.
>  Current PC-Write diskette pair and your unique registration number.
>  PC-Write support service for one year:  includes telephone support,
    our quarterly newsletter, and two free update or source diskettes.
>  A $25 commission when someone registers and gives your reg. number.
>  Sincere thanks; your support helps us continue to improve PC-Write!

Manual: hardbound $45, paper $35. Diskette pair $16.  Quantity pricing.
When you register, give above registration number, to credit its owner.
PO, COD, Rush add $5. Overseas add $20. WA orders add 7.9%. Visa/MC ok.
Quicksoft (R) Inc.  206/282-0452. 219 First N. #224, Seattle, WA 98109.
```

Figure 1.1: Opening screen and copyright notice for PC-Write.

PC-Write simply has no competition; its power, flexibility, speed and advanced features are only matched by programs listing at or near the $500 range. Yet, for all its flexibility and powerful features, PC-Write is remarkably easy to learn, in no small part due to the excellent tutorial documentation provided with the evaluation copy of the program.

PC-Write is a program which is well suited for most any user, from the occasional letter writer to the busy professional who needs to send out personalized mass mailings, produced multi-column page output like that found in magazines or newspapers, or turn out large, multi-page documents with footnotes or endnotes.

Although PC-Write is quite powerful, a user can become sufficiently proficient with its basic features within a matter of hours. This is due mainly to the excellent documentation which accompanies the program. The program comes with a 44-page manual on disk (users who register their program receive a 336-page printer manual) which covers most of the programs basic to advanced features. The documentation may, of course, be printed for the user's reference while she is evaluating the program, and it includes a detailed table of contents—an invaluable aid to any user learning a new program. In addition to the abridged manual, a 17-page tutorial covering 14 short lessons is also included in the distribution disk. The tutorial assists new and experienced users in configuring the program for use with their individual computer systems, and it also painlessly introduces users to the

```
Esc:Menu.Push Wrap+Sp- 20% Free.  0% Thru. Edit "B:\PCWRITE\work.doc"

                    What Price to Live the Dream?
                      Victor D. Lopez (C) 1988

     Ken  was tired, despondent and none too sober. He'd  learned
only two hours before that the Narcissus Project of which he  was
the head engineer was about to be cut, that funding would not  be
renewed  for the current fiscal year by the  intelligence  agency
for  which he worked. He saw the last fifteen years of his  life,
years  in which he was entirely absorbed in working on this  most
carefully guarded project and which had borne success beyond  his
most  optimistic  early dreams, rush by him in a  swirling  haze.
Gone were his well justified hopes for a Nobel prize in  physics,
along  with the once clear focus of his life, vanishing  like  an
evanescent  early  morning  springtime mist, burnt  away  by  the
unforgiving  rising  sun  of  a new day  (and  a  new  Washington
administration unfriendly to risky, high-priced covert projects).

     The  Phoenix project had been his life. He had conceived  it
while  an undergraduate student at MIT and it took on a  life  of
its   own  until  it  became  his  rason  d'etre.  He  used  his
considerable  power  of  persuasion,  and  political  connections
(being  the son of a powerful Eastern senator certainly  had  not
hindered his efforts, and he had not been shy about enlisting his
```

```
Esc:cancel.  F1-F1:help.  Alt/Shf/Ctl/Arrow:select.  Fn-key/Letter/Enter:action.
sF1:Fn-keys                                       sF7.Reform     sF9.Location
sF2:Merging    sF4:Shareware                      sF8.Center
Turn function key reminder on+ or off-



                                                  July 18, 1989



This is a sample file created with PC-CALC (tm). The screen is generally
uncluttered, with only the most crucial information being offered on the
topmost line on the screen.

Pictured here in this actual screen dump is the unobstrusive menu system. It
is accessed by striking the <ESC> key, and then options are selected through
use of the cursor control keys. There are more pull-down menus than are shown
on the screen at any given time; if one presses the cursor down past the last
line on the small help window, further menu choices will scroll up on the
screen. WordStar (tm)  commands and the ten function keys may also be used in
lieu of the menus; the choice is up to the user.
```

Top: **Figure 1.2: Actual screen of text imported from WordStar into PC-Write. Notice that only the topmost line is devoted to system messages, leaving 24 lines on screen for writing and editing text. The rather spartan display can quickly be enhanced by a plethora of pull-down menus and help screens when needed.** *Bottom:* **Figure 1.3: Actual editing screen from PC-Write.**

PC-Write program through a hands-on practice lesson. The user learns the essential features of the program by practicing, creating, editing and saving files, using formatting and editing commands, changing margins and other page formatting features, moving the cursor around the screen, learning the special keys utilized by the program, working with the help menus, performing search and replace functions and copying and deleting words, lines and blocks of text.

After spending an hour or two completing the tutorial exercises, the average user will be able to create a simple document using PC-Write, and will be familiar with the program's basic functions. The more advanced features of the program can be learned as they are needed. The user can use the program almost immediately for simple tasks such as writing a one-page letter, but he can also rest assured that the program will be able to meet his future needs as they arise.

The features offered by PC-Write are literally too many to enumerate. It incorporates every major feature found in most professional word processing programs. (The only exception is the lack of a thesaurus to look up words on-line, such as the ones offered by Word Perfect, WordStar and Microsoft Word, to name a few. But stand-alone thesauri are available from commercial software vendors for under $100.) In addition to the usual text formatting and editing capabilities, PC-Write offers excellent print enhancement capabilities, allowing documents to be enhanced by containing various type styles and type sizes. Printer support is also excellent, so that different fonts may be accessed by a user without having to go through painstaking (and often technically difficult) printer configurations. The program also allows for easy access to useful special characters, such as a wide variety of foreign characters. (This feature is one which should be available in every full-featured program, but seldom is; for anyone who writes in a foreign language, this feature is invaluable.)

A further helpful feature found in PC-Write is its combination of pull-down menus and multi-key commands. Users who like menus will find those in PC-Write useful and quite transparent. For users who prefer control-key sequences, the program also supports these (e.g., the authors of this text both prefer the WordStar command-driven approach as opposed to the menu-driven systems employed by programs such as Word Perfect or Multi Mate). Users familiar with WordStar will appreciate PC-Write's use of many of WordStar's classic commands to perform a wide range of editing functions.

Although, as has been previously noted, the program does not include a thesaurus, an excellent spelling checker is available. With it, a user may check any word, an entire document or any part thereof; the spelling checker words compare favorably with those of other full-featured professional word processing packages. Although the dictionary is not as large as

```
Esc:Cancel  F3.Guess  F10.Replace "uncluttered" with "uncomfortable"


                                                    July 18, 1989


This is a sample file created with PC-CALC (tm). The screen is generally
uncluttered, with only the most crucial information being offered on the
topmost line on the screen.

Pictured here in this actual screen dump is the unobstrusive menu system. It
is accessed by striking the <ESC> key, and then options are selected through
use of the cursor control keys. There are more pull-down menus than are shown
on the screen at any given time; if one presses the cursor down past the last
line on the small help window, further menu choices will scroll up on the
screen. WordStar (tm)  commands and the ten function keys may also be used in
lieu of the menus; the choice is up to the user.
```

Figure 1.4: PC-Write's spelling checker makes suggestions for proper spelling of words it cannot recognize. In this case, "uncluttered" is flagged as a suspect word and "uncomfortable" is suggested as a possible alternative. If the word is properly spelled, it can be added to the dictionary and will be recognized in the future. Note that no program will pick up properly spelled words which are incorrectly selected (here, PC-CALC is a valid word, but the writer meant PC-WRITE instead. No word processor can protect us from all our writing errors).

that found in the latest releases of WordStar, Word Perfect or Microsoft Word, it is quite adequate. And, since both the spell check and main word processing program run from RAM, large files may be checked quickly. If the program does not recognize the word, the user is prompted that it may be incorrectly spelled and has the option of correcting it or, if it is properly spelled, adding it to PC-Write's dictionary file so that it will be recognized in the future.

The program can even make suggestions for probable spellings for words it does not recognize; if a suggested spelling is acceptable to the user, the improperly spelled word will be automatically substituted by the chosen replacement. The program also includes the option to have spelling checked as one writes; if this option is selected, the program will beep every time it fails to recognize a word typed in by a user; this function may be favored by many users and is not found on many other leading word processing programs.

PC-Write incorporates a superb on-line help system which is extremely

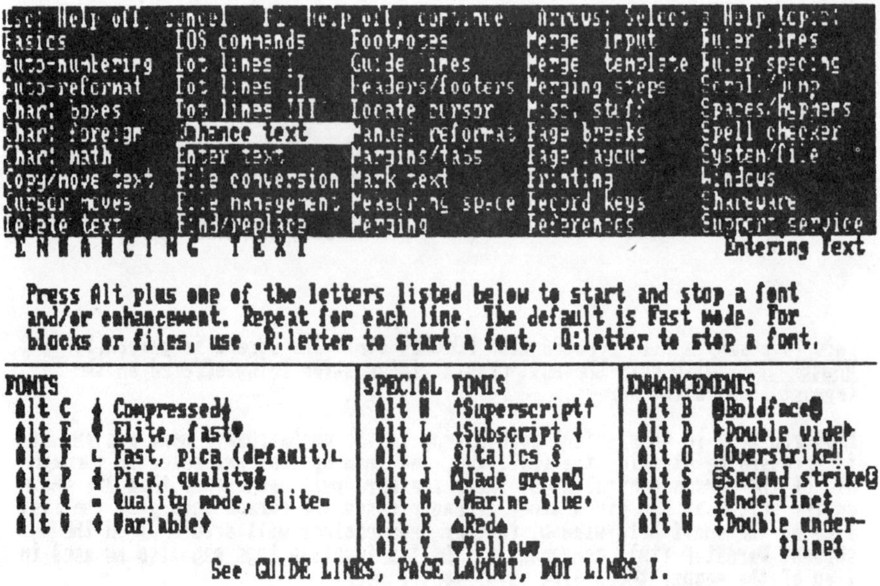

Figure 1.5: Actual help screen depicting some of PC-Write's built-in print enhancement capabilities. The program is able to reproduce various different fonts and print styles with a wide variety of printers.

useful for most users, in particular those new to the program. Help with most features of the program is always just a few keystrokes away. Also, since the program runs completely from RAM (Random Access Memory), the entire program—including its help screens—runs very quickly; there is no need to wait for annoying delays while the program accesses its disk drives at various parts in the program; this gives PC-Write a very noticeable speed advantage over many of its competitors—particularly during what are normally disk-intensive tasks, such as spell checks and access to help screens.

A price is paid for the program's speed, however, in that the need for RAM for loading and running the various parts of the program limits the size of files which can be worked on at a given time. The computers we own, both lap-top and desktop systems, all contain 640 kilobytes of RAM. So equipped, we were able to work on files of up to approximately 50 kilobytes in length (roughly 25 double-spaced pages of information). This is certainly sufficient for most applications; at worst, if one needs to work on a truly large file (such as this book), it could easily be broken down into smaller files, each not to exceed the 50-kilobyte maximum (e.g., a book could be broken down into separate chapters and then linked together for printing). PC-Write does give the user a running total of the percentage of space

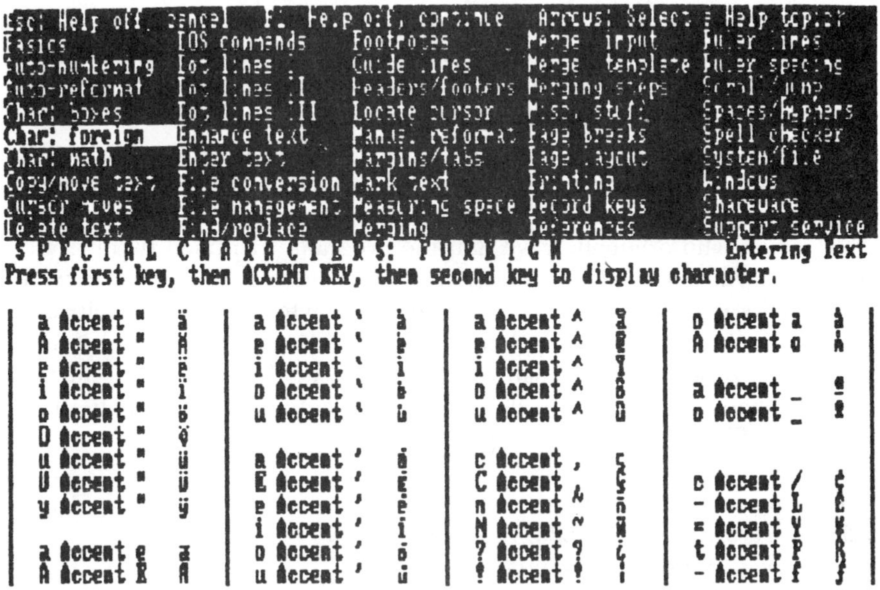

Figure 1.6: PC-Write offers excellent support of a wide variety of special graphics characters, giving the word processor the ability to create line drawings and special characters. In this screen, one can see the impressive array of special foreign characters which the program supports. Its ability to easily incorporate foreign characters and a wide array of special symbols without special programming by the user makes the program invaluable in many situations where these are needed.

remaining for data at any given time, so that there is always the opportunity to save a file once the memory buffer is approaching its full capacity and opening a new file.

Finally, the program supports advanced page formatting features such as headers, footers and footnotes. Through the use of embedded commands similar to WordStar's dot commands, the program achieves a high level of flexibility in text formatting and other advanced operations. When joined with the excellent support of different type sizes and styles (or fonts), PC-Write is capable of producing some very attractive printed results. This fact in combination with the plethora of available features makes PC-Write one of the best word processing programs at any price, and an unbelievable bargain at its $89 registration price.

Registration entitles the user to free support by phone and by mail, and brings the user a copy of the latest release of the program, in addition to a bound 336-page manual. Users who do not wish to register copies may still purchase the complete hardbound or softbound manual for $45 and and $35 respectively. And if these benefits aren't sufficient to convince those who try PC-Write to register their copies, registration brings with it one additional benefit to the user: the ability to earn commissions of $25 per copy for anyone who receives a copy of the program from him and then registers it. This is highly unusual—and effective—marketing strategy. Registered users get a copy of the program with a serial number reserved for them. They are then encouraged to give away copies of the program to friends and acquaintances. Whenever anyone given such a copy for their evaluation goes on to register the program for the usual $89 registration fee, the person who originally gave him the program (identified by his serial number) will get a $25 commission. In essence, while most shareware developers appeal to people's honesty to get them to register their software, Quicksoft, Inc., appeals to a much more effective motive: people's self-interest or profit motive. Whatever the appeal, PC-Write is one of the few truly successful shareware packages ever marketed and deservedly so.

Program: Pc-Write Ver. 2.7 © 1983–1986
Company: Quicksoft, Inc.
Address: 219 First N. #224, Seattle, WA 98109
Category: Word Processing
Registration Fee: $89

General Evaluation: PC-Write Ver. 2.7

	Excellent	*Very Good*	*Good*	*Average*	*Poor*
Ease of Use		***			
Ease of Learning		***			
Documentation	***				
Utility	***				
Overall Rating	***				

Galaxy™ Version 2.42

Anyone who has spent any significant amount of time working with various software packages can vouch for the fact that software can have personality traits not unlike those of human beings; there is a look and feel to each software package that distinguishes it from any other package in its category and gives it a character all its own. Like people, software can be flashy on the outside but lack any real substance; such software may be interesting to try out, but one seldom stays with it. Other software is dull on the outside but richly rewarding in its depth and substance; while this software tends to be difficult to learn and perhaps a bit frustrating to live with in the way it gets things done, it offers sufficient features to keep one interested for many years to come. Once in a long while, we find a package

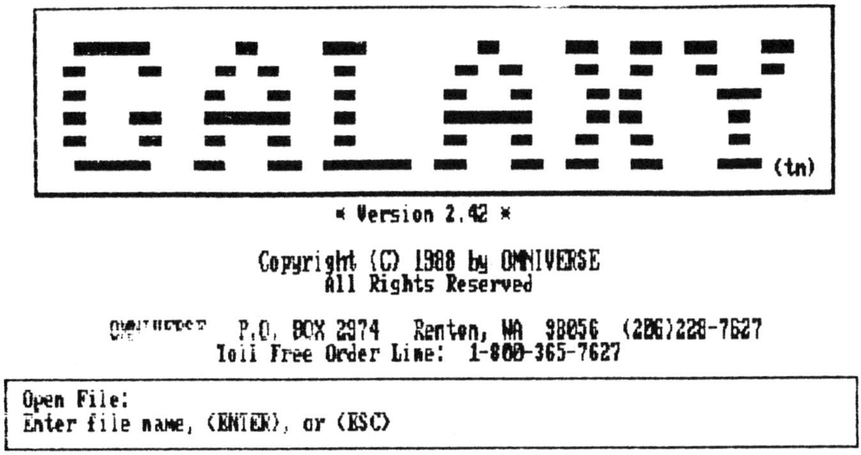

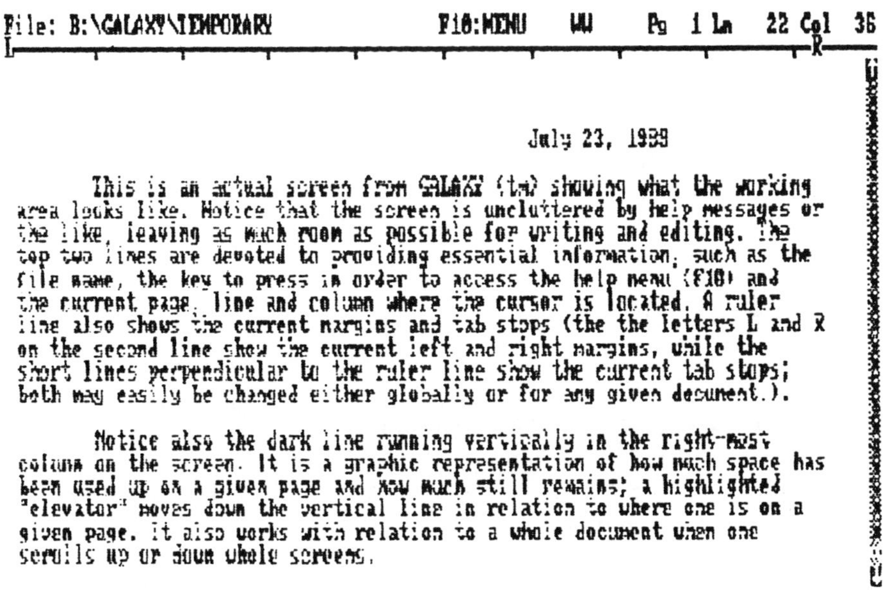

Top: **Figure 1.7: Opening screen for Galaxy. This powerful word processor features pull-down menus, compatibility with WordStar commands and its own command structure for ease of use and flexibility that are hard to beat.** ***Bottom:*** **Figure 1.8: Working screen from Galaxy showing a one-page document. Only essential information is displayed on the top two lines and on the vertical "elevator" slide bar at the right of the screen. Abundant help screens and pull-down menus are available at any time by pressing the F10 function key. (See Figure 1.12.)**

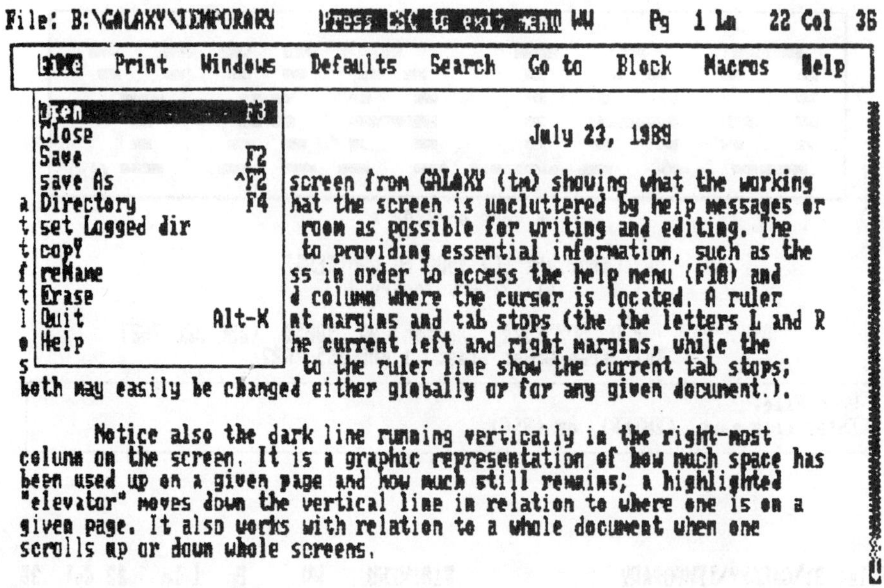

Figure 1.9: Pull-down menus are available at all times by pressing the F10 key. A menu bar appears on screen from which various categories of functions may be selected. A sliding highlight bar is moved over the menu choices by use of the cursor control keys, causing pull-down menus with choices on each highlighted category to automatically appear in a window superimposed on the screen. Available functions in each category can then be selected with the cursor control keys. In this way, no commands need be memorized in order to use even the most advanced functions of this versatile program.

which combines both interesting features and ease of use with sufficient depth so as to be useful for more than rudimentary applications. Such is the case with Galaxy, a package which seems to have been designed with a very important (and all too often ignored) concept in mind: that all users are not alike, and that a program's way of interfacing with the user—its ergonomics—is as important as its advanced features.

Galaxy is an impressive program for a variety of reasons, but what a new user will notice first is its flexibility and adaptability to different people's tastes. Most word processors currently released offer either a menu-driven or a command driven mode. There are as many arguments for the benefits of each user interface as there are people who subscribe to them. Pull down menus tend to be easy to learn and can be applied painlessly (at times nearly mindlessly) as one writes. If a user wants to perform a certain function, he need only touch a key, move his cursor through his menu and select the proper function therefrom. Some such systems use function keys

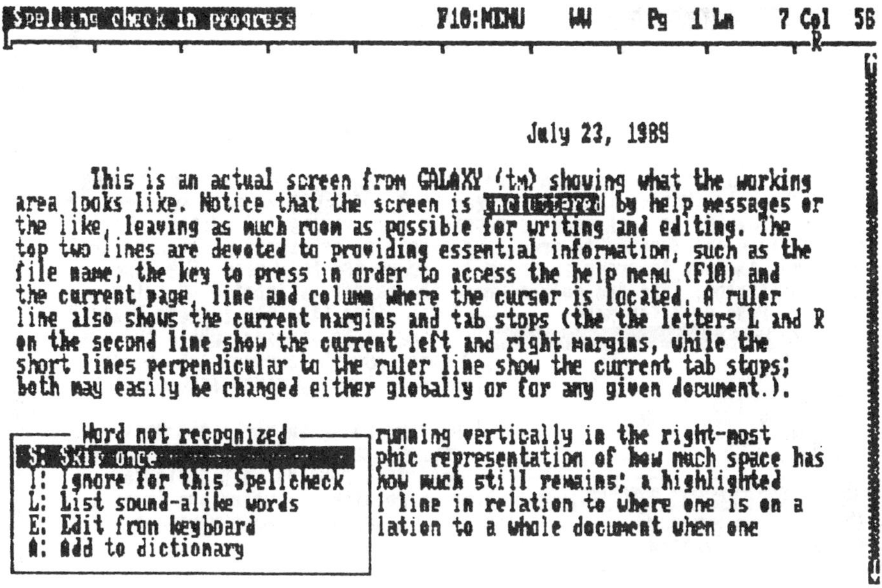

Figure 1.10: An excellent spelling checker is available with the program. Whenever the program encounters a word it does not recognize, it gives the user a choice of ignoring it, providing "sound-alike" suggestions, entering a correction from the keyboard or adding the word to the 45,000-word dictionary. The program runs from memory and is quite fast in its execution.

with various [ALT], [SHIFT] and [CTRL] key combinations to perform most word processing tasks, and offer an on-screen help system which shows what each key can do (e.g., the traditional WordStar command system). The latter system allows for faster typing by touch-typists, who can perform nearly any function without having their hands stray from the home keys; the latter is easier to learn. Some new software packages allow the user a choice of user interfaces (e.g., WordStar release 5.0). Galaxy also gives the user a choice, but of *three* different interfaces: A pull-down menu system which is nicely designed and a pleasure to use, a WordStar command system which utilizes over 54 of that word processor's classic commands (the program can also directly import WordStar data files from releases prior to ver. 5.0), and its own command system which is logical and relatively easy to remember. Nor is a user limited to a single interface; all three types of interfaces may be used simultaneously so that a user may use the faster command mode for commands he already knows, while using the menu mode for commands he is unfamiliar with. This leads to a very short learning curve for new users. In addition, a user may customize the program's default setting to suit a user's particular taste and needs. For ease

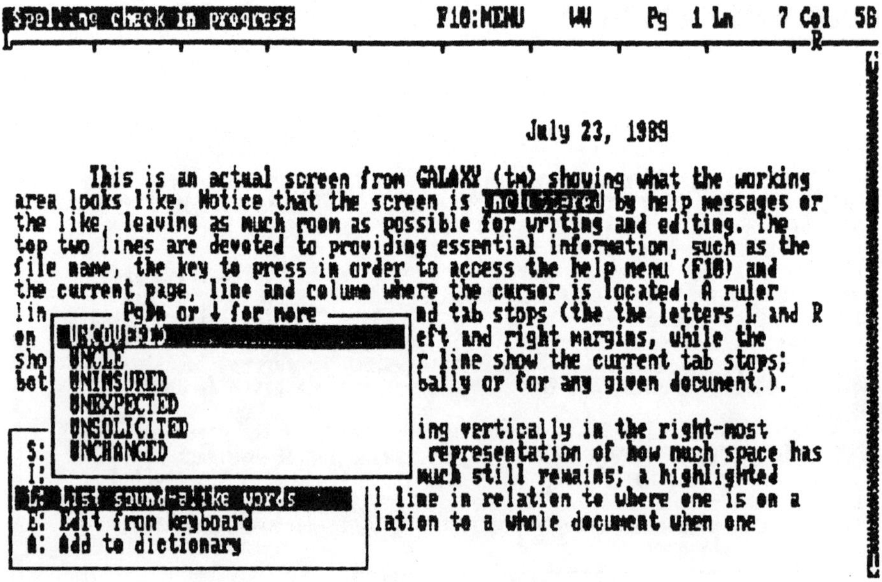

Figure 1.11: The spell-check program provides some valid suggestions for potentially misspelled words. In this case, it flags the word "uncluttered" as a potential misspelling, and provides 18 different possible suggestions for words the writer may have meant to use. These suggestions may be viewed in a separate window with six suggestions appearing at any one time. If one of these is adequate, the writer may select it by pressing the "enter" key while it is highlighted; the word will then be automatically replaced in the text.

of use, ease of learning, ergonomics and simple user-friendliness, this is probably the best word processing program that we have reviewed.

Galaxy runs completely from memory, which means it is fast. The annoying delays in program execution experienced by other programs as they need to access disk drives in order to perform given functions is obviated. As with PC-Write reviewed elsewhere in this text, Galaxy pays a price for its speed: there is a limit to the size of documents it can hold in memory at any given time, so that very large documents must be split up into two or more files and worked on piecemeal. The practical limit seems to be approximately a 50-kilobyte file, or approximately 25 double-spaced pages (provided a system contains 640K RAM; systems with less memory will accommodate smaller documents).

The program supports the usual features one expects from a serious package. Among its features not found in many competitors in the "under $100" category are a good 45,000-word spelling checker, windows capability (the ability to work on two documents at once and see both on the screen simultaneously) and the capacity to use macro definitions (the ability

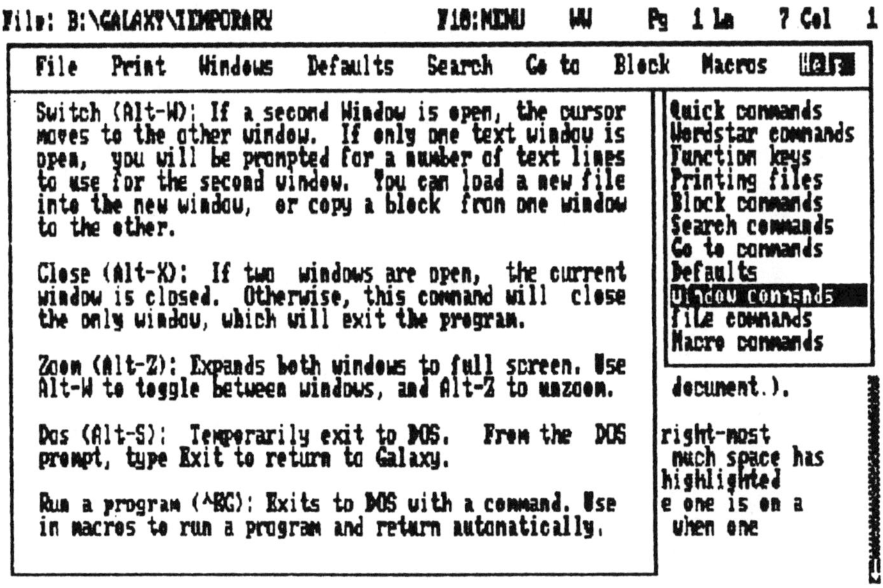

Figure 1.12: Galaxy includes excellent on-line help screens on almost every feature it provides. By selecting "Help" from the pull-down menu, a small window with categories of available help shows up on the upper right portion of the screen. By moving the highlighted bar to a given topic and pressing "Enter," a second, larger window appears on the screen with specific help text. This is an invaluable reference tool which greatly enhances the program's ease of learning and ease of use.

to have complex keystrokes programmed onto function keys for automatic execution).

The evaluation copy of the program includes an excellent 59-page manual in the distribution disk covering all of the program's main features. The manual walks the inexperienced reader through step by step instructions on setting up the program and running it. For the experienced user, the manual contains a good index covering all of the program's main features, as well as various appendices with command listings for easy reference. Like the program itself, the manual is quite user-friendly, and much thought has obviously gone into its planning.

Galaxy is a word processing package well suited for most light to medium duty uses. It is appropriate for home or office use for basic letter writing, preparation of memos and reports, and is nearly ideal as a tool for students (footnotes are supported, as well as various print enhancements). It is powerful enough for nearly any application, while retaining nearly unparalleled ease of use. When one factors in the modest registration fee of $59.95, which includes a printed reference guide and tutorial, as well as free telephone support, one would be hard pressed to find a better value anywhere.

Program: Galaxy Ver. 2.42 © 1988
Company: Omniverse
Address: P.O. Box 2974, Renton, WA 98056
Telephone: (206) 228-7627
Category: Word Processing
Registration Fee: $59.95

General Evaluation: Galaxy Ver. 2.7

	Excellent	*Very Good*	*Good*	*Average*	*Poor*
Ease of Use	***				
Ease of Learning	***				
Documentation	***				
Utility		***			
Overall Rating	***				

MindReader™ Version 2.0

One of the wonderful things about public domain and shareware is that authors are free to experiment with new ideas and incorporate these into their own software. Thus, while much of today's traditional commercial software packages tend to have a similar look and feel as smaller software developers try to emulate the leading software packages, public domain and shareware releases reflect their author's individual tastes and styles. At times, this can lead to radically different approaches to the way a software package should perform. And, whether one prefers the author's new method of doing the same old chore or chastises him for an awkward attempt to reinvent the wheel, the effect is generally to enrich the realm of applications software, if only in avoiding the bland "sameness" that characterizes much of the commercially released software today.

MindReader is a word processing program which attempts a radical divergence from the beaten path of traditional word processing packages. The program incorporates most of the major features one expects in a full-featured word processor, but it does so by means of an artificial intelligence engine which attempts to anticipate what a writer intends to write before she can finish writing it. The program comes with a list of most commonly used words and phrases which can be modified by the individual user. As soon as a letter is typed, the program tries to anticipate what is likely to follow, and gives the writer the option of accepting a given suggestion by depressing a "hot key" or simply ignoring the offered suggestions and continuing to type the rest of the word. As an example, if I were writing this review on MindReader and typed the letter "t", the program would immediately pop up a small window on my screen with the following suggestions:

; the
2 that
3 this
4 there
5 to the

If I intended to write "the," I could enter a semicolon at this point and the word "the" would be automatically completed, with a space inserted after it so that the next word could be typed. Thus, typing in "t;" would result in "the" and a space appearing on the screen. Typing in "t" and the number 5 would result in the phrase "to the" appearing on the screen, also with a space at the end of it so that the first letter of the next word could immediately be typed without need to depress the spacebar.

The net result achieved by the program is that text can be input with fewer keystrokes than through traditional means. If the suggestions are not accepted, new ones appear as one continues to type. In the above example, if I typed a "t" and did not accept any of the offered suggestions for completing my word but continued to type the letters "her," new suggestions would appear after I had input "ther" and these would be as follows:

; therefore
2 there is
3 thereafter
4 there are
5 thermometer

If my intended word was "thermometer," then all I need do would be to depress the number 5 which corresponds to it; in that way I would have written "thermometer" with just five keystrokes (t-h-e-r-5) as opposed to eleven (t-h-e-r-m-o-m-e-t-e-r). Obviously, the slower the typist, the greater the benefits to using this program. Undoubtedly, the typist who would benefit the most from this program would be one who utilizes the "hunt and peck," two-fingered typing technique. Typists who know the keyboard, however, can benefit in other ways. A fast but inaccurate typist would see his or her errors significantly reduced by allowing the program to complete words for him; the program will not misspell words it completes nor can it make typographical errors.

As mentioned before, the program utilizes artificial intelligence; the

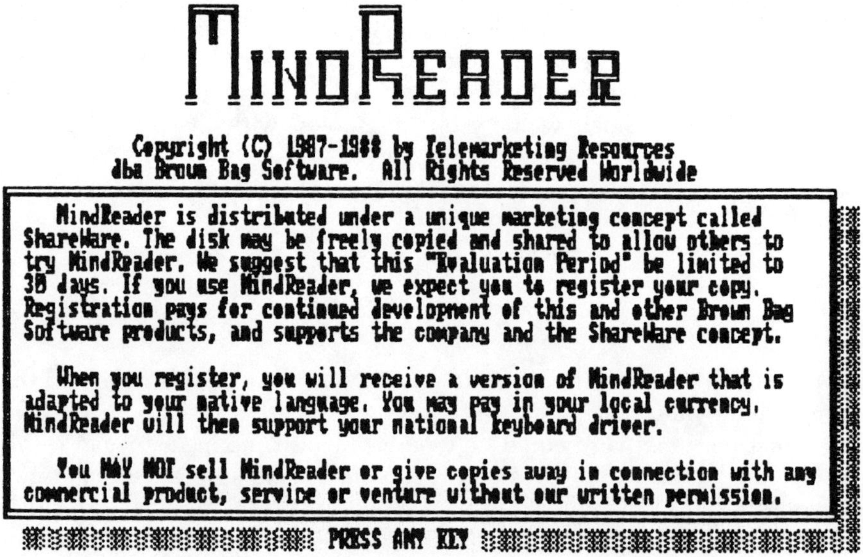

Figure 1.13: Opening screen and copyright notice for MindReader.

more one uses it, the better it can "learn" one's individual writing style and shift the choices offered for word completion to the order in which they are most likely to appear. For example, I am not likely to write the word "thermometer" very often, but I do write the word "thorough" a lot. If I were to make MindReader my primary word processor, I would replace "thermometer" with "thorough" as one of the five suggestions (a matter which can be accomplished with just a few keystrokes) the program will offer every time I type "t-h", and the program would eventually move it up from the fifth option to the first, activated by striking the semi-colon key (the "hot key" which contains the most-often-used words, and a key which is much more convenient to type than the number "5").

While many computer users could benefit from this program's WORDCOMPLETE feature, the program could be absolutely invaluable to a handicapped person who has limited use of (or missing) hands or fingers. A user who could not hope to obtain a relatively fast typing speed due to physical impediments could greatly improve his typing speed through MindReader's WORDCOMPLETE feature; for these users, MindReader could be a priceless commodity.

For users who are relatively fast typists, MindReader's WORDCOMPLETE option can soon grow tiresome. At even average typing speeds of 35 to 60 words per minute, the program's constant flickering "help" window, with the WORDCOMPLETE options which pop up on average after every three keystrokes, can be quite distracting and of little use. Fortunately, this

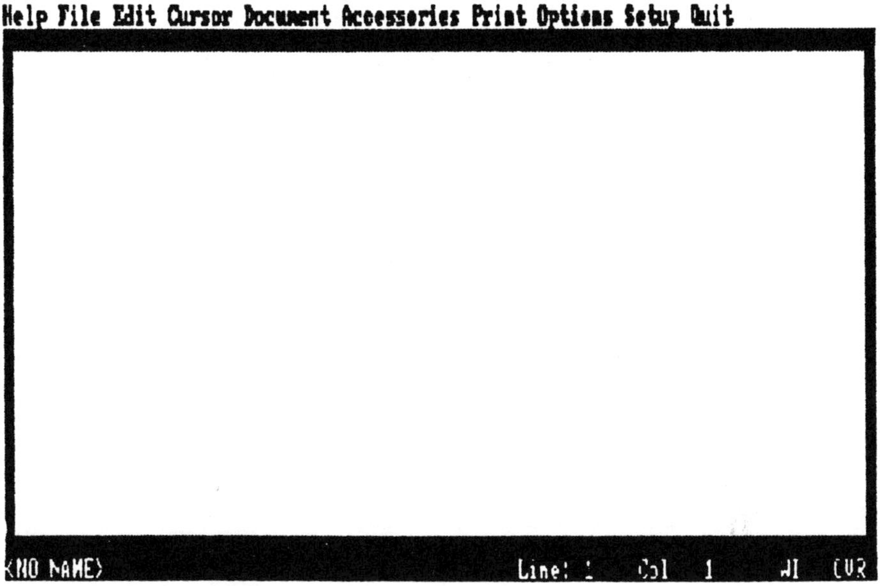

Figure 1.14: Editing screen for MindReader. Notice the uncluttered screen which leaves as much space as possible for editing.

feature *can* easily be turned off either temporarily or permanently with just a few keystrokes.

For a user who will definitely not use the WORDCOMPLETE help feature, MindReader may be somewhat overpriced at $89.95 registration fee. There are more powerful word processing programs within this price range in the shareware realm, such as PC-Write, reviewed elsewhere in this volume. The program is by no means short on features, however, and is capable of handling a wide range of word processing tasks.

The program handles the usual word processing functions flawlessly: inserting and deleting text, moving text around within a document or from one document to another, changing the format of a document (e.g., margins, page length, tab stops, line spacing), searching and replacing text and automatic word wrap at the end of each line are but a few of the usual features which are supported. The program offers many additional useful features which are not always found in word processing packages. These include both a usable spell-checking program and Insta Spell—a spelling checker which warns of possible misspellings while one is writing; if the program comes across a word it does not recognize, it highlights it and gives the writer the option of retyping it correctly, ignoring it or adding it to the dictionary so that it will be recognized in the future. A glossary function is also included which allows for often-used words or phrases to be saved and

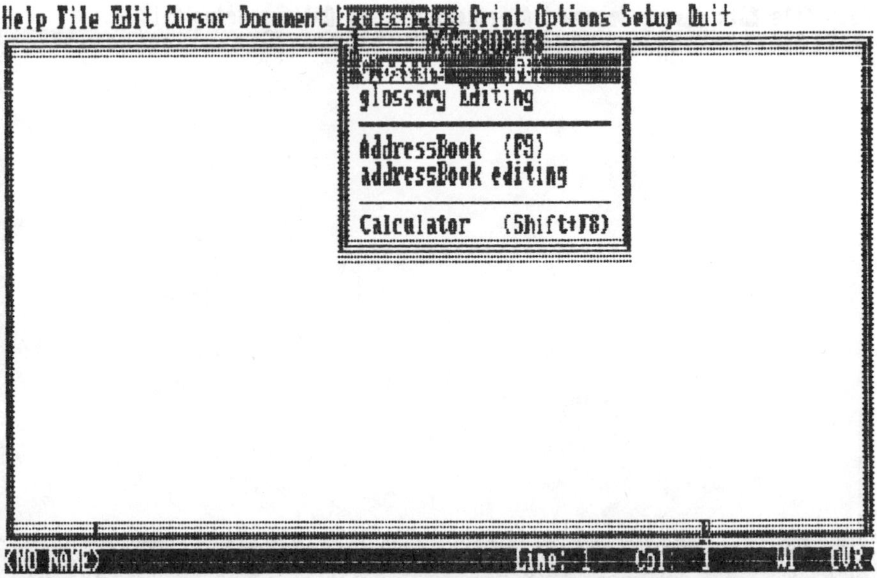

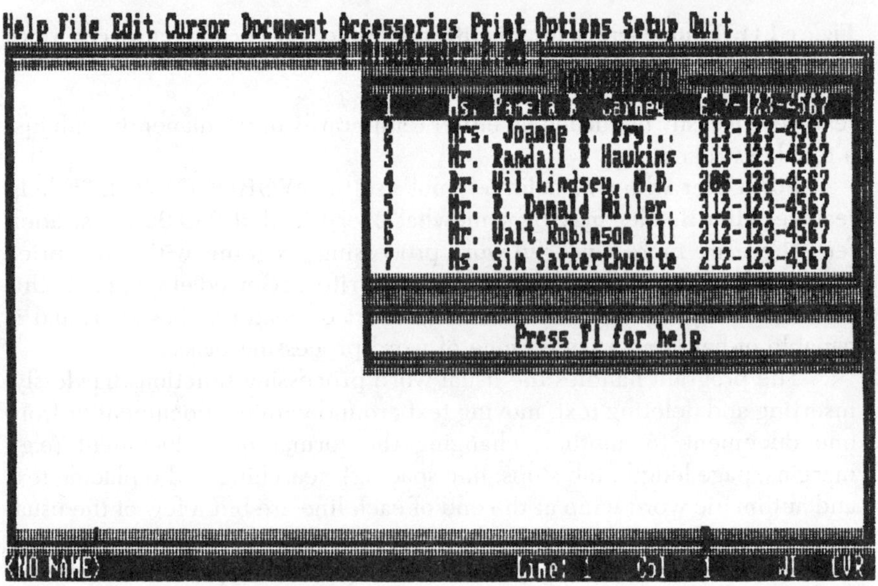

Top: **Figure 1.15: Pull-down menus make selecting from MindReader's available features an easy matter. The program is quite intuitive and has been designed with ease of use as a primary goal.** ***Bottom:*** **Figure 1.16: MindReader's ADDRESSBOOK feature is a mini-database program which can be used to store, sort and retrieve related information in a variety of ways. The information can also be used to create mail-merged correspondence with the program.**

Intro Scr Menu [illegible] WSKeys Dictionary AddrBook Glossary Calc Options

Alt+H	HELP MENU	Down	NEXT LINE	Home	START OF LINE
Alt+F	FILE MENU	Up	PREV LINE	End	END OF LINE
Alt+E	EDIT MENU	Right	NEXT CHAR	Home X2	START OF PAGE
Alt+C	CURSOR MENU	Left	PREV CHAR	End X2	END OF PAGE
Alt+D	DOC MENU	^Home	TOP OF PAGE	Home X3	START OF FILE
Alt+A	UTIL MENU	^End	BOT OF PAGE	End X3	END OF FILE
Alt+P	PRINT MENU	^Right	WORD RIGHT	Tab	INSERT TAB/WRITE TAB
Alt+O	OPTIONS MENU	^Left	WORD LEFT	Enter	SPLIT LINE/NEW LINE
Alt+S	SETUP MENU	^W	WORDWRAP	^F#	USER MACROS
Alt+Q	QUIT MENU	PgDn	NEXT PAGE	Alt+M	MACRO TOGGLE
Esc	QUIT MENU	PgUp	PREV PAGE	Ins	INSERT TOGGLE
Shift+F1	WORD TO DOC.	Alt+F1	UNDERLINE	F1	HELP
Shift+F2	UPDATE DIC.	Alt+F2	BOLDFACE	F2	PLURAL SUFFIX
Shift+F3	SEARCH/REPL.	Alt+F3	-	F3	ING SUFFIX
Shift+F4	INSERT LINE	Alt+F4	CENTER LINE	F4	PAST SUFFIX
Shift+F5	DELETE LINE	Alt+F5	PAGE BREAK	F5	SPELL CHECK
Shift+F6	-	Alt+F6	-	F6	DELETE PREV WORD
Shift+F7	SIGNATURE	Alt+F7	RULER SETUP	F7	PRINT SETUP
Shift+F8	CALCULATOR	Alt+F8	-	F8	GLOSARRY
Shift+F9	UNDO DELETE	Alt+F9	START BLOCK	F9	ADDRESSBOOK
Shift+F10	INFORMATION	Alt+F10	BLOCK MENU	F10	HELP MENU

Figure 1.17: MindReader offers extensive on-line help. Pictured here is a comprehensive help screen outlining special commands and the key sequences needed to access them.

retrieved for future use by pressing a few keys. Several safety features have also been built into the program: An OOPS! feature allows for text which has been accidentally erased to be restored; text can be set to be automatically saved after a given period of time (1 to 40 minutes); and text files can be encrypted to prevent unauthorized persons from gaining access to them and reading the information they contain (if a person forgets the password used to lock the files, there is no way to unlock them again).

MindReader contains a nice ADDRESSBOOK feature which functions as a mini-database program (see Chapter 3 for a full discussion of database programs); a user can set up a list of names, addresses and telephone numbers to function as an electronic Rolodex, and the names and addresses in the ADDRESSBOOK can be used by the program's MAIL MERGE feature to merge form letters with a list of names and addresses in the ADDRESSBOOK for personalized mass mailings. The ADDRESSBOOK file may also be searched, updated and printed at will.

A further nice feature found in MindReader is a built-in electronic calculator which contains the basic features found on most basic printing calculators and which can be made to print out mathematical operations onto a printer, in effect turning into one. In addition, the results of mathematical calculations can be directly imported into a word processing file for inclusion in it.

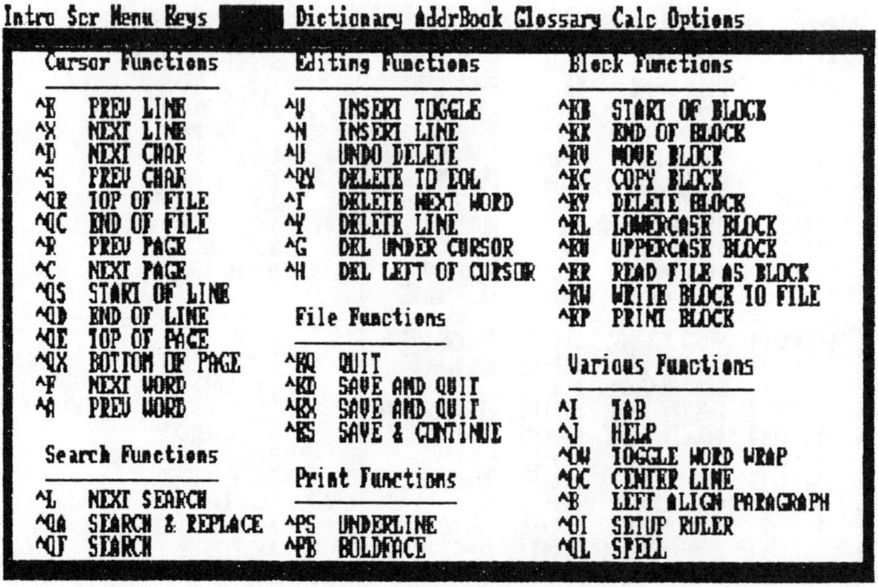

Figure 1.18: MindReader gives users the option of using many WordStar commands for users who are already familiar with that program. Pictured here is an actual help screen outlining some of the supported WordStar commands.

MindReader comes with a relatively brief but quite useful 22-page manual on disk. A full bound manual is available upon registration. While the short "manual" is by no means complete and lacks such niceties as a table of contents or index, it does highlight the basic features of the program and permits a user to get the program running with little difficulty. The fact that the program itself is relatively intuitive and easy to learn in part offsets the rather skimpy instructions distributed with the shareware evaluation copy of the program.

It is worthy of note that while MindReader utilizes its own command structure, it also permits users to use many of WordStar's commands as an option. Users who are already familiar with WordStar may use MindReader without having to relearn many new commands.

MindReader is certainly not a word processing package well suited to everyone's needs. Yet, for slow typists or physically handicapped users, it can be a priceless find. Even for fast touch-typists, the program has sufficient features to make it worthy of consideration.

Program: MindReader Ver. 2.0 © 1987–1988
Company: Brown Bag Software
Address: 2155 South Bascom Avenue, Campbell, CA 95008

Category: Word Processing
Registration Fee: $89.95

General Evaluation: MindReader Ver. 2.0

	Excellent	*Very Good*	*Good*	*Average*	*Poor*
Ease of Use		***			
Ease of Learning		***			
Documentation				***	
Utility			***		
Overall Rating		***			

FreeWord™ 1.0

For the beginning computer user, making the transition from writing on a typewriter to writing on a word processor can be a somewhat overwhelming experience. For this reason, many users who would undoubtedly greatly benefit from using even the simplest word processing program never make the transition. This is especially true for users who are introduced to a first-generation command-driven word processor by well meaning friends; I wonder how many users have experimented with, say, WordStar ver. 3.3 and given up on word processing because they perceived it to be "too complicated." While that program offered (for its time) extraordinary flexibility, it was certainly not meant for the occasional user who only intended to use it to write a letter to mom several times a year.

For the new user who wants a painless introduction into word processing and who does not need powerful features, a low-end program like FreeWord may be ideal. While it is unquestionably the least powerful program reviewed herein, FreeWord is one of the easiest to learn and use. The program offers only the most basic of features, and is missing what for many users will be crucial features, such as the ability to change margins, tabs, vary page lengths and the like. This makes the program useful only in limited applications, like letter writing or simple reports for school. But for the user who wants a "quick and simple" word processing package requiring practically no learning time at all, FreeWord may be ideal.

The program is extremely simple to use. Its opening screen gives the user the following choices, any of which may be accessed by depressing the [ALT] key in conjunction with the first letter of the desired choice: Help, Block, Directory, Load file, New page, Print, Quit, Find, Redisplay, Save file and Typewriter. When any of the above choices is selected, a menu of further choices appears, listing further options for the user to select. All functions available in this program must be chosen through this modified pull-down menu user interface.

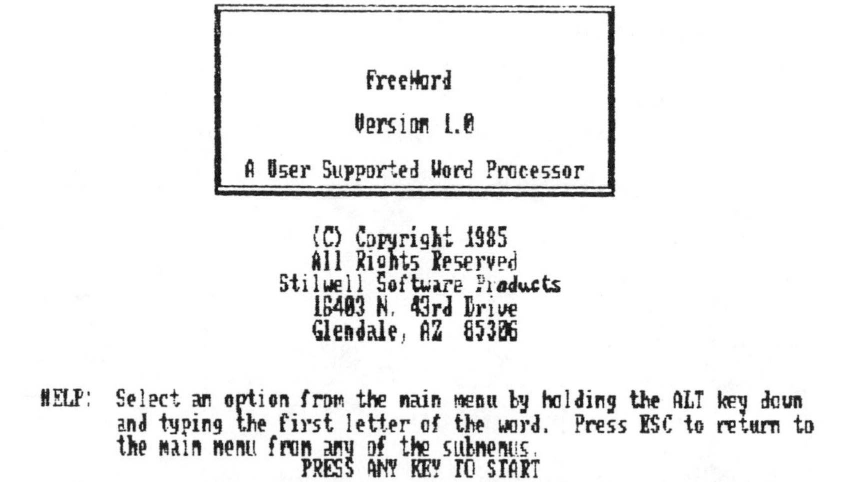

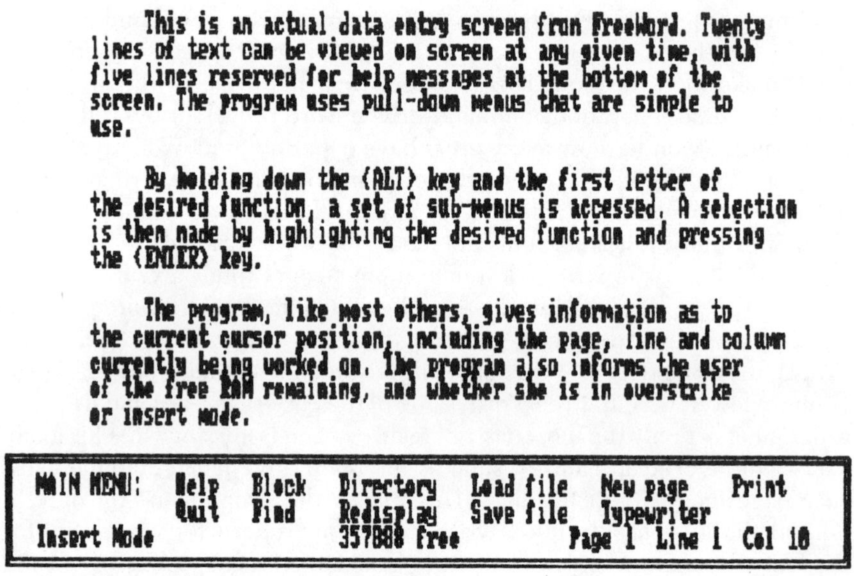

Top: **Figure 1.19: Opening screen and copyright notice for FreeWord.** ***Bottom:*** **Figure 1.20: Editing screen for FreeWord.**

The program offers an excellent on-line help facility which may be accessed at any time by depressing the [ALT]-H combination. The help feature works as an on-line reference and tutorial, giving specific information about all of the program's functions.

Along similar lines, the program comes with a detailed manual on disk which is 86 pages in length when printed. (Its length is somewhat deceptive, since it is formatted to 40-character margins and contains approximately half of the information normally found per printed page. The net result is the equivalent of a 43-page manual.) The manual is well indexed and quite helpful; in fact, its only fault may be overkill, since there is not much need for documentation in a program as simple as this one. The manual even includes a hands-on tutorial feature whereby text files included on the distribution copy of the diskette can be edited by the word processor to illustrate the program's features.

The program offers good cursor control, allowing for easy movement within the document by word, line, screen and to the top or bottom of a file. Find and replace options are also available, as are block operations for copying, deleting or moving blocks of text within the same document. (Multiple windows are not supported; a user is limited to working within a single document at any given time.) A spelling checker is available, but only upon registration of the program at the requested $49 price; a bound copy of the manual is also included in the registration price.

The program runs from memory, so that scrolling and text searches are relatively fast. The size of the file which can be worked on depends upon how much RAM is available on a given system (the program will run with a minimum of 256K RAM, one double-sided disk drive and either a color or monochrome monitor). On a system with 640K RAM, the program could load a maximum file of approximately 40 kilobytes, or approximately 20 double-spaced pages. Strangely enough, the built-in gauge which keeps track of available memory told us we could load a file of more than 200K, but we got an "out of memory" message with files greater than 40K; this may simply be a bug in the program. Whether the practical limit is 20 pages or not is of little consequence, since likely users of this program are unlikely to write files greater than several pages in length. Anyone needing to write extensive files would be ill advised to consider this program.

Among the program's most serious limitations are the inability to change margins, tab stops or to perform even rudimentary print enhancements such as bold-facing or underlining. These serious limitations in what is otherwise a very usable program are somewhat puzzling.

A nice feature of the program which is especially useful for users who are making the transition from a typewriter to a word processor is the ability of the program to emulate an electronic typewriter. By selecting this option from the main menu, a user is able to enter text one line at a time, making corrections of the entered text at any time prior to pressing the return key. (There is no automatic carriage return, however; one must manually insert a return at the end of each line.) This same feature can be used to send characters to one's printer for any print enhancements it supports. In this way, it is possible to tell the printer to print in near letter quality mode, or italics, or emphasized mode, for example, provided that it can support any

```
                    H E L P

   Please select the item you would like help with:

          1.  General editing
          2.  Cursor movement
          3.  Directory
          4.  Load file
          5.  Save file
          6.  Block move
          7.  Find
          8.  New page
          9.  Redisplay
         10.  Print
         11.  Quit
         12.  Color of screen
         13.  Typewriter
         14.  User Supported Software

         ESC  Return to main menu
```

```
              G E N E R A L   E D I T I N G
ESC KEY     - Return to main menu from submenu
BACKSPACE   - Delete text to left of cursor
DEL KEY     - Delete character at the cursor's location
CTRL & END  - Delete from cursor to end of line
ENTER KEY   - New line
INS KEY     - Used to toggle back and forth from insert to
              replace mode.
TAB KEY     - Double-arrow key used to move cursor five
              spaces to the right.
INSERTING   - Move cursor using arrow keys to position in
              text where you want to insert.  Check to see
              that you are in insert mode.  Start typing.
              Press ALT & R to redisplay (reformat) text.
REPLACING   - Move cursor using arrow keys to position in
              text where you want to replace.  Check to see
              that you are in the replace mode.  Start
              typing.  Press ALT & R to redisplay (reformat)
              text.
HYPHENATION - When warning sounds, move LEFT and RIGHT ARROW
              keys to move to appropriate place for hyphen;
              then press ESC.
FREE MEMORY - Number of bytes (characters) left in memory is
              displayed on the bottom line of main menu.
```

Top: Figure 1.21: Main help menu for FreeWord. _Bottom:_ Figure 1.22: Sample help screen for FreeWord. Specific help for major word processing functions is never more than a few keystrokes away. While the help screens are relatively basic in comparison with most other word processors reviewed in this text, they can be of great assistance, particularly for the new user.

such enhancement. The problem is that the user likeliest to want this program is least likely to be technically proficient enough to feel comfortable sending hexadecimal or decimal commands to the printer—a cumbersome procedure at best. Such capabilities are generally supported by other word processors through their built-in or programmable print enhancements, a feature not available with FreeWord.

FreeWord is a simple program best suited to users with simple word processing needs. Its most appealing feature is its ease of learning and use. It is a good first program to introduce the user to word processing in a safe, wholly unthreatening manner. The program will definitely be outgrown by a user at some point.

Program: FreeWord Ver. 1.0 © 1985
Company: Stilwell Software Products
Address: 16403 North 43rd Drive, Glendale, AZ 85306
Category: Word Processing
Registration Fee: $49

General Evaluation: FreeWord Ver. 1.0

	Excellent	*Very Good*	*Good*	*Average*	*Poor*
Ease of Use	***				
Ease of Learning	***				
Documentation	***				
Utility				***	
Overall Rating				***	

New York Word™ Version 2.2

New York Word is a full-featured, professional word processing program which combines some outstanding features with a remarkably low $45 registration fee (plus $2 for shipping and handling), making this one of the best software bargains.

The program's powerful features place it comfortably within the category of a professional word processing package. While New York Word is not as flashy as other commercial programs with which it can be compared (e.g., Word Perfect, WordStar, Microsoft Word, and Multi Mate, to name a few), it does share many of those programs' powerful features, and can actually be said to surpass them in a few notable areas, such as the number of windows it can access at one time (12) and its flexible mail merge program which incorporates some database functions not found in some of

```
NEW YORK WORD  V 2.2  (C) Copyright 1986  Marc Adler  All Rights Reserved
        NEW YORK WORD V.2.2  (C) COPYRIGHT 1984,1986  MARC ADLER

        If you find this program to be of use, please register your
        copy of New York Word. Registration is $45.00 plus $2 shipping.
        Registration gets you the users manual, latest disk, and NYW
        utilites, like the spelling program and mail merge. Mail to:

                    Marc Adler
                    Magma Software Systems
                    138-23 Hoover Ave,
                    Jamaica, New York 11435
```

```
Hit a key to start

This is an actual data entry screen from New York Word. While the screen
layout may seem somewhat Spartan with its single-line of useful information
displayed at the bottom of the screen, it is good to have 24 of 25 possible
lines of text reserved for data entry. Programs with lots of on-screen help
are wonderful for beginners, but such screen clutter soon gets in the way
of the writing process as a writer learns to use the program.◄
◄
Both authors like programs which make help available to the writer only
when it is requested. New York Word offers help at the press of a key (like
every other program reviewed herein). Pressing the <ALT> key and the H key
simultaneously brings up help menus. Pressing the <ALT> key and the M key
at the same time also brings up a pull-down menu system from which the
writer can select the function she wishes to execute. Like the help menu,
the command menu stays out of the way when it is not needed.◄
◄
The program also performs automatic backups as the writer writes--a feature
which can save the day in case of a power failure or a mistake which erases
the file being worked on from the computer's memory. This feature can be
switched off if it is not desired.◄
◄

col:  1  line  21 of  21  mode:O • fmt: 0  file temp
```

Top: **Figure 1.23: Opening screen and copyright notice for New York Word.**
Bottom: **Figure 1.24: Actual sample editing screen for New York Word.**

the leading packages. While its way of doing things may at times be a little more cumbersome, slower or not as thorough as some of its commercial siblings, one must keep in mind that the registration cost of the package is *less* than one tenth that of any of the programs mentioned above; and while we do prefer any of them to New York Word, they cannot be said to be ten times better than this fine program.

Although the program is at its best when accessed through its logical and easy to learn command structure, it does offer a menu-driven mode, allowing for all of its major functions to be accessed by means of pull-down menus and sub-menus. This, in effect, gives the user a choice: speed or ease of learning and use.

Among the program's most welcomed features is an excellent footnote-generating capability. As with other leading packages, footnoted text is marked as such, but the actual footnotes do not appear on screen unless one wishes to view them. Viewing existing footnotes is a simple matter, as is creating or changing them. Similarly, headers and footers are also supported.

The program also offers a very useful line drawing capability. Eleven different ANSI graphics characters are supported; these include horizontal and vertical lines, crosses, and corners, as well as various "T" shapes. With the line drawing capability, it is possible to design forms, do flow charts and otherwise enhance the printed page. Many otherwise powerful word processing packages do not include this valuable feature.

The program is also capable of generating an index and a table of contents for any given file. Text to be included in either an index or a table of contents is simply marked, and then its ultimate destination (e.g., as part of an index or a table of contents) is specified, all through a series of three simple keystrokes. This is a further feature not found in many competing packages.

New York Word also offers an excellent macro generating facility. With a macro-definition capability, it is possible to record a set of keystrokes and play them back later. Any sequence of keystrokes can be recorded and played back in the future by selecting it from a pull-down menu, or by using the macro replay command. Repetitive keystrokes which are used time and time again may be recorded and replayed with ease; in this way, a letterhead can be called up with two keystrokes, as can a salutation, or any such often-used boilerplate.

The program also offers a built-in calculator which allows for "on-the-fly" calculations without having to exit the program. It is also possible to incorporate the results of such mathematical calculations into the document currently being worked on.

Mail merge capabilities are also supported. This feature, available with most every professional word processing package available today, allows a

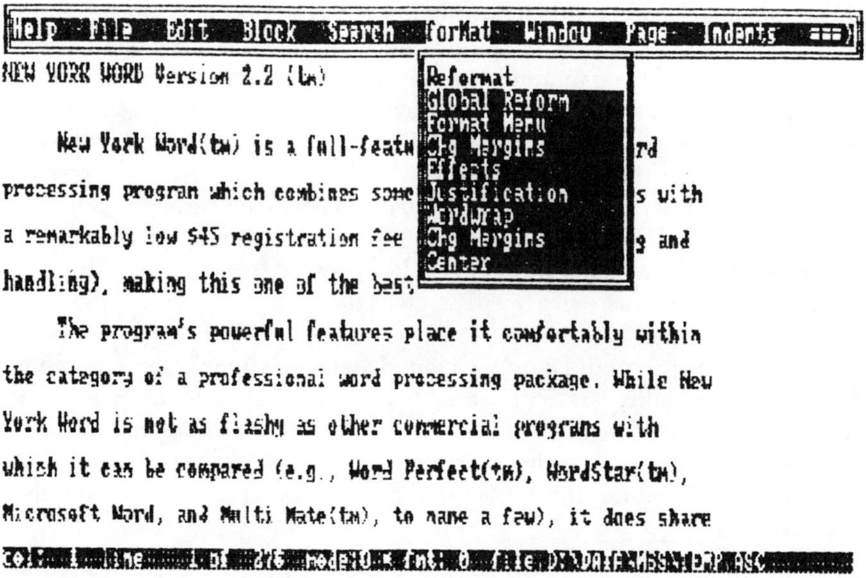

Figure 1.25: Pull-down menus and help screens remain out of the way until needed, when they can be called up by a simple two-key command ([ALT]-M for Menus and [ALT]-H for Help screens).

user to personalize letters or other documents for mass mailings. With this feature, a master document is created which provides for some "blanks" to be filled in by information contained in another file. In this way, it is possible to send, for example, a party invitation to any number of people which *appears* to have been written just for them, although only *one* master document has been written and later "merged" with a list of people meant to receive it; in this way, it is possible for companies who conduct contests as a means of boosting business to mail out millions of personalized letters which appear to have been individually prepared (i.e., Congratulations, Mr. John Doe, of 123-45 67th Street, Anytown, USA, you are one of 10 people from Anytown who may already have won $25,000,000,000 in the Read 'Em and Weep Sweepstakes . . .). The mail merge program available with New York Word is very versatile and includes some database capabilities such as the ability to select records for any given merged document through logical filters.

A spelling checker is also available with New York Word. The program flags suspect words and gives the writer the option of entering a proper spelling, ignoring the word or adding it (if it is properly spelled) to the built-in dictionary. Although it is not able to automatically replace misspelled words

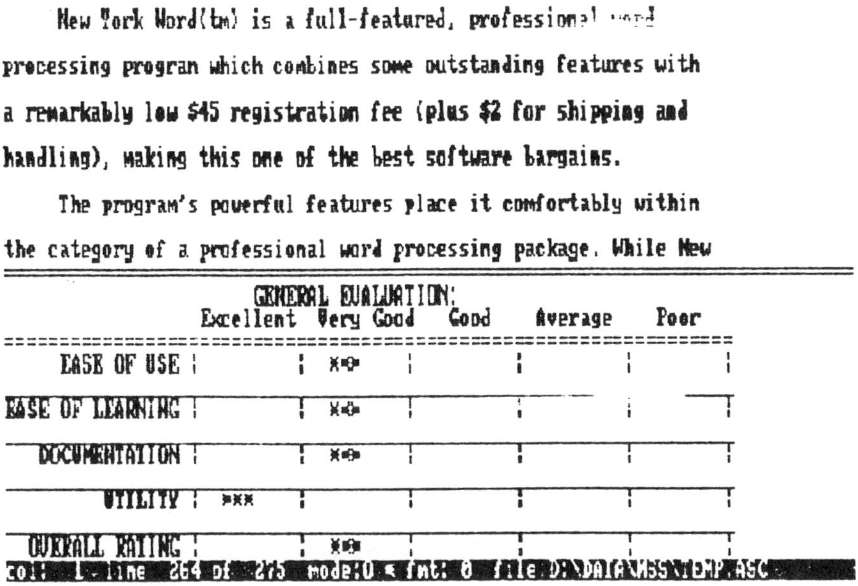

New York Word(tm) is a full-featured, professional word processing program which combines some outstanding features with a remarkably low $45 registration fee (plus $2 for shipping and handling), making this one of the best software bargains.

The program's powerful features place it comfortably within the category of a professional word processing package. While New

GENERAL EVALUATION:

	Excellent	Very Good	Good	Average	Poor
EASE OF USE		*+			
EASE OF LEARNING		*+			
DOCUMENTATION		*+			
UTILITY	***				
OVERALL RATING		*+			

col: 1 line 264 of 275 mode:0 < fmt: 0 file D:\DATA\M55\TEMP.ASC

Figure 1.26: Multiple windows are supported, allowing up to 12 different documents to be worked on at once—more than most other commercial programs. Here, different portions of the same file (the beginning and end) are being worked on at once.

with a selected replacement, it does offer helpful suggestions for proper spelling. This feature, while uninspired, is adequate.

Additional features supported by New York Word include auto alignment (useful for working with columns of numbers), optional auto hyphenation with several options, auto backup of work in progress, auto indent for new paragraphs and variable scrolling speeds.

A 46-page manual on disk is included with the distribution copy of the program. The manual, like the program, is well planned and implemented. There is a good table of contents which is very useful as a reference tool. There are also command summaries in each chapter. A comprehensive online help system is also available.

New York Word is a useful, flexible and quite powerful word processing program which incorporates most of the features found in the leading packages today in an inexpensive, easy-to-learn word processor. Because this is not a flashy system, it is easy to pass up when one is considering word processing packages. At first glance, it can seem at best adequate, if somewhat dull. But once one gets down to the business of writing, the program proves itself very quickly to be a powerful tool. Like a pencil, it may not be flashy or particularly exciting to use, but it can certainly get the job done.

Program: New York Word Ver. 2.2 © 1984, 1986
Author: Mark Adler
Company: Magma Software Systems
Address: 138-23 Hoover Avenue, Jamaica, NY 11435
Category: Word Processing
Registration Fee: $45 plus $2 for shipping and handling

General Evaluation: New York Word Ver. 2.2

	Excellent	*Very Good*	*Good*	*Average*	*Poor*
Ease of Use		***			
Ease of Learning		***			
Documentation		***			
Utility	***				
Overall Rating		***			

Outline!™ Version 3.14

While the computer has provided writers with an invaluable productivity tool, no machine or software package can actually write by itself—at least not yet, though that may change in years to come with the advent of ever more powerful computers and Artificial Intelligence programs. For the time being, though, the writer must still carefully organize his or her thoughts, selecting which ideas to develop, which to discard and choosing which words will best convey the selected ideas before finally committing them to paper. Word processors can be of tremendous help in manipulating text and enhancing its output, but they can do little by way of actually assisting with the organizational process. For assistance in that area, one can turn to an outline processor—a program designed to help in the outlining of ideas.

Outline! is a program designed to assist in organizing ideas into logical, hierarchical structures. The program is useful not just for writers, but also for people involved in planning (e.g., project managers) who need a flexible means of organizing information.

The program offers a great deal of flexibility both in the way it can process information and in its ability to interface with other stand-alone programs. It can access files created by other programs as well as write files which can be read by them. It can also access ASCII files and output in that format, so that it can easily be integrated into programs that it does not directly support (most any word processor can export and import text files in standard ASCII format).

Among its many features, Outline! offers a hierarchical outlining

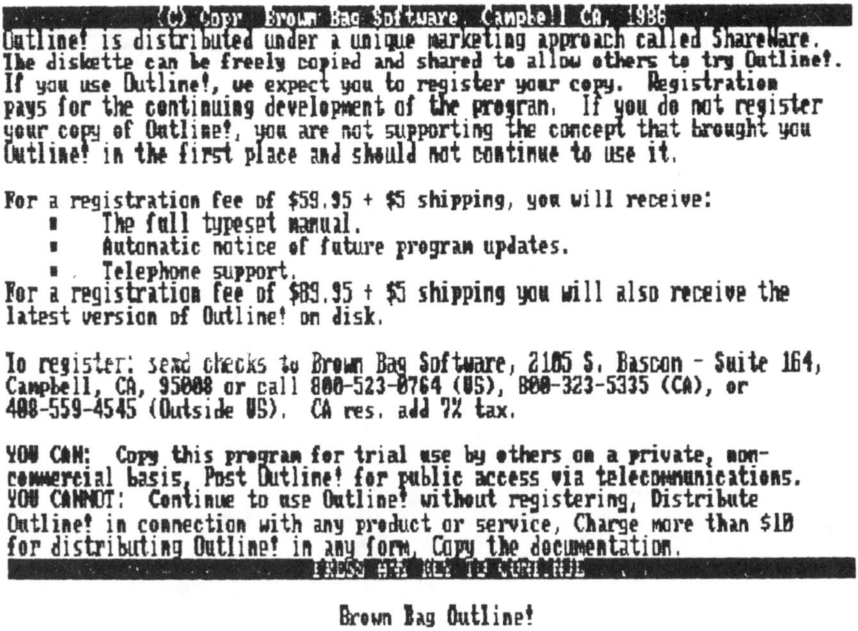

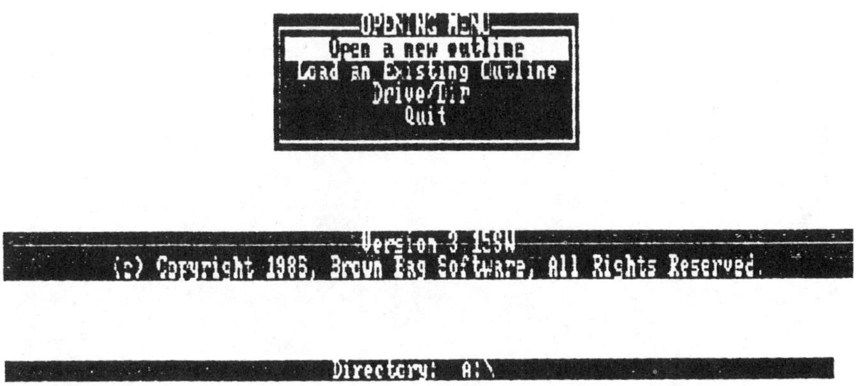

Top: **Figure 1.27: Opening screen and copyright notice for Outline!** *Bottom:* **Figure 1.28: Opening menu for Outline!**

structure, automatic indenting and numbering, full print enhancement and text formatting features, macro definitions, text search, replace and sort features, and the ability to incorporate textual material within outlines. The program also allows for access to selective areas of an outline at any given time, with only certain categories of ideas showing on screen or printed onto paper (designated portions of an outline with their subordinate

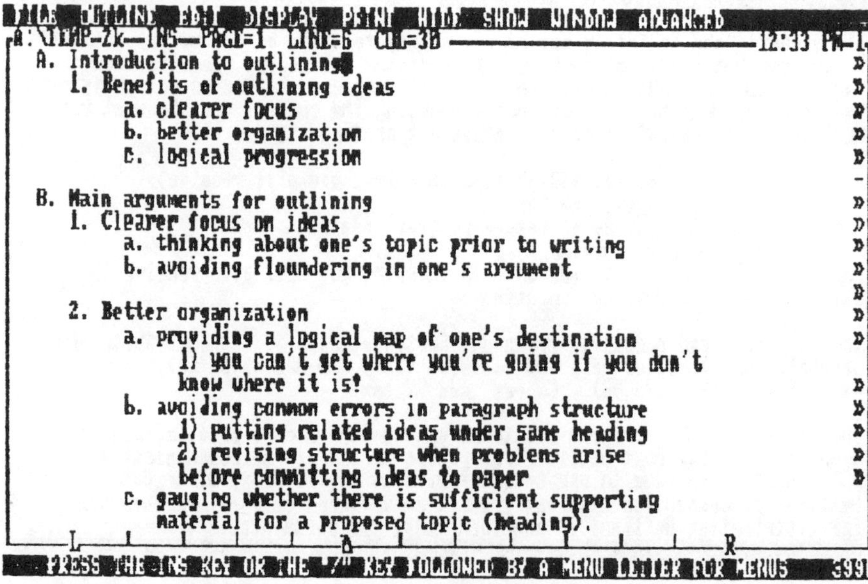

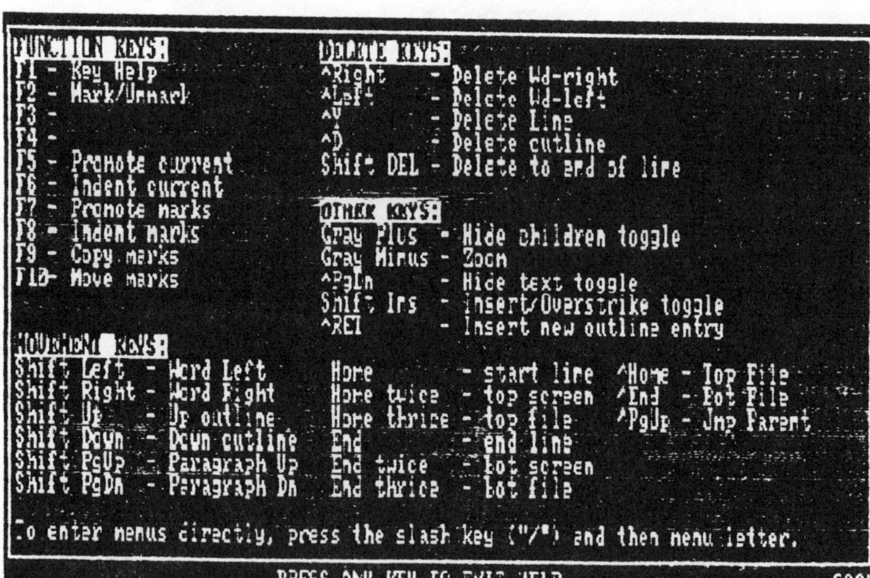

Top: **Figure 1.29: Sample outline being edited in Outline!** *Bottom:* **Figure 1.30: Main help screen for Outline!**

heading can be hidden at any time). Multiple windows are also supported, making it possible to simultaneously work with up to nine outlines at any given time, and to switch beteween them at will (copying blocks of text from one outline to another is also supported through the windows feature). The program can be used as a stand-alone system or run in memory resident mode, so that it can be called up from within any other applications program; if the memory-resident mode is selected, the program can be "popped up" from any word processor, permitting an outline to be called up at any time and referred to as the actual document it relates to is written—a feature most every writer will appreciate.

For all of its offered power and flexibility, Outline! is relatively easy to use. The program incorporates excellent on-screen help along with comprehensive pull-down menus. The 26-page abridged manual included with the evaluation copy of the program is clearly written, incorporates a good table of contents and includes a comprehensive command reference listing the major commands recognized by the program as well as functions assigned to specific keys. The net result is that a user is able to begin using the program after investing an hour or so in familiarizing himself or herself with the program's documentation and menu system. After that, the more advanced features can be learned gradually.

Outline! is included with some professional word processors, such as WordStar Ver. 5.0 as a stand-alone outlining program. That companies such as Micro Pro thought enough of this program to license it for inclusion with their leading word processing packages is interesting in itself. Fortunately, the program is also available through the shareware form of software distribution so that it can be tried by anyone for the modest copying cost charged by many user's groups or software copying services. Users who like and will continue to use the program can register their copies for a modest $59.95 plus $5 shipping and handling. Registration brings with it the complete bound version of the manual. (Outline! can be used with most any word processing package, including every one reviewed herein.)

The primary cause of weak writing (grammar and syntax aside) is poor organization; writers who begin writing without spending enough time *thinking* about where they intend to go with an idea (or how to get there) invariably get lost. An outline is as essential to writing as a roadmap is to driving in unfamiliar territory; while some drivers can invariably "find their way" just about anywhere without a map, most cannot and would be foolish to try. By using an outline, most anyone's writing can be better focused, more organized and, consequently, much improved. Outline! offers much welcomed assistance in "idea processing," as opposed to simple "word processing," where too much emphasis is often placed. As such, it is a program well worth exploring by anyone who could benefit from assistance in the organization of ideas, projects or tasks.

Program: Outline! Ver. 3.14 © 1986
Author: Marc Adler
Company: Brown Bag Software
Address: 2105 S. Bascom—Suite 164, Campbell, CA 95008
Category: Outline Processing
Registration Fee: $59.95 plus $5 shipping and handling
(Includes non-abridged, bound manual)

General Evaluation: Outline!: Ver. 3.14

	Excellent	*Very Good*	*Good*	*Average*	*Poor*
Ease of Use	***				
Ease of Learning		***			
Documentation		***			
Utility	***				
Overall Rating	***				

PC-Style™ Version 1.0

PC-Style is one of many fine programs from Jim Button of Buttonware. As its name implies, the program is a style checker. It has the ability to analyze text and make useful comments on the writer's style.

The program is so simple to use as to require no documentation, although a disk-based 17-page manual is included with it. Once the program is loaded, it prompts the user for the name of a file to be checked (it supports hard disk drives and subdirectories). The file name, along with its full path (if applicable) are typed in by the user, and the program then automatically loads the file and analyzes it. A graphics representation of the key areas checked for is shown on screen as the program checks through the document, with a sliding indicator shifting from one side of the scale to the other (best to worst) in key areas as the text is analyzed. Once the analysis is complete, a matter which takes only seconds for all but the lengthiest of documents, the results may be viewed on screen or sent to a printer.

PC-Style reports on the following areas: number of words per sentence, percentage of long words, percentage of personal words, percentage of action verbs, average number of syllables per word and readability level. Numerical scores are given in each area, as well as a graphic representation of the relative strength or weakness of the writing. The program, although useful as a general guide to the complexity of one's writing, is limited in its ability to recognize verbs or personal words (two categories in which writing is rated). Users can, however, expand the program's built-in lexicon.

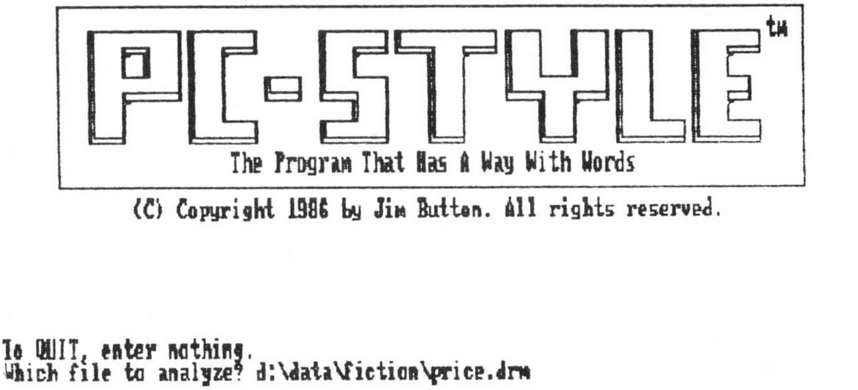

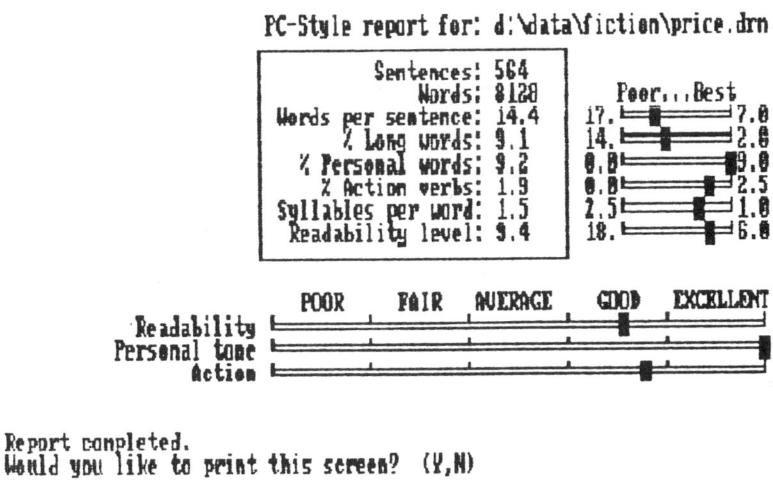

***Top:* Figure 1.31: Opening screen and copyright notice for PC-Style. *Bottom:* Figure 1.32: Actual report screen for a short story analyzed by PC-Style. The program is perhaps most useful for analyzing fiction, where personal tone, personal pronouns and action verbs are likeliest to be of importance. For factual writing, the program's evaluation may be misleading.**

As with any style or grammar checker, one should exercise good judgment in evaluating its reported results and be neither overly discouraged nor encouraged by its judgments. In general, however, PC-Style and programs like it which are available commercially can be quite useful in pointing out potential strengths and weaknesses in one's writing. And its results are not always predictable, even for the same writer. In trying out the program, I had it analyze three different files which I had written, each ranged in length between 25 and 60 double-spaced typed pages. Not surprisingly, a technical report on the law affecting timeshare ownership of coops and condominiums earned low grades in personal style, readability and action verbs. Sentence length was also judged poor (overly complex sentences). On the other hand, the program gave very high scores to a short story I'd recently written in all areas, and it was lukewarm with regard to portions of this book. (I also analyzed a half dozen sonnets, and the score was off the scale in the positive range in all rated areas.) The program obviously likes brevity and personal language, along with action verbs it can recognize. Where it finds it, such as in a sonnet or work of fiction with plenty of realistic dialogue, it awards high marks. When it does not, such as in technically complex material, it gives low marks. The ratings can, in any event, be useful in pointing out potential problems in the areas evaluated.

Program: PC-Style Ver. 1.1 © 1986
Author: Jim Button
Company: Buttonware, Inc.
Address: P.O. Box 5786, Bellevue, WA 98006
Category: Word Processing
Registration Fee: $29.95 plus $5 shipping and handling

General Evaluation: PC-Style Ver. 1.0

	Excellent	*Very Good*	*Good*	*Average*	*Poor*
Ease of Use	***				
Ease of Learning	***				
Documentation		***			
Utility		***			
Overall Rating		***			

2: Spreadsheet Programs

Introduction

When electronic calculators first appeared on the scene in the early 1970s, they seemed like wondrous devices. Although they cost several hundred dollars, they could do amazing things, like adding, subtracting, multiplying and dividing huge numbers—up to eight digits—in a flash, and they could perform floating point calculations. When true scientific calculators from Texas Instruments, Hewlett Packard and other leading companies arrived on the scene, many made a beeline for the nearest retailers to get their hands on these marvelous devices, wondering what technological wonders awaited them in the future, and hoping that such wonders would never cease.

Some 15 years later, we haven't been disappointed. There are now dozens of powerful spreadsheet programs which can crunch numbers faster and with greater ease than we could have envisioned in our most extravagant of those early silicon dreams. All of the programs reviewed in the following pages are far more powerful in their mathematical applications than any early hand-held calculator, and their price certainly cannot be beat.

Of all the marvelously diverse applications which a computer is able to perform, its ability to manipulate numbers is its strongest attribute. After all, numbers are the foundation upon which all computer operations rest, and the binary system which regulates the way a computer processes all information is its native language. Processing numerical data is, therefore, not surprisingly what a computer does best. And the program of choice for processing numerical data is unquestionably the spreadsheet. With it, it is possible to perform nearly any mathematical operation, from balancing your checkbook to keeping the books for any business.

Using a spreadsheet, it is possible to perform an almost limitless number of "what if" calculations. For example, if you are thinking about buying a house and would like to find out what the real monthly cost of a mortgage would be, a simple spreadsheet program can give you the answer in less than a minute—try finding out what a $200,000 mortgage at 11.5 percent for 30 years will cost you per month using paper, pencil and an amortization table! Not only can the computer perform calculations in minutes which would take hours or even days to figure out in traditional ways, but it can also allow you to change key numbers in an equation and get an almost instantaneous result. For example, what if you wanted to borrow only $150,000 with a payback period of 20 years? What if you factor in your federal and state tax savings on the interest paid on the mortgage? What if you rent part of the property and take a depreciation allowance on the rental portion of the home? The number of "what if" calculations are endless, and the answers are always just a few keystrokes—and minutes— away.

Once you explore the power of spreadsheet programs, you'll wonder how people have gotten along with pencil and paper (and their ten fingers and ten toes) for thousands of years without them. And you'll no more go back to the latter than you would give up your automobile in favor of a quaint pair of thongs.

AsEasyAs™ Version 3.01B

AsEasyAs is a full-featured spreadsheet program which incorporates both graphics and database capabilities. As its name implies, the program is similar in the way it looks and operates to the best-selling LOTUS 1-2-3 program. Users familiar with LOTUS 1-2-3 will have little difficulty using AsEasyAs without need for additional training. Both programs share similar file structure, so that spreadsheet files created with LOTUS are usable with AsEasyAs, and vice-versa.

The program is loaded by typing ASEASY followed by a carriage return at the system prompt. It is possible to set up the program to run under a variety of options when initially loading it to tailor AsEasyAs to the user's available graphics display. The available options are as follows:

- Q Quick screen options (speeds up screen input/output)
- E Enhanced graphics display (640 × 350 resolution)
- H Hercules graphics display (720 × 348—single page display)
- H Hercules graphics display (enables second graphics page)
- O Overlay file on disk (reads overlay file for the program from disk, instead of RAM, to save memory for systems with limited Random Access Memory)
- ATT Enables AT&T graphics display (640 × 400 resolution)
- M Menu color (for color monitors)
- G Graph color (for color monitors)
- F Foreground color (for color monitors)
- B Background color (for color monitors)

Under the above-noted options, a user who types ASEASY /O/H followed by a carriage return will enter AsEasyAs set up for a Hercules monitor and with overlays files accessed from disk to save limited Random Access Memory.

AsEasyAs offers extensive formatting capabilities for both spreadsheet cells, columns and print output. Cells may be formatted to display both numbers and text data. Numerical data may be displayed in a variety of formats, including the following:

Fixed:	123.45 (rounded to two decimal places)
Scientific Notation:	1.234E + 10
Comma:	1,234.0
Currency:	$1,234.56
Percent:	12.34
Text:	This is text.
+/−:	+ + + + + + + + + +
Date:	15 April, 89 (six different forms)
Hide:	[invisible cell]
Reset:	[return to global format]

Print output may also be formatted in a variety of ways. The program enables the setting of margins for the printed page, as well as headers, footers and line spacing. Printer controls may also be set to allow printers to output emphasized, double-strike, condensed and enlarged text. Line spacing may also be set to 1/8″, 7/72″ and 1/6″ for maximum flexibility. It is also possible to output data from a spreadsheet to an ASCII disk file instead of a printer; such data can then be imported into most any word processor and further manipulated or incorporated into written reports.

AsEasyAs also provides good graphics capabilities. Bar graphs, stacked bar graphs and pie charts, among others, may be created from spreadsheet files.

For ease of use, the program also permits the setup and use of macros—a means of programming certain keys to automatically execute given functions (ideal for executing complicated and repetitive key sequences automatically with only two keystrokes). The program also makes extensive use of function keys to minimize repetitive keystrokes. The combined use of macros and preprogrammed function keys increases the program's ease of use.

The program also offers logical functions and sorting capabilities. Ranges of cells may be sorted in a variety of ways, and logical operations (e.g., If-Then-Else statements) may be used both in devising spreadsheet formulas between cells and in text retrieval. With regard to the latter, the program can support basic database search and retrieval functions.

-•• AsEasyAs •• Version 3.01 B, (C) Copyright, TRIUS,Inc 1985,1986,1987,1988-

You may copy and distribute UNMODIFIED copies of this disk (BUT NOT THE MANUAL), provided that NO FEE or consideration is charged, and that this notice is not bypassed or removed.

AS-EASY-AS tm

If you find AsEasyAs useful, we expect you to register your copy. Registration costs $40.00 US (First Class or UPS is $45.00) and provides you with the current AsEasyAs DISK, printed, bound MANUAL and on-line HELP SCREENS. Site licenses and volume discounts are also available.

To register in the U.S. and Canada, send a Check/M. Order/P. Order to:
TRIUS Inc., 15 Atkinson St., Lynn, MA, 01905.
(International orders - Add $5.00 for S&H. Sorry, only US currency)

Copies in Europe can be registered with:
Shareware Marketing, 87 High Street, Tonbridge, Kent TN9 1RX, ENGLAND
Tel. (0732) 771344

See the Help Screens (press F1) for ready-made order forms and startup INFO.

Figure 2.2: Opening menu for AsEasyAs.

AsEasyAs also allows various date calculations similar to those supported by LOTUS 1-2-3 [e.g., @TODAY, @YEAR(×), @MONTH(×) and @DAY(×)]. Hence, elapsed days and future days may be automatically calculated based on either the system date or any given date entered from the keyboard.

Although the evaluation copy of the program does not contain a text-based manual (a printed manual is available only upon registration), it does incorporate a useful HELP feature. An on-line help may be called up at any time by depressing the F1 function key. The on-screen help text encompasses 58 screens of helpful information and includes many examples of how to implement the program's many features. The Help screens may be scrolled and read from beginning to end, or may be called up by a number of categories. Any given Help screen may, of course, be printed on paper by using the Shift-PrtSc screen-dump key sequence (pressing the Shift key and the PrtSc key simultaneously will dump the contents of any screen to a printer) for later reference.

AsEasyAs uses pull-down menus similar to those of LOTUS 1-2-3. The menus are logically organized and, for the most part, self-explanatory so that a user with some previous experience with any spreadsheet program will have little difficulty setting up a spreadsheet file without need to refer to the Help screens. Even users with no previous experience with spreadsheets will soon become familiar with the basic features of the program by reading the Help files and loading some of the included sample worksheets.

Opposite: **Figure 2.1: Opening screen and copyright notice for AsEasyAs.**

```
F1:Help 2:Edit 3:Macro 4:Abs     Ready !    5:Goto 6:Window 9:Calc F10:Graph
B4 [C2]: 25000

 ...........................A/.......................B/C/......................D/.....
  1 1988 FEDERAL INCOME TAX LIABILITY WORKSHEET                    21-Apr-89
  2
  3 ===================================================================================
  4 YEARLY GROSS INCOME:                     $25,000.00
  5 NUMBER OF DEPENDENTS:                             1
  6 STANDARD DEDUCTION:                       $3,000.00
  7
  8 ADJUSTED G.I.:                           $20,100.00
  9
 10 FED. TAX LIABILITY:                       $3,301.00
 11
 12 FICA TAX:                                      1875
 13 NEW YORK CITY/STATE TAX:                       2613
 14
 15
 16
 17
 18 NET YEARLY INCOME:                       $17,211.00
 19 NET WEEKLY INCOME:                          $330.98
 20 NET BI-WEEKLY INCOME:                       $661.96
   Free:99 % [304k]  Auto  [88FEDTAX.WK1]                              6:24:53 pm
```

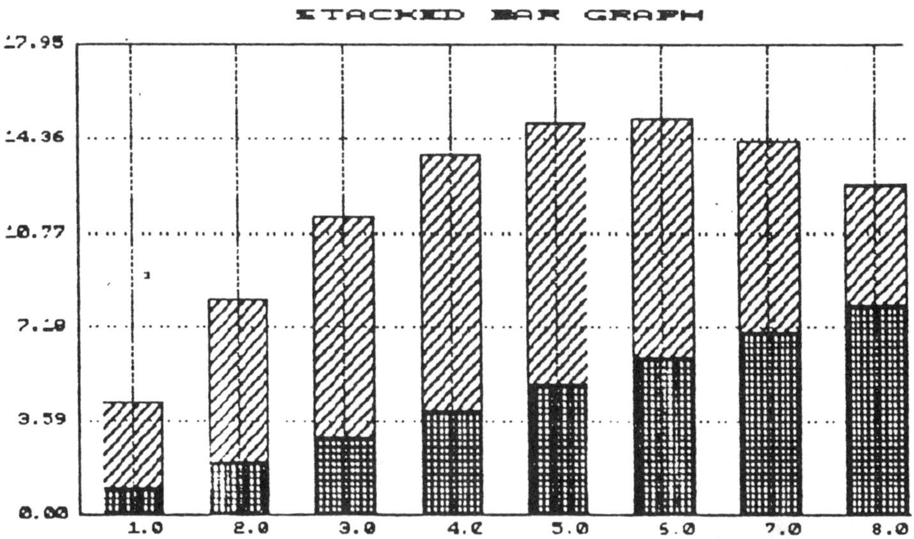

Figure 2.4: Stacked bar graph created with AsEasyAs. The program can create and print a wide variety of graphs, including line graphs, bar graphs and pie charts.

AsEasyAs is a powerful, full-featured and fast program which is relatively easy to learn and use. It has the additional benefit of file compatibility with LOTUS *.WKS files. This attribute makes available to users of AsEasyAs the hundreds if not thousands, of database files available in the public domain and through other sources for use with LOTUS 1-2-3. In addition to being an excellent stand-alone alternative to other leading spreadsheet programs listpriced for $500 and more, AsEasyAs is an ideal program for professionals who must use LOTUS 1-2-3 daily at work and who may wish to occasionally work on their LOTUS files at home without having to pay the relatively high cost of that program. For the modest price of the registration fee ($40 plus $5 for first class mail or UPS), these users will own a program with which they will feel immediately comfortable. And, as with all Shareware offerings, they need risk nothing to try it first. If it does not fit their needs, there is no obligation to register. They will lose only the $2 to $5 per disk copying charge which most user's groups and copying service companies charge for copies of any public-domain or shareware offering.

Program: AsEasyAs Ver. 3.01B © 1985, 1986
Author: N/A

Opposite: **Figure 2.3: Simple spreadsheet running in AsEasyAs.**

Company: TRIUS, Inc.
Address: 15 Atkinson Street, Lynn, MA 01905
Category: Spreadsheet
Registration Fee: $40 (U.S.). Add $5 for 1st class mail or UPS (international orders $5 additional for shipping and handling). Copies in Europe may be registered with Shareware Marketing, 87 High Street, Tonbridge, Kent TN9 IRX, England.
Telephone: (0732) 771344

General Evaluation: AsEasyAs Ver. 3.01B

	Excellent	*Very Good*	*Good*	*Average*	*Poor*
Ease of Use	***				
Ease of Learning		***			
Documentation			***		
Utility	***				
Overall Rating	***				

FreeCalc™ Version 2.0

FreeCalc is an easy to use, entry-level electronic spreadsheet program with some interesting features. It supports spreadsheets of up to 250 rows and 50 columns, for a total of 12,500 cells. These limits, while smaller than many professional spreadsheet programs, nevertheless allow FreeCalc to be used for some rather extensive applications.

The program uses a pull-down menu system which is intuitive and easy to implement. It allows a user to choose from the program's many options by typing the first letter of the command they wish to implement; all commands are listed on screen and are, for the most part, self-explanatory.

FreeCalc offers features found in most good spreadsheet programs. Commands for inserting data and formulas into a spreadsheet, erasing, copying and reformatting either whole spreadsheets or any portion thereof, loading and saving work files, manual and automatic recalculation of spreadsheets and report generation are all supported. In addition, the program contains a simple word processor which can be used to write memos, letters or reports with relative ease. The built-in word processor, while by no means a full-feature one, allows for inserting, deleting, copying and moving blocks of text, as well as changing margins. Some basic features found in even modest word processing programs (such as automatic text wrapping at the end of a line) are, however, missing from what is essentially a very basic text editor.

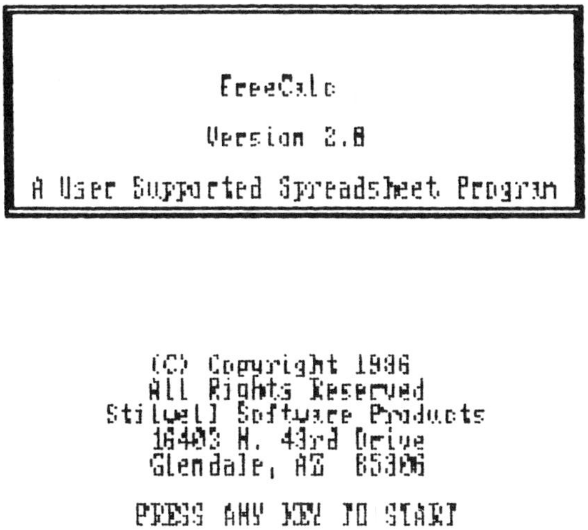

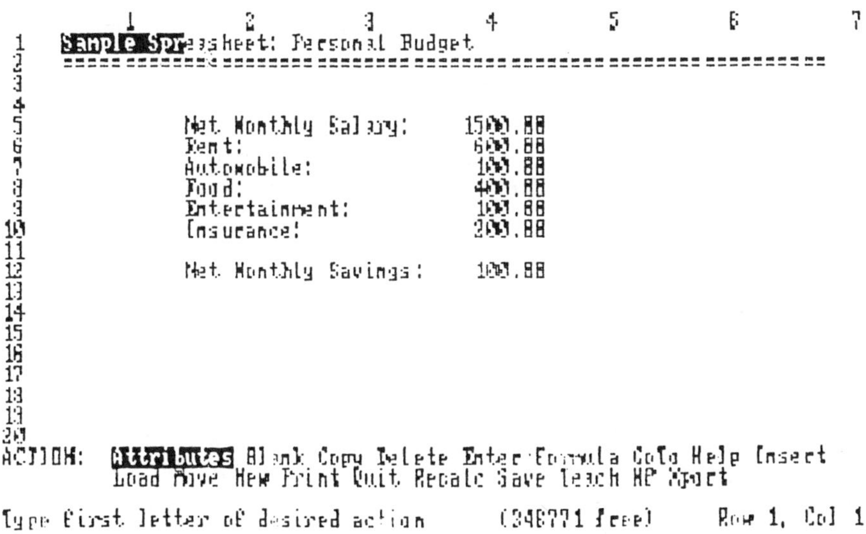

***Top:* Figure 2.5: FreeCalc opening screen and copyright notice. *Bottom:* Figure 2.6: Simple spreadsheet created with FreeCalc.**

A rather interesting feature of the program is its ability to assist users with the creation of formulas for their spreadsheets. Two modes for formula creation are supported: a "user supplied" formula mode, and a "system supplied" mode. The former mode is similar to most other spreadsheet programs; a user manually enters formulas into given cells in the spreadsheet, and may relate these to other cells in the same spreadsheet. The latter

HELP

Please select the item you would like help with:

1. Attributes	12. Load
2. Blank	13. Move
3. Color of screen	14. New
4. Copy	15. Print
5. Cursor movement	16. Quit
6. Delete	17. Recalc
7. Directory	18. Save
8. Enter	19. Teach (Macros)
9. Formula	20. The FreeCalc Auditor
10. GoTo	21. User supported software
11. Insert	22. WP (Word Processing)
	23. Xport

ESC Return to main menu

Figure 2.7: Help menu for FreeCalc (accessed with F1 at any time).

("system supplied" formula mode) is an unusual and useful method of creating formulas with the aid of the program; built-in mathematical operations such as Sum, Minus, Average, Greatest Value, Least Value and Count are selected from on-screen menus and the program fills the mathematical formulas into a chosen cell for the user. For inexperienced users, this feature can be quite handy. It works somewhat like the "Assist" mode in dBase III Plus. As selections are made from the on-screen menus, the program automatically writes the formula equivalent on whatever part of the spreadsheet is selected to accept these formulas.) As an example, if a user wishes to add the values contained in three spreadsheet cells, she may write out the formula where she wants it to appear in the spreadsheet as: SUM R1C1 THRU R3C1. The program will then add whatever numbers it finds in the cells R1C1, R2C1 and R3C1 and give an answer. Through the "system supplied" formula method, the user may select the SUM option from the on-screen menu and then enter the cells to be added when the program asks for that information; the program will then write the formula for the user and perform the requested mathematical operations automatically. In a sense, the user is walked through the formula writing process systematically, making it more difficult for a mistake to be made in the creation of formulas.

The evaluation copy of FreeCalc contains a 108-page manual on disk. Like most shareware programs, the disk-based manual may be printed for easy reference. It is well written and covers all of the program's functions. Examples are used throughout, allowing readers to better understand how

It is possible to do limited word processing using FreeCalc (if you find you need additional word processing features you might want to look at Stilwell Software Products' word processor called FreeWord).

To perform word processing with FreeCalc, change the width of column 1 (see the help section for the Attributes option if you are uncertain how to do this) to be whatever you want for a left margin (e.g., 7). Next, change the width of column 2 for the width of the document (e.g., 65). Select the WP option from the Main Action Menu. Normally when entering a cell defined as "Alpha", FreeCalc will automatically move you to the next column once the cell if filled if that next column is empty. By selecting the WP option and entering a "Y" to enter the WP mode, you can turn that feature off. FreeCalc will then beep when you have reached the end of the cell.

Select the Enter option from the Main Action Menu, and then select to enter Alpha data. You can now start typing. When you get to the end of the cell, FreeCalc will beep. You can press the DOWN arrow key to move to the next row and remain in the enter alpha data mode. You can also select to center the text you are typing, to alien flush on the left side, or to alien flush on the right side.

Figure 2.8: Sample help screen on word processing feature.

to use the program. Furthermore, FreeCalc includes on-line help screens which are indexed to the program's main features; most users' questions will be answered in the help files which can be accessed at any time without need to exit the program. Along with the informative help screens and printable manual, the program includes three ready to use demonstration files: DEMO1.FC, DEMO2.FC and DEMO3.FC. The first two of these provide users with personal budget files, and the third contains a sample budget forecast spreadsheet for an imaginary business. The manual covers these three demonstration spreadsheets through some tutorial applications so users may manipulate data in the three spreadsheets and add some additional formulas to get a good feel of how spreadsheets are constructed and used. After examining all three files and making the changes suggested in the disk-based manual, even users with no prior exposure to spreadsheets will be able to set up their own electronic spreadsheet with ease.

The program diverges slightly from the accepted standard of naming rows and columns. In most basic or full-featured spreadsheet programs, rows are assigned numbers and columns letters. For reasons known only to the program's author, FreeCalc assigns numbers to both rows and columns. Thus, where the first cell on other spreadsheets is normally assigned the name A1 (the intersection of Column "A" with Row "1"), the same column would be called R1C1 in this program (Row "1" Column "1"). This is by no means a problem, since the program does otherwise adhere to other spreadsheet conventions. For an advanced user, however, the designation of numbers to both rows and columns takes a little getting used to.

Among the program's advanced features are a simple to learn macro definition program for assigning simple or complex functions to any key in the keyboard, and support for the Intel 8087 or 80287 math chips for dramatically improved performance in large spreadsheets for users who have added the optional coprocessor chips to their systems.

Registration cost for the program is $47.50. Users who register their programs will receive a bound copy of the manual, and an additional program, the FreeCalc Auditor, which assists in finding errors in any FreeCalc spreadsheet. Users who choose to register also qualify for telephone support.

FreeCalc is a program which works well, is relatively simple to learn and use, and contains many of the advanced features of leading spreadsheet programs. While it is not as powerful as LOTUS 1-2-3, Super Calc 4.0 or AsEasyAs, it contains ample features to meet most users' needs.

Program: FreeCalc Ver. 2.0 © 1986
Author: N/A
Company: Stilwell Software Products
Address: 16403 North 43rd Drive, Glendale, AZ 85306
Category: Spreadsheet
Registration Fee: $47.50 (Printed manual, supplemental error-tracing program and phone support are all available with registration at no additional cost.)

General Evaluation: FreeCalc Ver. 2.0

	Excellent	*Very Good*	*Good*	*Average*	*Poor*
Ease of Use		***			
Ease of Learning		***			
Documentation		***			
Utility			***		
Overall Rating		***			

PC-Calc™

PC-CALC is one in a notable series of distinguished programs from Jim Button of ButtonWare. The program incorporates a rare combination of ease of use and power not available in many of its high-priced commercial counterparts. It is available at a fraction of their cost.

```
PC-CALC (tm)

Version 3.0
October 1, 1985

(C)Copyright CALC, 1984
(C)Copyright ButtonWare, 1984
Portions (C)Copyright Microsoft Corporation, 1983
All Rights Reserved

Jim Button
P.O. Box 5786
Bellevue WA 98006 USA
```

Figure 2.9: Opening screen and copyright notice of PC-Calc Ver. 3.0.

Although the program comes with a 35-page printable *Evaluation Guide* on the distribution disk, users with previous exposure to spreadsheets will be able to use it immediately without reading the abridged manual; its well-designed user interface is easy to learn as are the commands. Users familiar with Super Calc versions 2.0 through 4.0 will find the command structure of PC-Calc evocative of that leading program.

The user's manual, an abridged version of the 155 typeset user's guide, is available upon registration. The brief manual is an excellent one which provides a good overview of the powerful features of PC-Calc. A person with little computer exposure will be able to set up and use a simple spreadsheet by simply reading and following along with the manual. An experienced user will find useful brief coverage of every PC-Calc command and samples of their use. It will serve both as a good introduction into PC-Calc and a quick reference guide until a user decides to register his copy and receives the more expansive and detailed printed *User Guide.*

The general features of PC-Calc include:

- —Maximum spreadsheet size: 64 columns by 256 rows
- —Support of up to 14 significant decimal places
- —Linking with other spreadsheets for three dimensional calculations (no limit to possible number of spreadsheets which can be accessed at one time)
- —Maximum contents in a cell: 75 characters
- —Math functions supported:

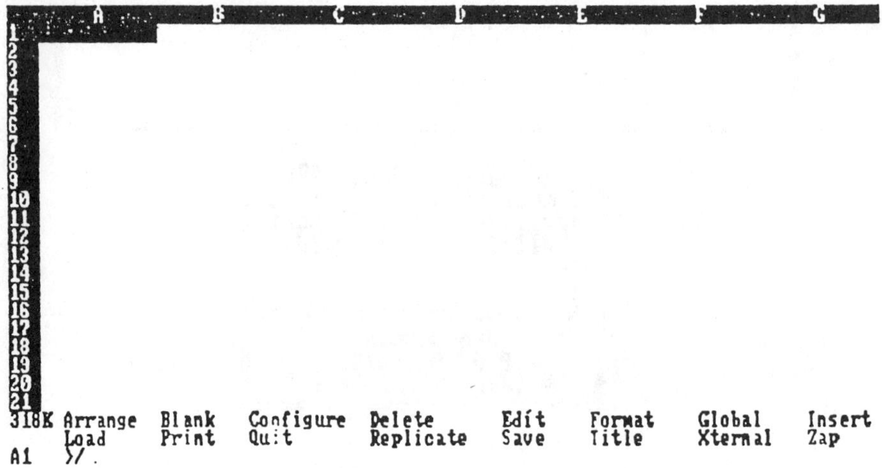

Figure 2.10: Opening menu for PC-Calc Ver. 3.0. Note the various functions available at the bottom of the screen. The menu is accessed by typing a slash [/] and the first letter of the function to be performed.

addition	[+]
subtraction	[−]
multiplication	[*]
division	[/]
exponents	[↑]
percentage	[%]
logical	[AND], [OR], [NOT], [IF], [THEN], [ELSE], [<], [>], [=]
remainder (modulo)	[/]
absolute value	[ABS]
arctangent	[ATN]
average	[AVERAGE]
cosine	[COS]
tangent	[TAN]
standard deviation	[STDEV]
fixed and floating decimals	
scientific notation	

Bar graphs

LOOKUP features

MAX	[Searches blocks, rows or columns and returns the largest number in a given range.]

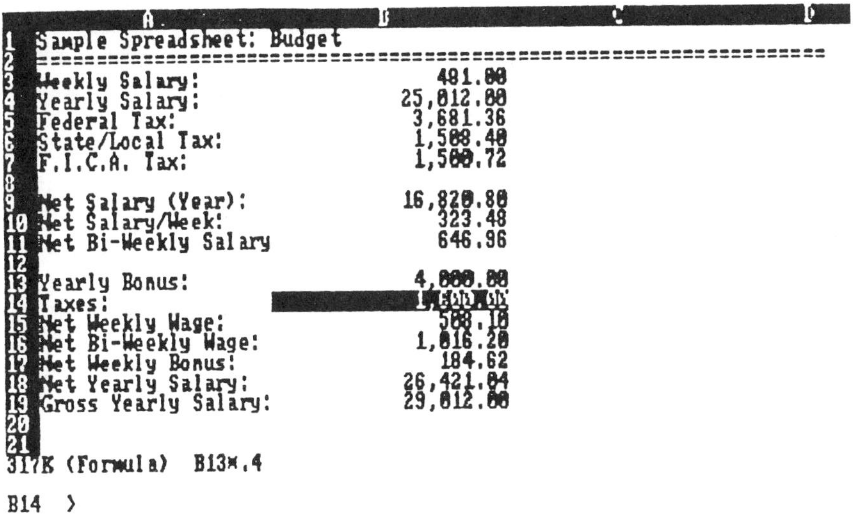

Figure 2.11: Simple spreadsheet running in PC-Calc.

Printer formatting	[10, 12 or 17 characters per inch]
Hide	[hides cells from screen or printed output]
Protect	[protects cell or range of cells]

System requirements for running PC-Calc:

- —IBM PC or compatible with minimum of 256K RAM
- —MS/DOS or PC/DOS version 2.0 or later
- —Monochrome or color card and monitor (40- or 80-column display. Can be configured for displays of a minimum of 8 lines—very useful when using older laptops with limited line displays)
- —A minimum of one double-sided, double density drive. Hard drives and electronic drives (RAM disks) may also be used.
- —May be configured for most any printer. Formatting options for Epson compatible printers are available.

Like other software offerings from ButtonWare reviewed elsewhere in this text (e.g., PC-File+, PC-Write, PC-Outline and PC-Style, PC-Calc is a useful, powerful and reasonably priced package which will nicely fill the needs of most users, be they beginners or advanced computerists. In addition, PC-Calc has the useful ability to interface with other ButtonWare products, so that an integrated software package capable of sharing files may be built, one module at a time, by a user for a relatively low cost. PC-Calc can import database files created with PC-File III Plus and perform mathematical calculations on numerical fields with ease. Likewise, PC-Calc files can be exported to PC-Write and incorporated into reports with that word processing program. (Printed reports may, of course, be directly printed from PC-Calc, just as they can from PC-File III Plus.) As a result, a user wishing to register all of his ButtonWare products will build a solid, interactive software library which will offer free support and low priced future updates for a total price well below the retail cost of a single software package such as LOTUS 1-2-3, Word Perfect Ver. 5.0 or dBASE 4.0. And, for the average user, these programs will provide all the power, flexibility and ease of use they are likely to ever need.

Program: PC-Calc © CALC 1948, 1985
Author: Jim Button
Company: ButtonWare, Inc.
Address: P.O. Box 5786, Bellevue, WA 98006
Category: Spreadsheet
Registration Fee: $59.95 plus $5 for shipping and handling
(Checks payable to: Jim Button)

General Evaluation: PC-Calc

	Excellent	*Very Good*	*Good*	*Average*	*Poor*
Ease of Use	***				
Ease of Learning	***				
Documentation		***			
Utility	***				
Overall Rating	***				

3: Database Management Programs

Introduction

One of the most powerful and useful attributes of the computer is its ability to quickly and easily manage information, particularly when large amounts of data are involved. Prior to the ready availability of personal computers in the 1980s, information had to be managed manually. In an office environment this meant that all records had to be kept in file cabinets, microfilm or other similar storage media. Information retrieval was a slow and cumbersome process which required clerical employees to manually search and retrieve needed information for reports, billing, and simply to maintain the daily flow of business. If an executive of a company involved in the sale of widgets wished to compile a list of all clients who had done business with the company in excess of $20,000 throughout the previous year, hundreds of personnel hours would be required to compile that report; file checks would have to retrieve every file, search it for the net yearly purchases of each client, compile data on every client falling within the stated sales figures and then turn over the information to a secretarial pool to type up the required report. Once all the data was gathered, files would have to be refiled. The process would be repeated every time a similar report was needed. The preparation of such reports was a costly and time consuming project which would not lightly be undertaken.

Once computers became widely available to businesses and individuals at a reasonable cost, the logistics of preparing such reports, and of record-keeping in general, changed drastically. Once a computerized system was set in place to keep track of a company's records, data retrieval and report preparation became a simple matter requiring minutes or hours, not days or weeks. And the whole process could be accomplished by a single computer operator with ease. In our example, a computer operator using a database management program could retrieve the needed sales figures in minutes by entering a few simple commands. Analysis of data, thus, has become an important business tool affordable by even the smallest company. Today, a company which retains a manual record-keeping system is the exception, not the rule. Computers are used in almost every department for data storage and retrieval. Personnel records, client lists, inventory, mass mailings, and most data-intensive tasks can be done by a computer faster, cheaper and more effectively than by any manual means.

The use of database programs is not reserved for business. There are dozens of applications from which the average home computerist can benefit. A user can set up a computerized personal phone directory, personal home inventory, record or tape collection, videotape guide, Christmas list file and so on. As an example, for those who exchange Christmas or Channukah greetings yearly, the repetitive addressing of envelopes can be a frustrating chore. Through the use of most any database program, the task can be automated and gummed labels can be generated yearly in minutes (or complete envelopes typed out directly from any dot-matrix, daisy wheel or laser printer). Names can be added or deleted in seconds, and a record of greeting cards received can also be kept. It is even possible to set up a database which automatically prints labels or envelopes only to friends who returned greeting cards last year (or once in the past three years, etc.). In the same way, it is easy to keep a computerized phone and address database which can access any person's name in seconds, or sort and print a hard copy of every person listed in alphabetical order by their first or last names. It is even possible to do mail merge mailings of letters to employers, friends (e.g., for party invitations) where every person on a given database file is sent the same letter with their name, address, mailing date, greeting and salutation included. (Why print out 100 cards to 100 different people when you can type out a single note and merge it with a database file to print out 100 personalized notes—and envelopes—automatically?)

Regardless of how basic or exacting your data-management needs are, you will find at least one of the following database management programs to be a wonderful productivity tool tailor-made to fit both your intended use and computer skills.

WAMPUM™ Version 3.2B

WAMPUM is a full-featured, professional database management program which is fully compatible with Ashton Tate's best-selling dBase III Plus program. Advanced users and programmers familiar with dBase will appreciate WAMPUM's menu-driven system. Using WAMPUM is not too different from using dBase III Plus in the Assist mode.

Unlike dBase, WAMPUM does not give the option of using either a command of menu mode; only a menu mode is available. Nevertheless, the menu system is sophisticated enough as to be transparent for most applications, and, at least for this writer, seems much more intuitive than that of dBase.

WAMPUM comes with a complete 81-page manual on disk. Although the program's available on-line help feature has been deleted from the evaluation copy by the author to allow the program to run on floppy-disk systems, the missing files are sent to users upon payment of the quite reasonable $25 registration fee. Even without on-line help, the evaluation copy of the program is fully functional. The manual provided on disk is an excellent one, and even users without extensive knowledge of database programs will be able to set up and run complicated databases within hours, not weeks, of acquiring the program (something not generally true of dBase III Plus). It is clearly written and direct, and it contains a comprehensive two-page index which is quite useful when searching for specific information. In addition, Ward Mundy, the program's author and owner, has taken the time to provide many useful examples of the implementation of WAMPUM's many features in the manual.

One of the most important attributes of any program is its flexibility (what we call "utility" or general usefulness in the review tables in this book); in general, the more features a program possesses, the higher its utility rating, since it will lend itself to a greater number of applications than its more limited counterparts. In this area, WAMPUM truly stands out. Its long list of sophisticated features and supporting programs allow WAMPUM to be useful in a veritable limitless number of applications. It can, for example, easily be adopted for use in any business (small, medium or large) as a stand-alone relational database system to keep employee records, track inventory, send out mass mailings to clients (it has both mail merge and label generating capabilities), keep tax records, maintain client lists, handle client billing, and generate a wide variety of business reports using multiple databases.

Although an in-depth look at all of WAMPUM's features is beyond the scope of this volume, its most salient features should at least be noted. These include:

—The ability to create and use dBase III Plus compatible databases, labels and reports;
—Network support (including password protection, audit trail, transaction logging, file locking and customized configurations for users in a network environment);
—Mail merge capabilities (letters, labels, etc.) with manipulation of up to five databases for each merged form;
—Support for up to ten printer fonts;
—Various field types, including: Char, Numeric, Date, Logical and Memo. (It also supports calculated fields);
—A library of preformatted output forms;
—Macro support (library of pre-defined macros is included);
—Global search and replace of up to ten elements in a single operation;

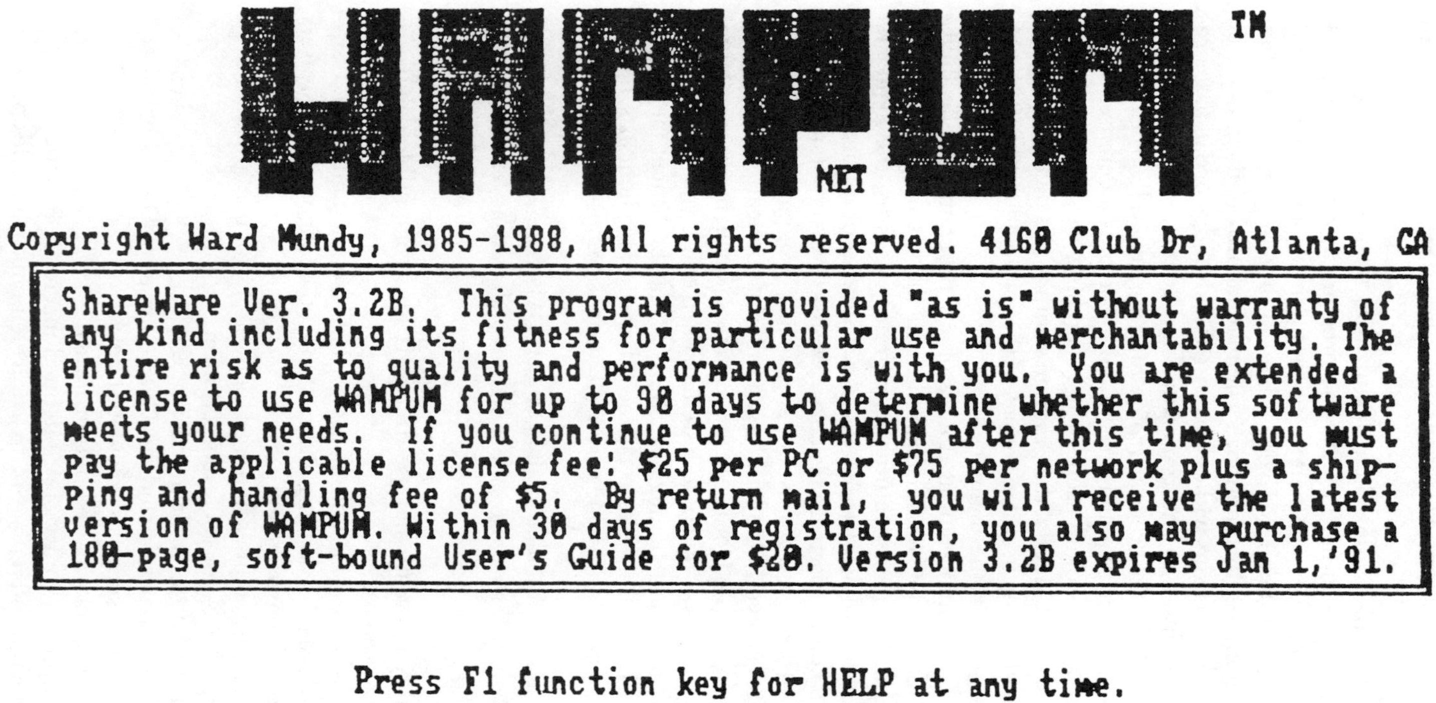

Figure 3.1: Opening screen and copyright notice for WAMPUM Ver. 3.2B.

—Field specification for file search requests;
—Configuration and use of up to seven indexes per database file.

WAMPUM supports two different modes: an End User Edition and a Developer's Edition. The End User mode is accessed by typing WAMPUM at the DOS prompt (or WAMPUM MONO for users with a monochrome display). In this mode, an end user may add information to an existing database, change information in an existing database or retrieve information from an existing database. The Developer's Edition, on the other hand, allows an end user to set up new databases and access the program's advanced features, such as generating form letters or labels. The latter mode is accessed by entering WAMPUM VOODOO (or WAMPUM VOODOO MONO for systems with a monochrome display) at the DOS prompt. Under the Developer's Edition, a database containing up to 400 different fields may be set up, although one is limited to a maximum of 128 different fields if dBase compatibility is desired. It is possible to set up some rather complicated databases with WAMPUM. Furthermore, the fact that up to seven different indexes may be used with any given database allows for a great deal of flexibilty in generating reports from any database, regardless of its relative simplicity or complexity. In addition, under the Developer's Edition, it is possible to change a database's existing file structure by altering existing field names, field lengths and field decimals, as well as adding new fields to existing database files. (If a field name or field type is changed, however, the data in the replaced field will be lost.)

With regard to dBase III Plus compatibility, databases, reports and labels are fully compatible, but indexes are not. Therefore, if a dBase file is used by WAMPUM, it must be reindexed. This is by no means a serious limitation, especially in view of the speed enhancement that WAMPUM provides over most dBase applications largely due to its indexing structure; generally, retrieval time for records is under one second, even when using rather large databases.

WAMPUM also provides excellent printer support which extends to laser printers. Up to nine different fonts may be used in any given report, letter or label applications. The program also allows for extensive use of keyboard macros; up to 39 different macros may be programmed into function keys to automatically execute lengthy, repetitive or time-consuming data entry tasks. Every program retains macro definitions set up for it, so that up to 39 different macros may be used in every separate database application.

The registration fee for WAMPUM is an indisputable bargain at $25 per individual user or $75 per computer network. With registration, users receive an expanded version of the program which runs on either a floppy-disk system (two floppies are the minimum required, as well as at least 420K

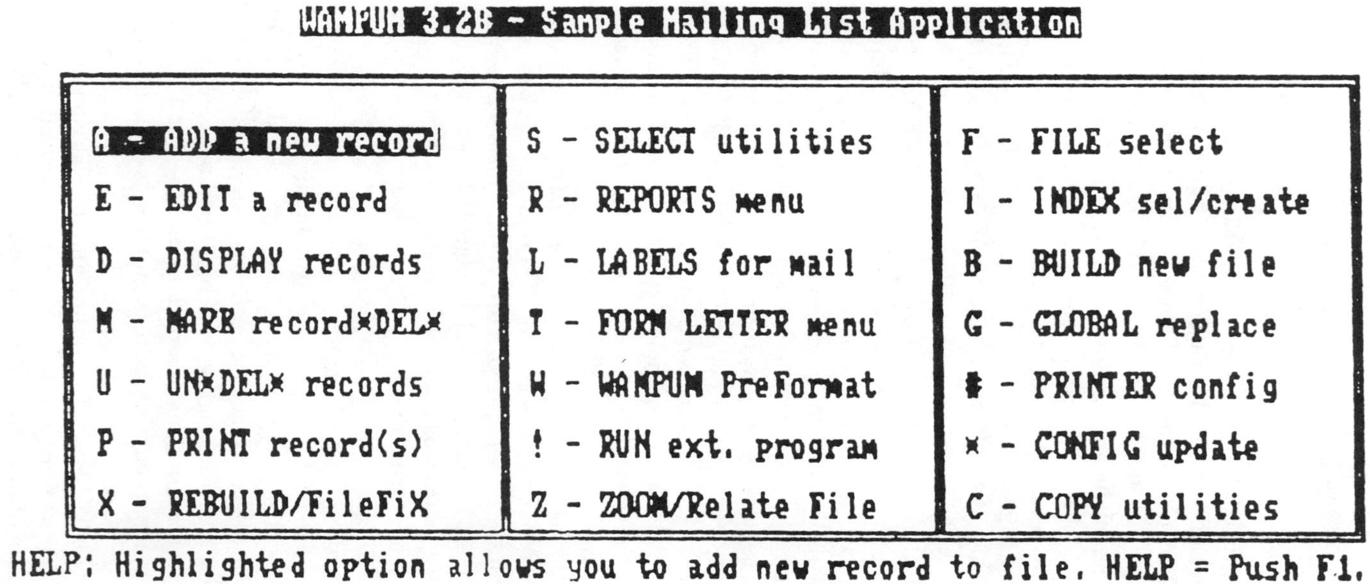

Figure 3.2: Opening menu for WAMPUM. This dBase III Plus compatible, full-featured database management program is completely menu driven.

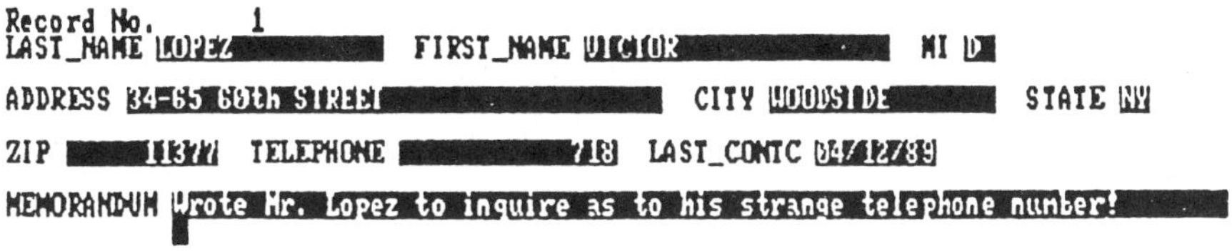

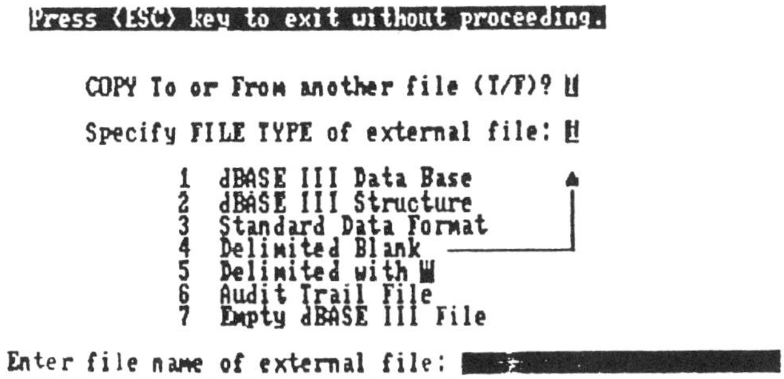

Top: **Figure 3.3: Sample data entry screen in WAMPUM.** ***Bottom:*** **Figure 3.4: WAMPUM's file importing and exporting utility. The program allows for the importing and exporting of data files in a variety of formats, and can access database programs and files created with dBase III Plus directly.**

of available RAM with systems running DOS 3.1) or a hard disk, with the latter being highly recommended for ease of use and speed. The registered version includes programs and files deleted from the evaluation version due to limitations of disk space, such as the on-line help feature. Nevertheless, the Shareware version of the program is fully usable as is. A 180-page soft-bound *User's Guide* is also available from the author within 30 days of registration for an additional $20 fee. (As previously noted, the disk-based manual included with the evaluation copy of WAMPUM is an excellent one and the only reference most users will ever need.) The author provides a generous 90-day evaluation period for users to learn and use the program prior to registration. After that time, users are honor-bound to register the program if they find it useful and intend to continue using it. The modest price asked for registration of this powerful, well-designed and easy to use software package is, by any measure, truly an incredible bargain; as the author himself quips in the evaluation program's on-screen general information message: "If you like WAMPUM and use it, please give the author a break and PAY YOUR DUES! The alternative is more $695 packages and no more WAMPUM's!"

Program: WAMPUM Shareware Ver. 3.2B © Ward Mundy, 1986–1988
Author: Ward Mundy

Company: N/A
Address: 4160 Club Drive, Atlanta, GA 30319
Category: Database
Registration Fee: $25 per individual user, $75 per computer network

General Evaluation: WAMPUM Ver. 3.2B

	Excellent	*Very Good*	*Good*	*Average*	*Poor*
Ease of Use	***				
Ease of Learning		***			
Documentation	***				
Utility	***				
Overall Rating	***				

PC-File + ™

PC-File + is a powerful database program that combines speed, ease of use and advanced features found only in programs costing hundreds of dollars more.

The program is completely menu-driven; users need not learn complicated commands or a new programming language in order to set up and run simple or complex applications. Although the evaluation copy comes with a 107-page manual on disk, a user with some computing experience can run the program and set up some rather complex applications without spending a single minute with the manual (although careful study of the program is highly recommended in order to fully utilize its advanced features). Menus are thoughtfully implemented so that they are nearly transparent as they assist a user in setting up a new database. Unlike many menu-driven programs, PC-File + is neither slow nor cumbersome, even when dealing with some extensive applications. A very useful feature for new users is PC-File + 's Teach Mode, whereby a user is prompted through an optional window as to every option available at any given point in the program. Thus, a very detailed electronic tutor is available at a moment's notice; whenever a question arises, extensive help is never more than two keystrokes away.

PC-File + contains many useful features not found in many leading database programs. Among these is the ability to define a database by typing in field names and lengths on the screen as one wishes them to appear on the data entry screen. A user is given complete control as to the appearance of the data entry screen, field length, and the sequence in which fields will be accessed for data entry. In addition, field names need not be limited to a fixed maximum length (e.g., eight characters) as with most database

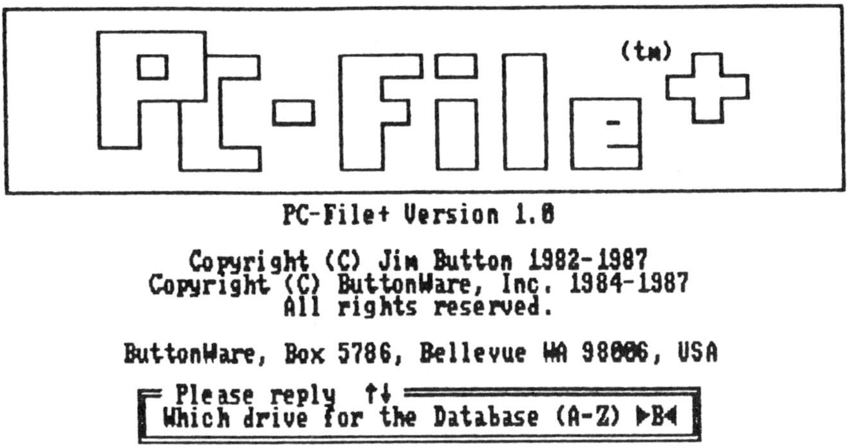

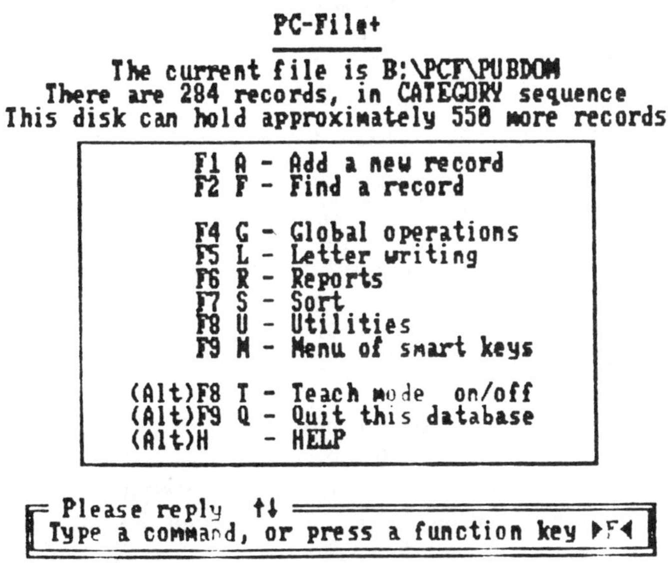

Top: **Figure 3.5: Opening screen and copyright notice for PC-File + Ver. 1.0.**
Bottom: **Figure 3.6: Opening menu for PC-File + Ver. 1.0. This powerful program is completely menu-driven and very easy to learn.**

programs and may contain more than one word; hence, a cryptic (and confusing) field name such as "C__LAST__N" can become "Client's Last Name." PC-File + also offers powerful sorting, indexing and retrieval functions. Sorting by up to ten fields in ascending or descending order by field is possible. Indexing is both automatic and quick. And information retrieval offers many useful choices, such as use of wild cards and the ability

```
Record number 1                                                        A
PROGRAM NAME ▸                    ◂   AUTHOR'S NAME [                  ]
    CATEGORY [                    ]   STREET ADDRS  [                  ]
   VOLUME NO [   ]                    CITY, ST, ZIP [                  ]
        DATE [        ]               COMPANY NAME  [                  ]
                                      PROGRAM TYPE (PD / SW): [  ]

BRIEF DESCRIPTION: [                                                   ]
      DESCRIPTION: [                                                   ]



 Please respond. Press (F10) when complete.
```

Figure 3.7: Sample data entry screen in PC-File + .

to search for information phonetically when one is uncertain as to correct spelling.

In addition, PC-File + can export its databases for use with other programs and import files created with other programs for use by a PC-File + defined database. Data can thus be shared with many popular programs, such as Mail Merge (WordStar), Lotus 1-2-3, PC-Calc, dBase II and III, Visi Calc and others. The conversions are carried out quickly and effortlessly. In evaluating the program, several large files created with Lotus 1-2-3, dBase III + and WordStar's Mail Merge were converted. The largest of these, a 550-kilobyte file created by dBase III +, required approximately 16 minutes to complete using a hard disk drive; but the transfer time was considerably less than that required by dBase III + to export the same file to Mail Merge format (28 minutes).

Finally, PC-File + includes the ability to generate mailing labels and merged letters from its databases. The procedure for both is simple and works flawlessly. In fact, the label-generating aspect of the program may in itself be worth the registration fee for users needing that function; labels of various sizes and up to three across on a sheet are supported. It is also possible to create a database with PC-File + to later be transferred to WordStar's Mail Merge program. Doing so permits simple updating, sorting and generating of reports with the stored data. In addition, entering information in a PC-File + database file is easier than creating a Mail Merge data

```
PC-FILE+ UTILITIES MENU

C.  Clone (change the database definition)
D.  Duplicate records (find and list)
E.  Export the current database
I.  Import a PC-File+ database or other file
M.  Maintenance - Copy, Delete or Rename a PC-File+ file
N.  Name of field, mask, constant or calc (modify)
P.  Profile files (set up configuration)
S.  Smart keys (modify)
U.  Un-delete records

Q.  Quit Utilities - Return to Master Menu

Please reply ↑↓
Enter your selection. ▶Q◀
```

Figure 3.8: PC-File+ contains many useful utilities which allow a user to customize any database, even after it has been created. File import and export utilities are also included.

file through WordStar, and prevents common errors such as missing commas between fields, empty fields, etc. The actual conversion from PC-File+ to Mail Merge–usable files takes only seconds for all but gargantuan files.

The evaluation copy of PC-File+ comes in two 5.25-inch floppy diskettes and includes a printable manual. The manual itself is over 100 pages in length and covers all the features of the program. There are some sections covering advanced functions which are deleted from the evaluation version; even without these sections, however, a user can get extensive use out of the program. For those who find the program useful and intend to continue using it, the author requires registration, which costs $59.95 (plus $5 shipping and handling). Registered users get a printed copy of the complete manual, as well as a registered copy of the latest version of the program by return mail.

For all its "user-friendliness," PC-File+ is a remarkably flexible and powerful tool: one which allows a novice to set up an electronic phone book or other simple database within minutes, not months, while delighting an experienced user with its many functions and efficient design long after its acquisition.

Program: PC-File+ © Jim Button 1982–87, © ButtonWare 1984–87
Author: Jim Button
Company: ButtonWare, Inc.

Address: Box 5786, Bellevue, WA 98006
Category: Database
Registration Fee: $59.95 (plus $5 shipping and handling)

General Evaluation: PC-File +

	Excellent	*Very Good*	*Good*	*Average*	*Poor*
Ease of Use	***				
Ease of Learning	***				
Documentation			***		
Utility	***				
Overall Rating	***				

File Express™

File Express is a full-featured, menu-driven database management program which is simple to use, easy to learn and powerful enough for any but the most complicated applications.

The program includes the following features:

—Maximum number of records: 32,767
—Maximum number of characters per record: 2,400
—Maximum number of fields per record: 40
—Field length: 1–60 characters
—Maximum number of sorted fields: 10 in ascending or descending order
—Minimum system requirements: IBM PC/XT/AT or 100% compatible computer with at least 128K of Random Access Memory (RAM), at least one SSDD floppy disk drive (2 drives or one drive and a hard disk are highly recommended), MS/DOS v. 1.1 or newer.

The evaluation copy of the program is a full-featured one; unlike many user-supported software releases, File Express comes complete in a two- or three-disk set (two disks for users with double-sided, double density 5.25-inch drives [360K maximum data storage capacity], and three disks for users with the older [and, by now, functionally obsolete] single-sided, double-density drives [180K maximum data storage capacity]).The program includes a 70-page manual on disk which is well-written, logically organized and contains a comprehensive two-page table of contents for easy reference to the program's many features.

Although the program's documentation is very informative and should

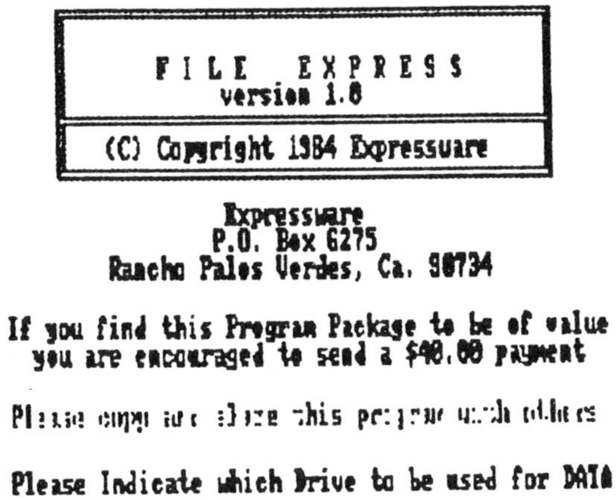

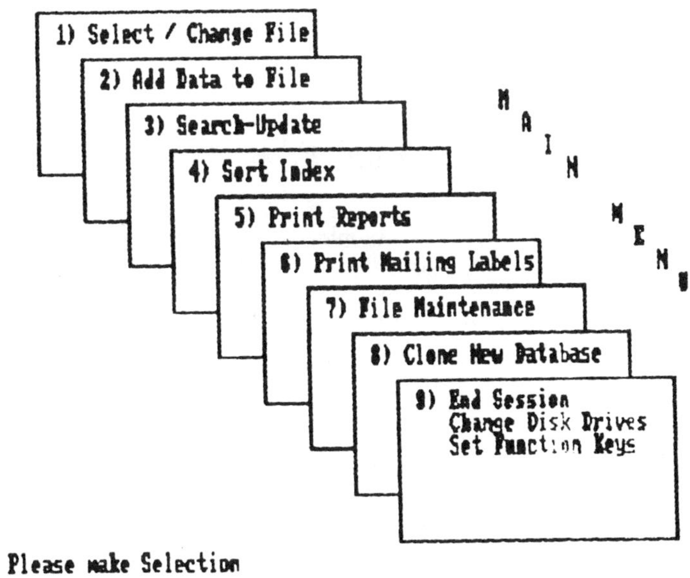

***Top:* Figure 3.9: File Express opening screen and copyright notice. *Bottom:* Figure 3.10: Main menu screen for File Express. This powerful program is intuitive, easy to learn and offers sufficient flexibility for a wide variety of database applications.**

be read through at least once even by advanced users in order to take advantage of the program's many useful features, File Express has been designed with an excellent pull-down menu system so that most users can immediately use the program without having to first read the manual.

In setting up a new database, a user may choose from various field types to include in the database definition. One may choose from Numeric,

Define Fields for a:TEMP File Page 1

	-field name-	-type-	-length-	-calc field-
1	First Name	A	15	No
2	Middle Init	A	1	No
3	Last Name	A	15	No
4	Street Addrs	!	45	No
5	City	A	12	No
6	State	A	2	No
7	Zip	N	5	No
8	Memo	-		

+=positive >=whole #=decimal $=dollar A=alpha N=numeric !=anything

Figure 3.11: Defining a database is a simple matter with File Express. Fields may be designated to contain positive numbers, whole numbers, dollar amounts, alphabetic entries, numerical data or a catch-all "anything" category (numbers, alphabetic data, symbols, etc.). As with most database programs, a wide variety of mathematical functions may be performed on fields containing numerical or dollar amount data.

Alphabetic or Mixed fields. Numeric fields may be positive or negative numbers, decimals or dollar amounts of up to 14 digits in length. Mathematical operations may be performed on Numeric fields, and these may be either manually or automatically recalculated any time data is added or changed in the database.

Altering an existing database is a simple matter with File Express. Fields may easily be added, deleted, or altered in an existing database. An additional nice feature is the ability to program a number of keys to automatically perform certain functions (macro capability).

File searches in an existing database may be performed by field number, field contents or last record entered. Once a record is found, its contents may easily be altered on the screen. Sorting the database is just as simple; it may be sorted by up to 10 different fields in ascending or descending order. Additionally fields may be sorted either by their entire contents or a part thereof (e.g., if a field is 60 characters in length and

```
      Add Data to TEMP     File         [illegible] #        1 - Page  1


 1 First Name   Victor
 2 Middle Init  D
 3 Last Name    Lopez
 4 Street Addrs 12-34 56th Street
 5 City         Woodside
 6 State        NY
 7 Zip          11377
 8 Memo         Mr. Lopez seems to have a rather strange street address!




Press - <S>ave  <C>hange  <R>e-enter  <Esc> to quit
```

Figure 3.12: Sample data entry screen in File Express.

contains many different words, it may be sorted in its entirety or by, say, the first character only, or the first 10 characters, etc.).

Report generation, labels and mail merge functions are also supported. Reports may be produced either in rows (usual format, and the only one supported by most database programs) or in different columns. As an example a list of clients for a company may be reproduced in the following two report formats assuming the field's Customer's Name, Address, City, State, Zip, Last Order Date and Amount Past Due:

(Traditional "row" report listing: single row per record)

Name	Address	City	ST Zip	L__Ord	Pst__D
John Smith	123-45 60th Street	Anytown,	NY 00000	1/1/89	$10.00

This is the optional "column" listing: multiple rows and columns per record.

Name:	John Smith
Address:	123-45 60th Street
City ST ZIP:	Anytown, NY 00000
Last Order:	1/1/89
Amount Past Due:	$10

In addition to a flexible report generator, the program includes an excellent label generating program. Users may easily print various kinds of labels using their existing database files. The program supports gummed labels up to three across per sheet and up to 50 characters wide and 15 lines in height. Lines of predefined text to be repetitively printed on each label in addition from the data in each database record may also be used.

The program also supports mail-merge printing. A standard business letter or similar document may be merged with a database file to produced personalized documents with a minimum of effort. For example, a database of potential employers may be created with File Express and merged with a form letter produced to send out personalized employment queries to selected employers. Fields from the database may be placed in the preprinted document to produce personalized letters without having to retype the same information more than once.

To facilitate the creation of merged documents, File Express allows files created with many word processing packages to be imported and used by the program. Files from some other database programs may also be imported (e.g., programs which can export files in delimited ASCII files can be directly used by File Express through the included IMPORT.EXE program). The program also includes a printer definition program to allow for different print widths to be printed on each label, report or mail-merge printouts.

While File Express does not contain all the high-level features of either WAMPUM or PC-File +, it is a useful and powerful program in its own right, offering an excellent mix of flexibility, advanced features and an easy to learn menu system.

Program: File Express © 1984
Author: David M. Berdan
Company: Expressware
Address: P.O. Box 6275, Rancho Palos Verdes, CA 90734
Category: Database
Registration Fee: $40 (Latest version of program shipped with registration.) Printed manual available for $15. Users who send two formatted diskettes with a prepaid mailer to the author at the above address will receive a copy of the latest version of the program for their evaluation. (Three disks are required for single-sided drive users.)

General Evaluation: File Express

	Excellent	*Very Good*	*Good*	*Average*	*Poor*
Ease of Use		***			
Ease of Learning	***				
Documentation	***				
Utility		***			
Overall Rating		***			

3by5™

3by5 is a free-form information management system which allows a user to search, index and retrieve various kinds of data. It is unlike most standard database management systems in that it does not require data to be entered or retrieved in accordance to strict criteria, but rather functions much like its name applies: a "three by five" set of index cards which may be structured, organized and used in ways limited only by the imagination of its user.

The key concept in 3by5 is *flexibility*. The user is allowed to input data in any way she chooses, and then search such data for strings of text appearing in it. Logical operators (e.g., "and" / "or" expressions) are supported, as are the ability to work with up to three different files simultaneously. In addition, the program is not limited to using files created only with it: ASCII files created with any text editor, database or spreadsheet program which is capable of saving text in such a format are also supported. It can also access files created with WordStar or Word Perfect.

3by5 incorporates a text editor as part of the program. While the editor is not a full-blown word processor, it is by no means a stripped-down line editor. The program's documentation notes that its editor is based on the Wang and Symphony word processors. Its features include word wrap, cut and paste operations on blocks of text, text insertion and deletion with automatic text alignment and quite adequate cursor control commands. A maximum of 60 lines of text may be inputted into a given record using the text editor. For a user writing a two-page letter, the features of 3by5's text editor would be quite sufficient, and the program, though not intended for this use, is adequate as a "fast and simple" word processing tool. The fact that it can access up to three different files at once through its useful windows system makes it a wonderful tool for outlining and organizing ideas, as well as a data management program.

The program's documentation is a pleasure to read through and use. It is a combination reference manual and hands-on tutorial which leads the user through every step in learning to use the program. The 59-page manual

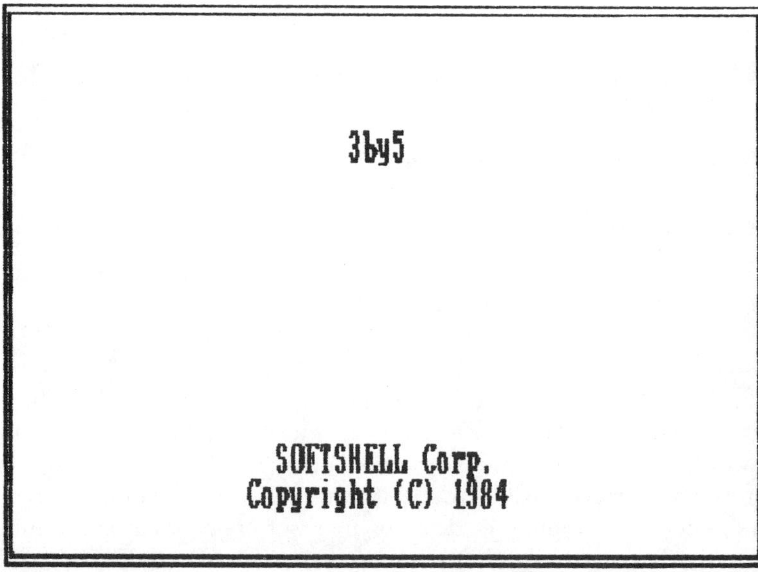

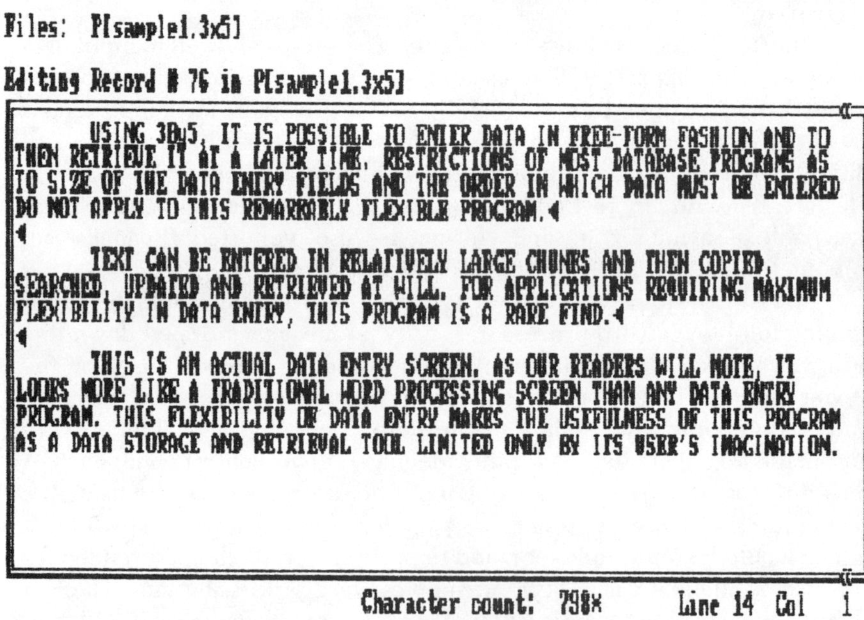

Top: **Figure 3.13: Opening screen and copyright notice for 3by5.** ***Bottom:*** **Figure 3.14: Sample data entry screen for 3by5. This is a free-form database management program. As its name implies, one enters data as in a 3″ by 5″ index card. There are no complicated data entry parameters to set up. A file is named and information may immediately be entered in any form one wishes. Once entered, information may be searched in a variety of ways.**

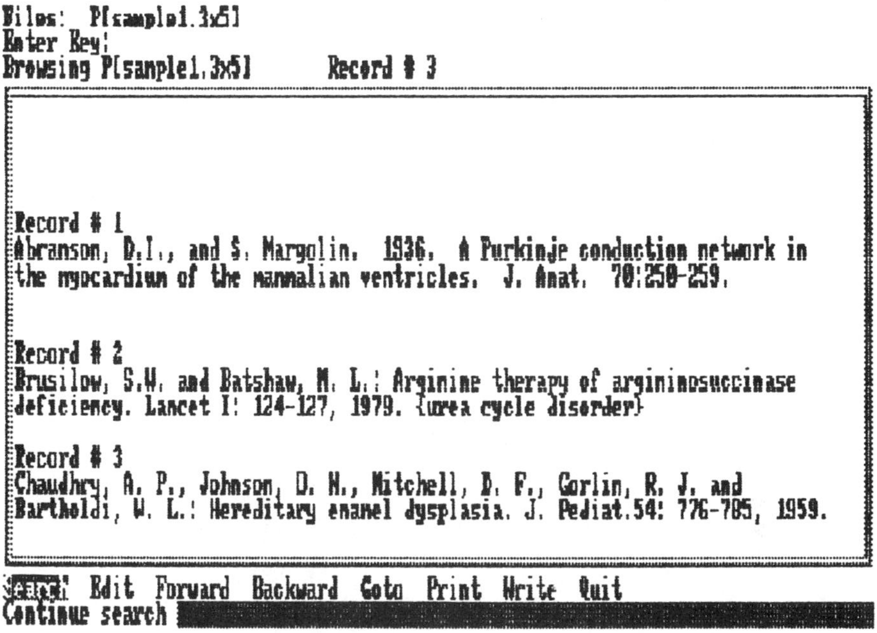

Figure 3.15: Sample search screen for 3by5. Records may be searched by browsing through the database one record at a time (forward, backward or through specific record numbers). The database may also be searched in its entirety for records containing specific information.

on the distribution disk contains a detailed table of contents and an index, as well as detailed examples of how the program works. It is both well written and informative.

3by5 is neither a full-fledged database management system nor a word processor; yet it combines useful features of both to provide the user with a flexible, easy to learn program readily adaptable to many uses. These can range in complexity from a filing system for patient records in a doctor's office to research notes for a scholar to recipes for a gourmet. All can easily be input, related, searched and organized using this software.

Program: 3by5 © 1984
Author: N/A
Company: SoftShell Corp.
Address: P.O. Box 18522, Baltimore, MD 21237
Category: Database
Registration Fee: None specified. (May not be the case for subsequent releases of this software.)

General Evaluation: 3by5 – 1984

	Excellent	*Very Good*	*Good*	*Average*	*Poor*
Ease of Use		***			
Ease of Learning	***				
Documentation	***				
Utility		***			
Overall Rating		***			

4: Communications Programs

Introduction

Some of the best deals available in user supported software are the communications programs. Here you can find programs that are not only superior to commercially available programs in ease and capability, but are available for a fraction of the cost. The small investment needed to get you started (a modem and communications package can be obtained for less than $100) will greatly expand the usefulness and potential of your computer.

All good communications programs can handle the most basic needs. This includes communicating directly with other users, accessing information services, and uploading and downloading files to and from bulletin boards. The more advanced programs will allow users to access their system from outside computers, create their own bulletin board, and design their own applications.

The programs described in this chapter were selected for their multitude of features, as well as their ease of operation relative to their level of sophistication. All contain directories with auto-redial functions capable of cycling through series of numbers, scriptwriting for automating log-on procedures, pop-up help screens, keyboard macros for defining often used commands and phrases, access to the operating system, and full file transfer capabilities.

The features and capabilities of the programs included here should satisfy the needs of most users. The deciding factor in selecting a program should be the level of sophistication the user hopes to attain since, as a rule with most communications programs, the more advanced the features, the harder the program is to master. Regardless of the program selected, the user is guaranteed sophistication and relative ease of operation at a price far below that of commercially available packages.

ProComm™ Version 2.4.2

ProComm is a sophisticated, professional level, communications program designed to handle a broad variety of telecommunications tasks.

PROCOMM (tm)

Version 2.4.2

(C) 1985, 1986 Datastorm Technologies, Inc. (Formerly PIL Software Systems)

This is a user supported product. It is not public domain, and it is not free software. You are granted a limited license to use this product on a trial basis. If you wish to continue using the product after the trial period you must register by sending: (a) $25 for registration only (no disk), (b) $35 for registration plus the latest version on disk, or (c) $50 for registration, disk and printed, bound manual to the address below. Missouri residents please add 4.3% sales tax.

ProComm support BBS: (314) 449-9401 24 hours per day, 7 days per week.

Thank you for your support!

=== Datastorm Technologies, Inc. PO Box 1471 Columbia, MO 65205 ===

ProComm Help

MAJOR FUNCTIONS	UTILITY FUNCTIONS	FILE FUNCTIONS
Dialing Directory . Alt-D	Program Info ...... Alt-I	Send files ...... PgUp
Automatic Redial... Alt-R	Setup Screen ...... Alt-S	Receive files ... PgDn
Keyboard Macros ... Alt-M	Kermit Server Cmd . Alt-K	Directory ...... Alt-F
Line Settings ..... Alt-P	Change Directory .. Alt-B	View a File .... Alt-V
Translate Table ... Alt-W	Clear Screen ...... Alt-C	Screen Dump .... Alt-G
Editor .... Alt-A	Toggle Duplex ..... Alt-E	Log Toggle Alt-F1
Exit .... Alt-X	Hang Up Phone ..... Alt-H	Log Hold Alt-F2
Host Mode .... Alt-Q	Elapsed Time ...... Alt-T	
Chat Mode .... Alt-O	Print On/Off ...... Alt-L	
DOS Gateway Alt-F4	Set Colors .... Alt-Z	
Command Files Alt-F5	Auto Answer .... Alt-Y	
Redisplay Alt-F6	Toggle CR-CR/LF .. Alt-F3	
	Break Key Alt-F7	

Datastorm Technologies, Inc.

Top: **Figure 4.1: Opening screen and copyright notice for ProComm.** ***Bottom:*** **Figure 4.2: ProComm command help screen.**

Its features and ease of operation rival, and in many cases surpass, the capabilities of many commercially available communications software.

Included with the normal telecommunication functions standard with most packages are the kind of advanced features one would expect to find in more sophisticated programs. These include the ability to emulate many popular terminals, a dialing directory containing search and automatic redial facilities, several popular file transfer protocols, keyboard macros, command language, remote access, and much more.

ProComm requires 130K RAM and can be used with color or monochrome displays. The default settings in ProComm are established for use with Hayes compatible modems. Noncompatible modems can be used, but you will need to consult your owner's guide for various settings and limitations.

After loading ProComm, the user is entered into the terminal mode. The screen is blank except at the bottom, where the status line displays the settings of various status indicators, such as baud, parity, duplex, capture, etc., as well as the help command. Communications generally take place in this mode. Commands are executed here and are accessed through pop-up windows that leave your original screen intact, even during on-line transmissions. The command help screen can be accessed at any time by typing ALT-F10.

ProComm's utilization of pop-up command windows greatly facilitates learning and usage. Once in the terminal mode, typing ALT-F10 brings up the command help screen which lists all of ProComm's available commands, categorized by function type. Commands can be executed from the terminal mode. Changing settings or executing functions in ProComm takes only one or two steps. Most commands will bring up an individualized window which clearly lays out that function's available options. Typing any non-command key returns you to the terminal mode.

The experienced communications user should have no problem establishing communications and immediately taking advantage of ProComm's many features. Simply loading the program and running through the various help commands, whenever convenient, or as the need arises, will result in a solid working knowledge of the program without benefit of the manual. Of course, for those who want to take full advantage of ProComm's features, we do recommend that you read applicable sections of the 100-page manual. It is extremely well documented, and will help guide you through the advanced features.

The communications novice, armed with minimal knowledge of their own equipment and information supplied by their communication partner, should be able to manipulate their way through most transmissions. A limited amount of communications skill, however, will not be enough to satisfy all applications. As is the case with most communication packages, the reference manual, though very detailed and thorough, does not serve as a tutorial on general communications. ProComm offers assistance through their BBS network, with priority given to registered users. But in order to take full advantage of the software, the novice should plan on doing a minimal amount of research on data transmission.

The ProComm user's ability to perform standard communications

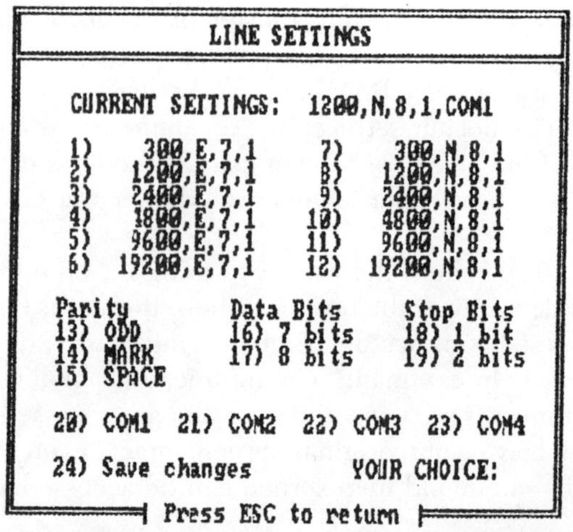

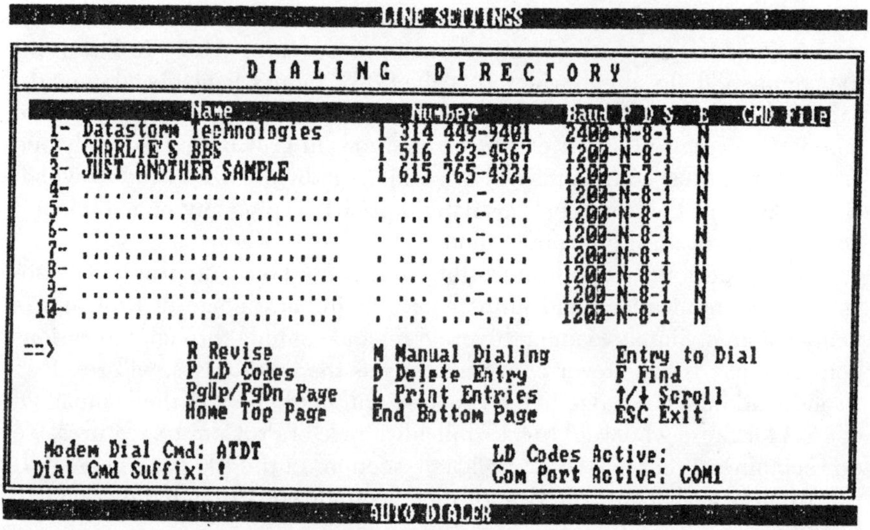

Top: Figure 4.3 Parameter settings in ProComm. Baud settings go as high as 19,200. _Bottom:_ Figure 4.4. The ProComm dialing directory can accommodate up to 100 entries. The user can search for entries by name or by phone number.

functions is greatly simplified by the program's many features. ProComm's directory is capable of handling 100 entries and includes a search function for quickly accessing desired listings. The search can be performed by phone number or name. The auto-redial feature has the added ability to continuously dial a series of hard-to-access phone numbers until a connection is made.

Command files are user-created text files that contain ProComm commands. They can be used to automatically perform tasks such as log-ons

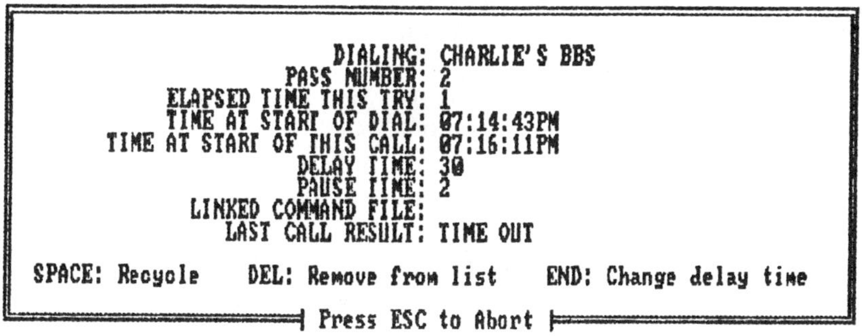

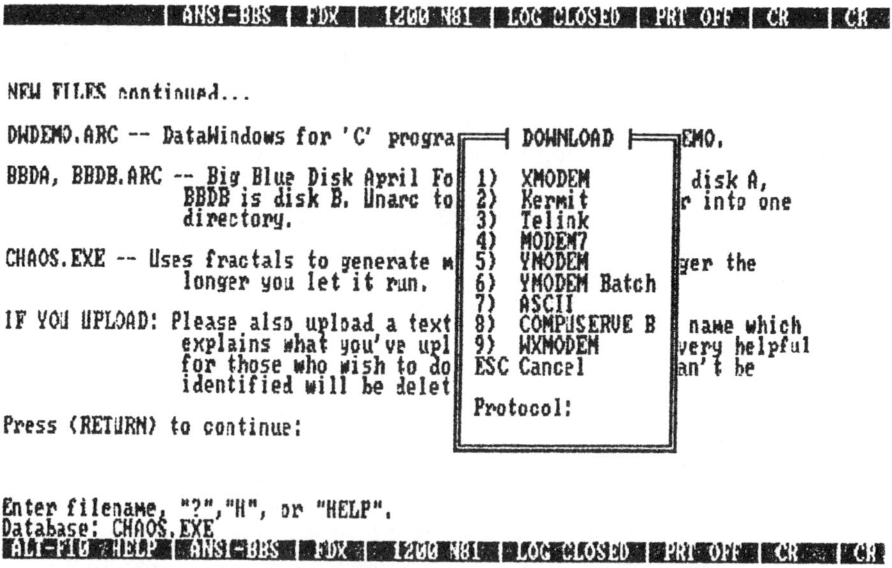

Top: **Figure 4.5: After activating the dialer, ProComm will keep you informed of the calling status until the connection is completed or the attempt is aborted.** ***Bottom:*** **Figure 4.6: While online, ProComm will allow you to change or select settings including upload and download protocols.**

or unattended file transfers and can be optionally linked to directory entries to automate the entire dialing and log-on procedure. Command files can be executed from within ProComm or as a command line option when you first invoke the program, causing it to be executed immediately upon program startup.

Writing a command file, especially to perform more advanced operations, can be quite a challenge. For that reason, many users ignore this powerful feature. ProComm has made the process much easier by combining excellent documentation with excellent command language. ProComm would be a fine choice for the command language novice looking to expand their communication capabilities.

It should be noted that a glaring omission from ProComm's command language capabilities is time-scheduling, the ability to start a series of commands at a scheduled time. A program of this level of sophistication should include this feature, and its absence restricts the programs overall capabilities.

Host mode allows the user remote access to their computer from an outside source. Uses for this include file transfers, DOS functions, etc. Host provides for two-level password security, with the second password needed to access the system level. Host mode can issue log-on messages and provide you with an access history.

ProComm gives you nine choices of protocols for uploading and downloading files. The functions are accessed from the terminal mode by typing PgUp for uploading or PgDn for downloading. With several protocols available, including ASCII, XMODEM, YMODEM, and KERMIT, you should be able to exchange files with virtually any system.

A number of popular terminals can be emulated by ProComm. Most standard features, and many extended features, can be handled. Functions of nonemulated terminals are still processed to insure that all control codes are handled properly.

Other impressive features of ProComm include the abilities to "capture" or "log" data appearing on your screen to disk or printer, to dump any screen image to file, and to scroll back 10,000 characters.

ProComm supplies the user with a fully operational, professional level communications software program that can efficiently and conveniently handle most communications needs. The modest registration fee ($25) is well worth the benefits, which include mailed notification of updates, and priority support on ProComm's private BBS for registered users only—available 24 hours a day, seven days a week. Of course, users who find the program not suitable to their needs, are under no obligation to register; however, for the user who elects to continue usage, the program and support received will far exceed what is being offered by many commercially available communication packages costing considerably more.

Program: ProComm Ver. 2.4.2 © 1985, 1986
Author: N/A
Company: Datastrom Technologies, Inc.
Address: P.O. Box 1471, Columbia, MO 65205
Category: Communications Programs
Registration Fee: $25 (MC/VISA/U.S. checks) Add $5 conversion fee for checks not drawn in U.S. currency.

General Evaluation: PROCOMM Ver. 2.4.2

	Excellent	*Very Good*	*Good*	*Average*	*Poor*
Ease of Use	***				
Ease of Learning	***				
Documentation	***				
Utility		***			
Overall Rating	***				

Qmodem™ Version 2.0

Qmodem is a sophisticated, advanced level, communications program designed to handle a broad variety of telecommunication tasks. It has features only somewhat beyond that of the most rudimentary programs, yet enough to satisfy the limited needs of most users without the confusion sometimes caused by a multitude of functions unnecessary to most. The registration price of only $10 certainly helps to make this program an excellent buy.

Features beyond the standard telecommunication functions include a dialing directory capable of handling 200 entries, automatic redial facilities with the ability to cycle through several numbers, a well-documented, easy to use, macro system, and the ability to time-schedule log-ons.

At 192K, Qmodem requires an unusually large amount of RAM to operate. It can be used with color or monochrome displays, but requires running an install program before operating. The manual warns that Qmodem sometimes does not work when background software, such as a screen clock, is running. We used Qmodem with several background programs, including a screen clock, and never had a problem. Qmodem supports two multi-tasking environments: Topview from IBM and Desqview from QuarterDeck Systems. Both let Qmodem run in window mode, where it can write directly without affecting other windows. You will need one of these two programs, however, to take advantage of this feature.

Loading Qmodem enters the user into the terminal mode. There is no permanent status line on screen to remind you of the help command and various parameter settings, but a message on the screen after log-on informs you of the help screen command "HOME," which, as opposed to the usual two-key help command, is easy to remember. Typing the "HOME" key accesses a pop-up window which displays the commands executable in Qmodem. A lack of a status line means you will have to use the command keys to remind you of current settings. This is not a significant inconvenience, however, since most commands are easy to remember (ALT-P for parameter settings, ALT-D for dialing directory, etc.); and help is just a keystroke away.

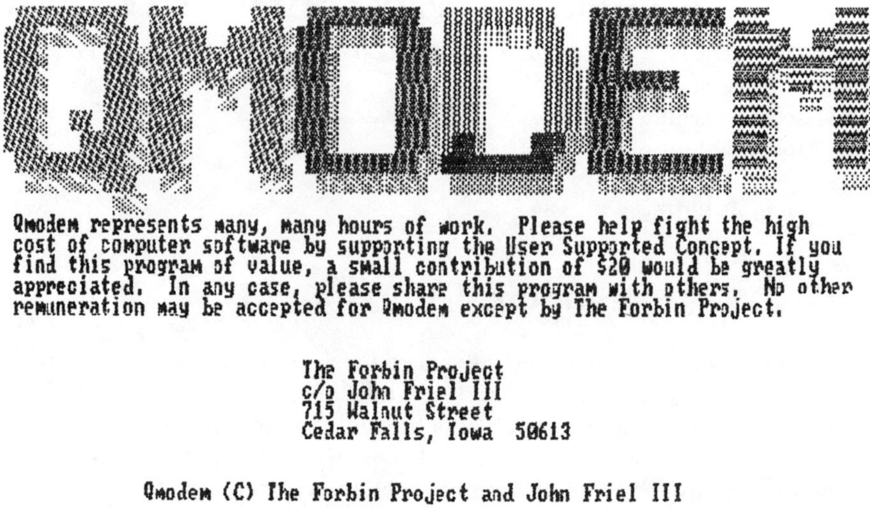

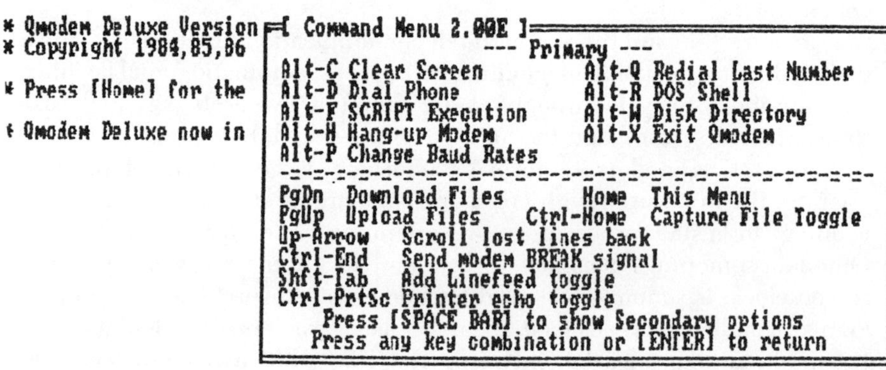

***Top:* Figure 4.7: Opening screen and copyright notice for Qmodem. *Bottom:* Figure 4.8: The HOME key brings up the command menu in Qmodem. The user will need to press the space bar from here to display "secondary" options such as viewing a file or changing sub-directories.**

Most default settings are changed at the window. Qmodem handles all the standard parameter settings and can be set to transmit at any of five different baud rates. Special settings, such as the time wait between redials, must be done at the Install level. Qmodem can emulate the standard ANSI-BBS terminal and includes amongst its commands a Graphics mode toggle.

Qmodem's sophisticated dialing directory can handle 200 entries, and includes a quick dial function which enables you to begin communications without entering the directory. The auto-redial function has the added

```
* Qmodem Deluxe Version 2.00E Production.  Compiled on 7 March 1986.
* Copyright 1984,85,86 -- The Forbin Project Inc. and John Friel III

* Press [Home] for the Command Menu.
    ╔[ Set Modem Speed ]═══════════════════════════════════
* Qm║ Current setting is      :      1200,N,8,1
    ║ Available Settings are  :
    ║ A) 300 ,E,7,1    B) 300 ,O,7,1    C) 300 ,N,8,1
    ║ D) 1200,E,7,1    E) 1200,O,7,1    F) 1200,N,8,1
    ║ G) 2400,E,7,1    H) 2400,O,7,1    I) 2400,N,8,1
    ║ J) 4800,E,7,1    K) 4800,O,7,1    L) 4800,N,8,1
    ║ M) 9600,E,7,1    N) 9600,O,7,1    O) 9600,N,8,1
    ║
    ║            Selection [CR=no change] ?
    ╚══════════════════════════════════════════════════════
```

```
╔[ Qmodem Phone Book ]═════════════════════════════════════════════════
║ Page  1
[D]                     Name                     Number       Comm       Script
  1 The Forbin Project - Home of Qmodem 1-319-277-0044 2400-8-N-1
  2 InfoWorld                           1-516-653-0967 1200-8-N-1
  3 Auto-Source                         1-212-327-6764 1200-8-N-1 Auto-on
  4 Factsheet Five                      1-518-479-3879 1200-8-N-1
  5 Easy Link                           1-800-325-4112 1200-8-N-1 Link-up
  6                                                    1200-8-N-1
  7                                                    1200-8-N-1
  8                                                    1200-8-N-1
  9                                                    1200-8-N-1
 10                                                    1200-8-N-1
╠[ Options ]═══════════════════════════════════════════════════════════

          C - Clear entry(s)          R - Revise an entry
          D - Dial number(s)          X - eXit Phone Book
          E - rEvise prefix codes     PgDn - Show Next page
          M - Manual dial a number    PgUp - Show Previous page

              Choice ?
╚══════════════════════════════════════════════════════════════════════
```

Top: **Figure 4.9: Selecting parameters in Qmodem.** ***Bottom:*** **Figure 4.10: The Qmodem dialing directory can accommodate 200 entries.**

capability of continuously dialing a preprogrammed series of numbers until a connection is made.

The process of setting parameters, dialing another computer, logging on with a user name and password, retrieving and saving information, and logging off, can be automated using Qmodem's command language, Script. Script is one of Qmodem's most powerful features, enabling you to direct an entire log-on procedure to start at a specific time—something many of the more advanced programs cannot do. Scripts can be linked to run automatically when a specific entry in the phone directory is accessed; or, they can be started by typing the Script command and selecting the one you wish to run. Learning how to use Scripts will take a little time, but Qmodem provides the user with excellent documentation and a command language that is easy to interpret.

Once you are logged-on to another system, Qmodem will allow you to "capture" data appearing on your screen to disk or to printer, but the function must first be activated in Install. Scroll-back can access the last 50 lines on screen. The user defines the limit but must be careful not to over-allocate since the scroll-back function is in direct competition with the DOS shell for RAM space.

One of the basic functions of a communications program is the ability to upload and download files and Qmodem allows you the option of six different file transfer protocols, including ASCII and XMODEM in three different versions. This should be sufficient for the user to exchange files with almost any system. The function keys for retrieving and sending files are industry standards: PgUp for uploading and PgDn for downloading.

In Qmodem the user possesses a fully operational, advanced level communications software package that will efficiently handle most communication needs. It is not the most powerful program available and lags somewhat behind in ease of use and learning, thanks to the lack of a status line and inadequate documentation which, outside of the command language instruction, is actually a reference manual. Its advantages, however, are notable, such as an excellent command language, time-scheduling capabilities, a full-featured 200-entry dialing directory, and, not least of all, a ridiculously low registration cost of $10. The registered user is not promised user support, but benefits include notification of updates and new releases, and a copy of QMLOAD, a utility program for building large Qmodem phone directories by extracting "Name" and "Number" information from almost any ASCII formatted file. With its very nice array of features and capabilities, Qmodem is an excellent buy.

Program: Qmodem Ver. 2.0 © 1986
Author: John Friel III
Company: The Forbin Project, Inc.
Address: 715 Walnut Street, Cedar Falls, Iowa 50613
Category: Communications Programs
Registration Fee: $10 non-commercial users ($20 suggested)
$25 commercial

General Evaluation: Qmodem Ver. 2.0

	Excellent	*Very Good*	*Good*	*Average*	*Poor*
Ease of Use			***		
Ease of Learning				***	
Documentation				***	
Utility			***		
Overall Rating			***		

Telix™ Version 3.11

Telix is a sophisticated, and extremely powerful, professional level communications program. It is designed to satisfy the complex requirements of more advanced users without sacrificing the ease of operation required by users needing only the basics.

Telix's advanced features include expanded parameter and baud capabilities, multiple dialing directories holding up to a thousand entries each, a usage log, many popular file-transfer protocols, extensive command language and a Host or remote access mode with operator paging.

Telix requires 170K RAM and can be used with color or monochrome displays. It can support up to eight defined comm ports and any number of disk drives. The baud rate can be set as high as 115,200 and there are five different possible parity settings. Compatibility with most hardware and system capabilities are virtually assured.

Negotiating through Telix's complex series of options is not a problem. In the terminal mode, Telix's optional status line displays a wealth of important information. Included are the help command, current parameter settings, "capture" or "log" status, script file activated, online or offline status, and more. The status line can be displayed at the top or bottom of the screen or not at all. ALT-Z activates the help screen showing you all available commands. More information is located at the bottom of the screen such as time, date, parameter settings, current directory, etc. Typing a command will either perform a function or pop-up another menu with choices that can be selected with a single keystroke or by highlighting your selection and hitting return.

Telix emulates four terminals: TTY, ANSI-BBS, VT102, and VT52. While it would have been preferable to have more, these four represent the most popular and should be enough to satisfy all conditions.

The powerful Telix dialing directory offers the user many options and capabilities. The user can set up as many directories as desired, each capable of holding up to 1,000 entries. Each listing can hold many items of information. In addition to basic information like parameter settings and script names, Telix will keep the date of the last call and the number of successful calls completed to that number. You can also set defaults for terminal emulation, protocol, echo, password for the remote server, etc. The auto-redial function can continuously dial a series of hard-to-access phone numbers until a connection is made. The numbers can be taken from "marked" entries in the directory, or from a user created "list" using the directory's LIST command. The directory has a search function and a usage log, which when activated, appends to a given file a log of all phone calls made and subsequent files transferred.

Telix's command language, SALT (Script Application Language for

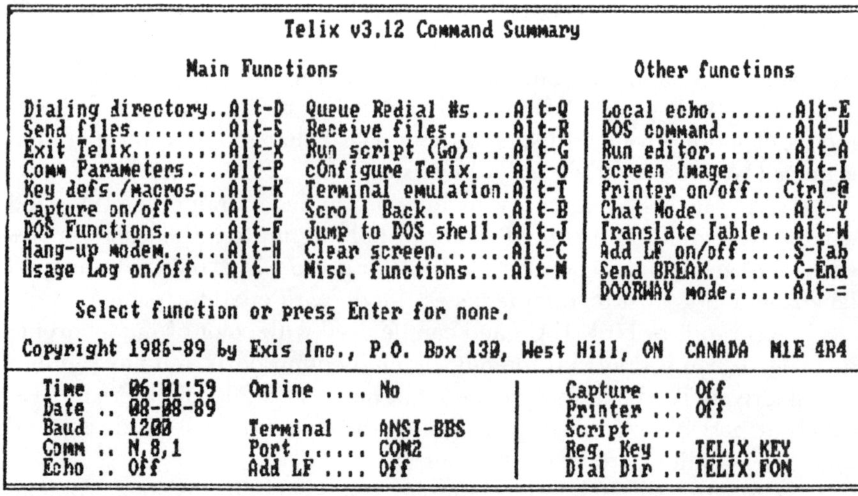

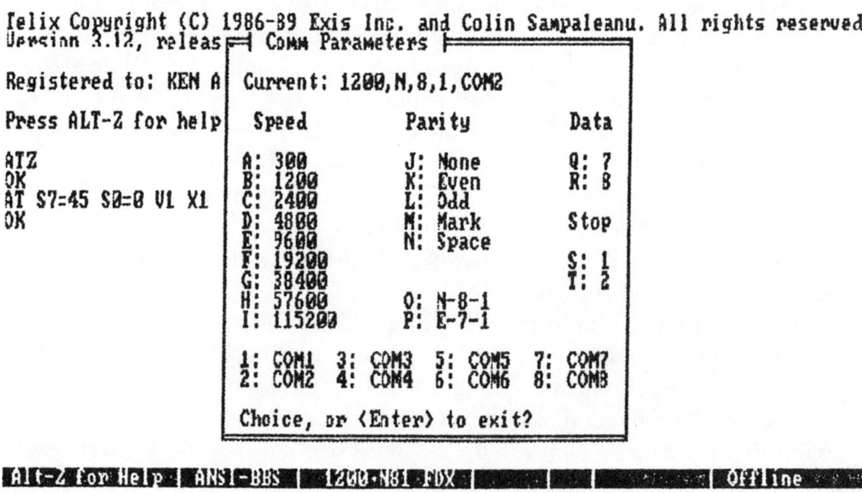

Top: **Figure 4.11: The Telix command summary menu also displays the time, date, parameter settings, and other useful information.** ***Bottom:*** **Figure 4.12: Parameter settings in Telix. Options include 8 baud settings, 5 parity settings, and a choice 8 Commports.**

Telix), is incredibly powerful, but enormously complex. The user inexperienced in command language and programming concepts will find SALT difficult to learn and will need to spend a fairly sizeable amount of time familiarizing himself with it in order to make full use of Telix's power and capabilities. This is time well spent, however, and made a bit easier by a separate and thoroughly comprehensive 100+ page manual describing SALT, its syntax and uses.

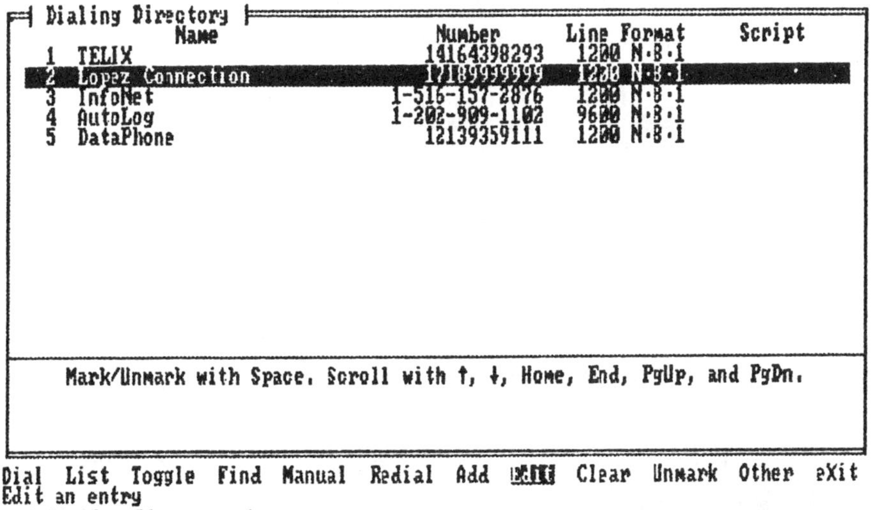

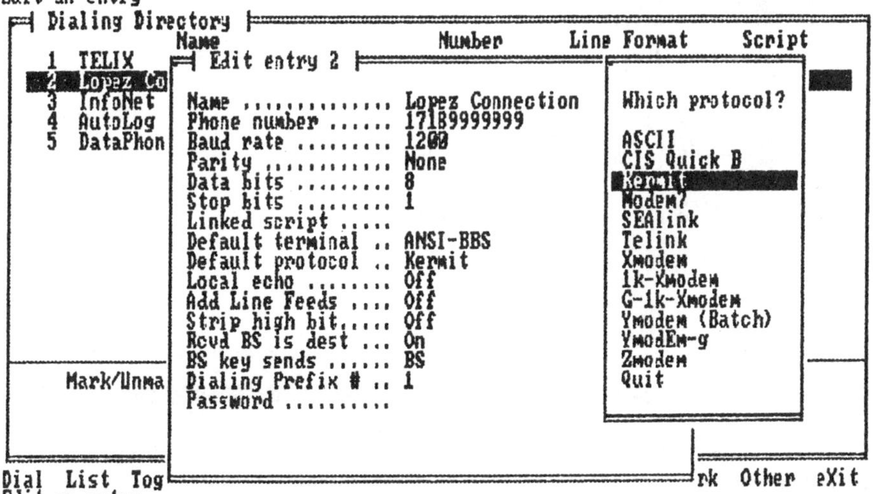

Top: Figure 4.13: A Telix dialing directory. The user can set up as many directories as desired, each capable of holding 1,000 entries. _Bottom:_ Figure 4.14: Each Telix directory entry has its own default settings as well as an optional password for restricted use.

The program's remote access function, Host, is so powerful it can act as a small bulletin board system. Others will be able to access your system to "chat" with you, or to upload or download files, depending on their assigned password level. The user will have full access through a four-level password system, preventing unauthorized access to areas not designated by you as open. Directories can be set up to be used strictly for uploading or for downloading files. A welcome message can be prepared for the caller

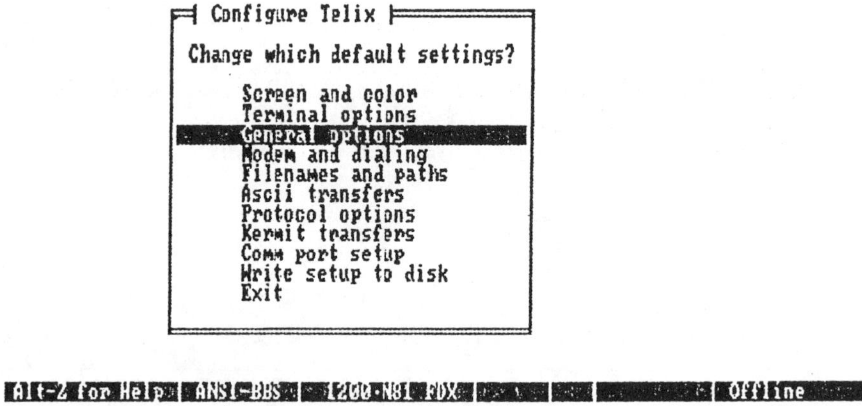

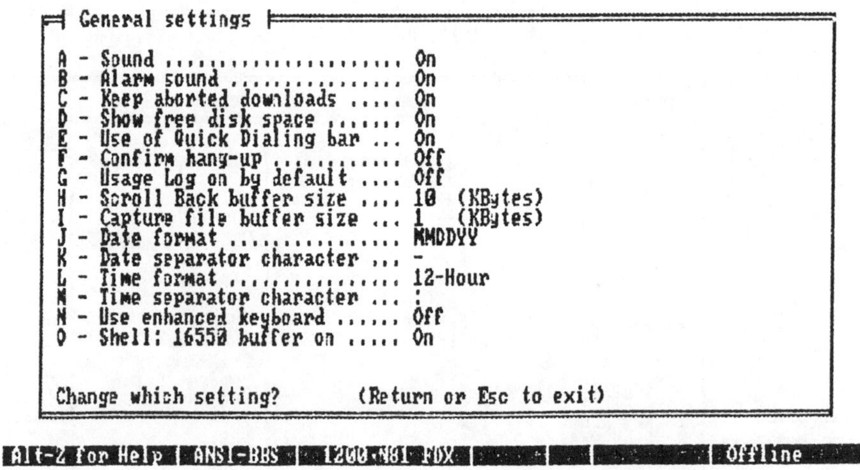

Figure 4.15 & Figure 4.16: System defaults are easily changed through Telix's menu system giving the user control over a vast number of functions and settings.

as well as a menu of options such as Upload, Download, Chat, Goodbye, etc. If the caller selects CHAT, the host operator is paged for 20 seconds with the option of entering the "chat" mode for direct communication with the caller. Host is a full-featured remote access system which, when combined with command language programming, can act as a limited bulletin board.

Telix offers 12 choices of popular file transferring protocols. The user is even allowed to define up to four external protocols, making compatibility with any system virtually assured.

Other features include "capturing" information coming in from the comm to disk or to printer, screen imaging which dumps the screen contents to disk, and scroll-back which allows you to move back through the last 1,000 to 64,000 characters received.

Telix is an extremely powerful communications program that probably looks and sounds more overwhelming than it really is. The basic and advanced functions of other communication programs are generally handled the same way here except that Telix offers the user far more capabilities and features. The enhancements make the program more complicated. The documentation is concise and very well written, however. The only major drawback is the difficulty in learning the command language, SALT. It is something that might be considered prohibitive to the user who wants the power of command language but does not possess, or want to spend considerable time learning, programming principles.

Overall, the program offers advantages to all users: providing easily applied basic operations without sacrificing the potential for more advanced applications. When you consider the modest registration cost of $35 and having the Telix Software Support BBS available 24 hours a day, one may find that the added time and effort needed to master this program is well worth the while.

Program: Telix Ver. 3.11 © 1986, 1987, 1988
Author: N/A
Company: Exis, Inc.
Address: P.O. Box 130, West Hill, Ontario M1E 4R4, Canada
Category: Communications Programs
Registration Fee: $35 ($44 CND)

General Evaluation: Telix Ver. 3.11

	Excellent	*Very Good*	*Good*	*Average*	*Poor*
Ease of Use		***			
Ease of Learning			***		
Documentation	***				
Utility	***				
Overall Rating	***				

5: Financial Programs

Introduction

In our travels, we have come across three types of financial management programs: very basic ones, suitable for not much more than home finance; bigger, more elaborate, semiprofessional programs, for advanced home management and small businesses; and the monster, "professional" management programs, that the layman could not begin to comprehend.

These professional level programs are for a specialized audience and are not being addressed here. Amongst the others, we were looking for two types of programs: a very capable but simple, easy to understand home financial management program that was not too simple, but also did not go overboard with complex accounting principles; and a more advanced home or small business financial manager, that would satisfy the needs of those looking for a little more than simple transaction recordkeeping, but would help that person along if he did not fully understand basic accounting principles.

Checkmate is unburdened and uncluttered with advanced accounting principles; yet it is not simplistic, is very capable, very efficient, and has some surprising features. Finance Manager II is far more sophisticated, more complex, though not overly so, and dives into basic accounting principles. The effort to bring the beginner along is genuine and effective and will be appreciated (they practically insist that you register).

However far you want to go with your financial management, one of these programs will fit the bill.

Checkmate™ Version 1.03

Checkmate is a very basic but very capable bank accounting program. It cannot compete with powerful commercially available home financial programs, but it is nicely planned, easy to use, and has some excellent and useful capabilities and features.

The program is designed to help the user keep track of their banking activity. It will record and maintain transactions, print reports, and help

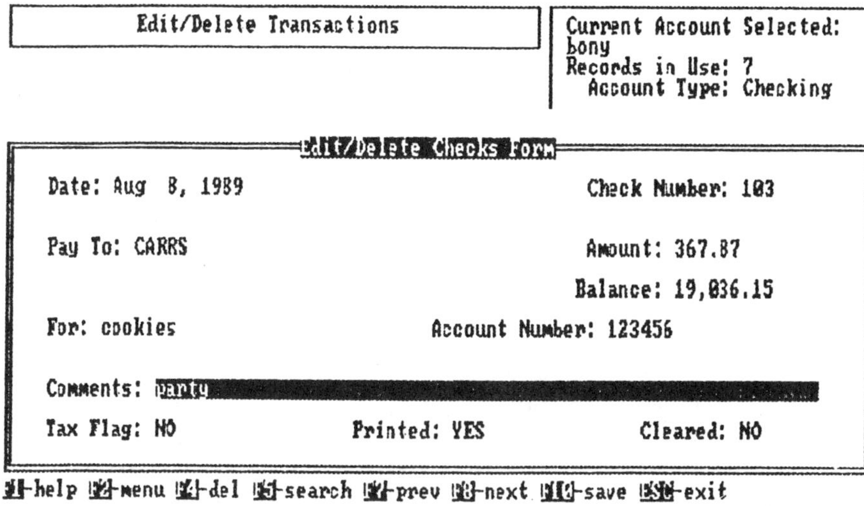

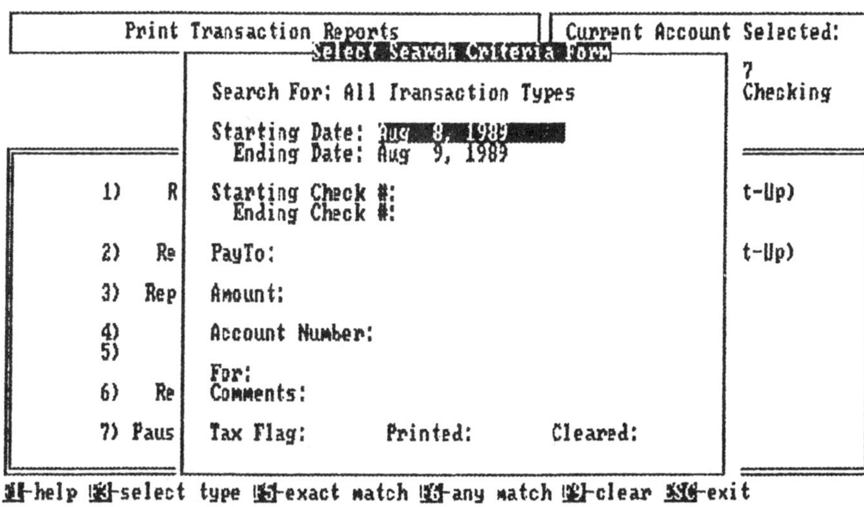

Top: Figure 5.1: A sample transaction in Checkmate. The program's scheme of financial management is to thoroughly manipulate a minimal amount of user supplied information making for an efficient but easy to use financial tool. _Bottom:_ Figure 5.2: Checkmate can access data using a variety of search criteria.

reconcile your statements. It can also be programmed to print checks. Balances are updated after every transaction, enabling the user to instantly track her bank account status.

The program needs 256K of RAM to run. One floppy drive is all that's needed, though two floppy drives or a hard drive is recommended.

The program's functions are well organized under pull-down menus and are categorized into five major groups: Accounts, for account setup and maintenance, Transactions, Reports, Setup and CALC.

Checkmate can support up to eight checking or savings accounts simultaneously, though the total number is limited only by your disk space. When defining an account, the user sets the name, including a short one for menu access, the account type, account number, opening balance, and next check number. Even after transactions have been entered, maintenance, such as a name change, can be performed. Changing the opening balance is no problem; Checkmate will update the entire data file.

The user has a choice of four types of transactions: Check, Deposit, Bank debit and Bank credit. After your selection, a form appears requesting information such as transaction date, payee or payer, the amount, the reason and comments. An optional "tax flag" is included to help you maintain your tax records. Another helpful item is the "cleared flag." If a transaction you enter already appears on your statement, you would indicate "yes." Otherwise, the flag remains "no" until you reconcile your entries with your statement and indicate otherwise, using the "Reconcile" function. Entries are added to the account by pressing F10. You can also delete an entry and Checkmate will automatically update the transaction file and the account.

Checkmate allows you to predefine often used transactions. When entering a transaction, you can select one you've predefined and it will be inserted automatically on the entry form. If you have a blank field in the predefined entry, the cursor will move to that field upon entry. Most users have often used transactions, thus this proves to be a very helpful function.

At any time, the user can generate one of three reports: a transaction report, listing all transactions; an account report, which prints a general record of all accounts; and a reconcile report, generally used to reconcile when you receive your statement. With transactions, you have the option of listing all transactions or selecting a "search criteria" for printing selective transactions. The criteria can be combined in any manner and include date range, check numbers, pages, amounts, and flags. Totals for the selected transactions will be printed.

Account reports can be selected to generate quick, one-line glances at account transactions, or a multiple-line comprehensive view of each transaction. Only the transactions for the specified account are generated.

The reconcilement report prompts the user, transaction by transaction, to indicate whether or not an entry has cleared on the statement. Checkmate will then print a report listing remaining outstanding transactions, actual balance, outstanding balance, and what the statement balance should be. If that figure does not match his statement, he can review and edit his entries to correct the problem.

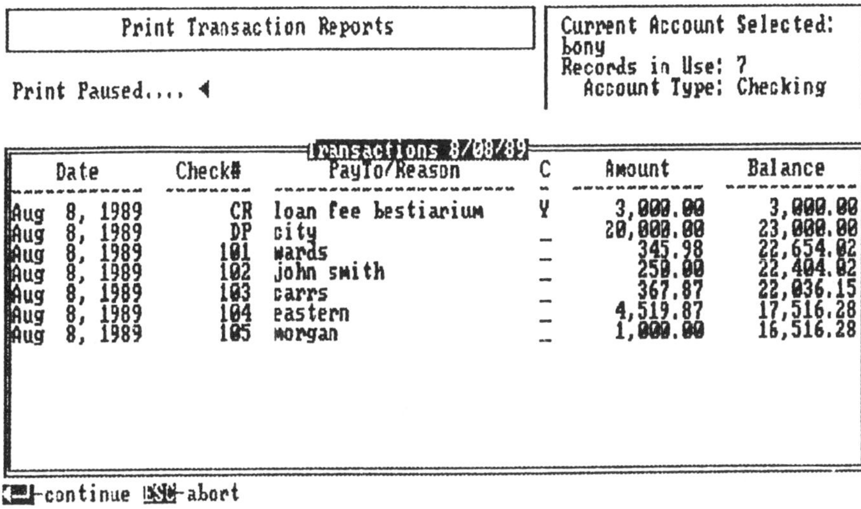

Print Transaction Reports

Print Paused....

Current Account Selected: bony
Records in Use: 7
Account Type: Checking

Transactions 8/08/89

Date	Check#	PayTo/Reason	C	Amount	Balance
Aug 8, 1989	CR	loan fee bestiarium	Y	3,000.00	3,000.00
Aug 8, 1989	DP	city	_	20,000.00	23,000.00
Aug 8, 1989	101	wards	_	345.98	22,654.02
Aug 8, 1989	102	john smith	_	250.00	22,404.02
Aug 8, 1989	103	carrs	_	367.87	22,036.15
Aug 8, 1989	104	eastern	_	4,519.87	17,516.28
Aug 8, 1989	105	morgan	_	1,000.00	16,516.28

-continue ESC-abort

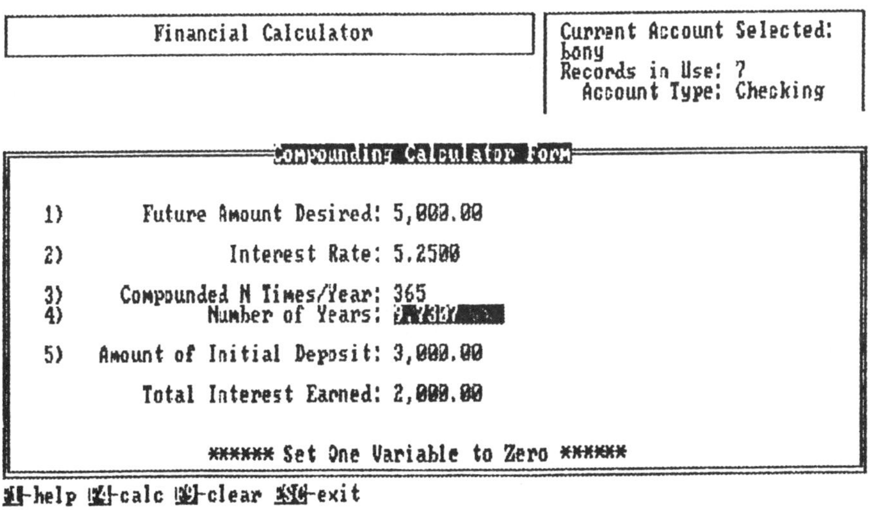

Financial Calculator

Current Account Selected: bony
Records in Use: 7
Account Type: Checking

Compounding Calculator Form

1) Future Amount Desired: 5,000.00

2) Interest Rate: 5.2500

3) Compounded N Times/Year: 365
4) Number of Years: [illegible]

5) Amount of Initial Deposit: 3,000.00

Total Interest Earned: 2,000.00

****** Set One Variable to Zero ******

-help -calc -clear ESC-exit

Top: Figure 5.3: An abbreviated transaction report organized by date. _Bottom:_ Figure 5.4: A compounding interest module. Checkmate comes with several "CALC" functions which enable the user to calculate an interest- or percentage-related variable from information the user supplies.

Checkmate also includes a facility for printing checks. An optional flag is included in the transaction form to indicate which check has been printed. The user prints out an elaborate graphical template which is used to set the parameters needed to print her check in the proper alignment. Setting up the parameters requires trial and error and is very time-consuming, but the facility works quite well, and is worth the time and effort required to set up.

A nifty addition to the program are the "CALC" functions which will calculate a missing variable from information you supply to accrued interest or percentage modules. For example, in the Loan function, you can calculate the number of years it would take to pay off x loan, at x interest rate, at x payments per year, at x dollars per payment. You supply the x values. Or you can calculate the amount of payment, when you supply the other variables. Other functions include Regular Deposits and Compounding Interest.

Checkmate is a very efficient, easy to use personal banking manager. The needs of most users will not go beyond this program's capabilities. Registration is $25 and includes the Checkmate manual which goes into greater detail than the shareware manual and includes tips and hints for better utilizing the system. You will also be placed on the mailing list to receive notices of updates and other products.

This program would be an excellent choice to handle basic bank accounting needs.

Program: Checkmate Ver. 1.03 © 1986
Author: N/A
Company: Custom Technologies
Address: P.O. Box 10096, Panama City, Florida 32404
Category: Financial Programs
Registration Fee: $25 (Florida residents add sales tax)

General Evaluation: Checkmate Ver. 1.03

	Excellent	*Very Good*	*Good*	*Average*	*Poor*
Ease of Use	***				
Ease of Learning	***				
Documentation		***			
Utility		***			
Overall Rating	***				

Finance Manager II™—General Ledger Version 1.2

Finance Manager II—General Ledger, henceforth referred to as FMII-GL, is a sophisticated, menu-driven, double-entry bookkeeping system suitable for personal or small business use. It is designed to be an effective and easy-to-use tool for the individual with a minimum of bookkeeping experience. It is capable of managing individual or small business finances.

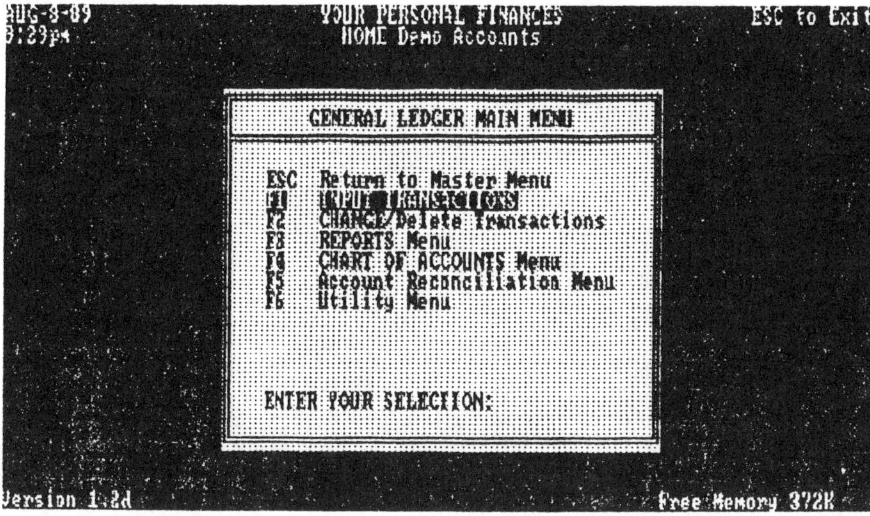

Figure 5.5: The FMII-GL main menu.

The program achieves a level of sophistication that can be difficult for those without some knowledge of basic accounting principles. Unlike other programs in its class, however, a genuine attempt is made to familiarize the beginner with enough principles to allow her to make effective use of this system. This fact, as well as the program's sophistication and relative ease of use, makes FMII-GL worth examining.

Finance Manager II is actually a full-featured, personal/small business financial management system. The program consists of several "modules" one of which is the General Ledger. Since FMII-GL is fully functional independently of the other modules, and the others, not included in the original package, have to be purchased separately, we will only be dealing with FMII-GL and not the other modules. Additional information on the other modules is available from the manual.

Amongst the many features and capabilities of FMII-GL is the ability to store and maintain nearly 2,000 accounts, maintain multiple books such as for home and work, allow 32,000 transactions per year, permit multiple debit and credit transactions, enter transactions from the previous month or year, prepare a full range of reports, perform automatic fiscal year out accounting, create graphs and more.

The system can operate with a monochrome or color monitor and requires 256K bytes of memory. Two floppy drives, or one high-density drive, or a hard disk drive is required.

The new user's first task will be to enter a "Chart of Accounts," a detailed listing of all financial accounts. These accounts are the basis for the

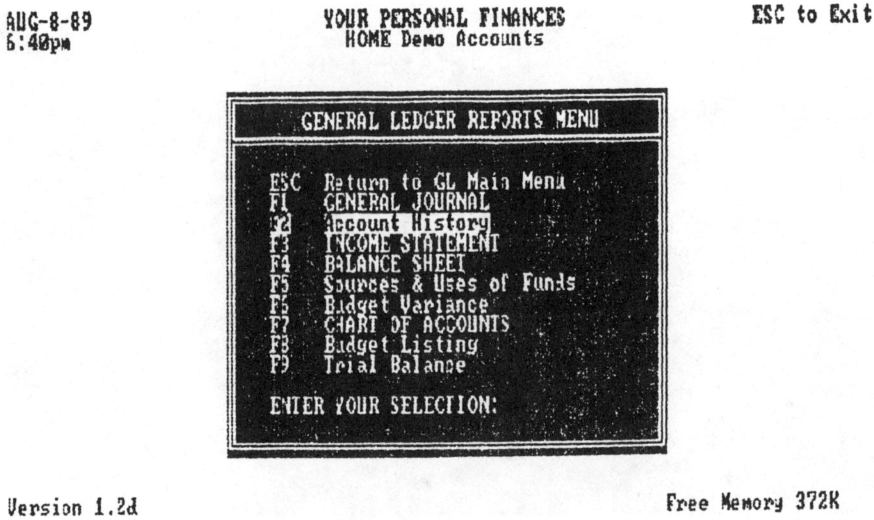

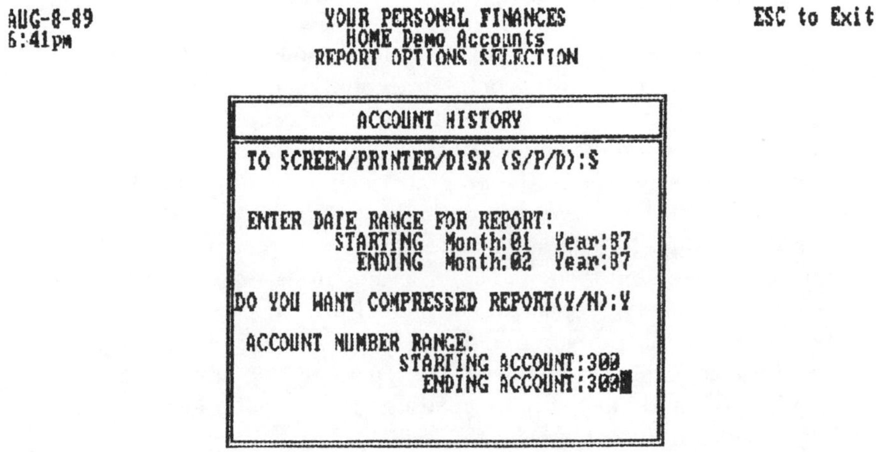

***Top:* Figure 5.6: The different report title available with FMII-GL. *Bottom:* Figure 5.7: FMII-GL reports can be organized by date and/or account and can be compressed for summarizations or non-compressed for more detail.**

entire management system and it is essential that the accounts be accurate and logical. FMII-GL provides two sets of sample account charts (home and work) with transactions and summaries for review. The documentation and samples are extremely beneficial to the user who is trying to start his own accounts chart.

Accounts are suborganized by account number types representing capital or equity, liabilities, assets, income and expenses. Each consists of

```
AUG-8-89                 YOUR PERSONAL FINANCES                     PAGE 1
6:42pm                    HOME Demo Accounts
                           ACCOUNT HISTORY
                        JAN-87 Through FEB-87

  DATE          DESCRIPTION            CL CHECK      DEBITS        CREDITS
-------- ----------------------------- -- -----   -----------   -----------
300 Checking account #2
-----------------------
         Beginning Balance                           2,000.00
01-02-87 car #2 payment                 * 1003                       150.00
01-15-87 paycheck                       * DEP          600.00
01-31-87 paycheck                       * DEP          610.00
02-02-87 car #2 payment                 * 1004                       150.00
02-05-87 The Denver                     * 1005                       350.00
02-15-87 Visa bill in full                1006                       118.25
02-15-87 paycheck                       * DEP          600.00
02-19-87 home furnishings                 1007                       295.35
02-28-87 paycheck                       * DEP          610.00
                                                  -----------   -----------
         Ending Balance                              3,356.40

                                                  PRESS ANY KEY TO CONTINUE
```

```
AUG-8-89                 YOUR PERSONAL FINANCES                     PAGE 8
6:50pm                    HOME Demo Accounts
                           GENERAL JOURNAL
                        JAN-87 Through DEC-87

  DATE    ACT#       ACCOUNT NAME      CL CHECK      DEBITS        CREDITS
-------- ---- ------------------------ -- -----   -----------   -----------
02-16-87 2100 Car loan #1                               55.00
          200 Checking account #1       * 1019                       200.00
         5100 Car loan #1 interest                     145.00
                 car #1 payment
02-17-87 5480 Gasoline                                  85.25
          200 Checking account #1       * 1020                        85.25
                 texaco bill
02-19-87 1350 Paintings                                295.35
          300 Checking account #2         1007                       295.35
                 home furnishings
02-21-87 5650 Dry Cleaning                              32.00
          200 Checking account #1       * 1021                        32.00
                 dry cleaning
02-22-87 1180 Boat                                   6,000.00
          200 Checking account #1       * 1022                     1,000.00
         2050 Bank loan                                            5,000.00
                 purchase used boat
                                                  PRESS ANY KEY TO CONTINUE
```

Top: **Figure 5.8: A compressed account history report organized by date and specific account.** ***Bottom:*** **Figure 5.9: An FMII-GL general journal report organized by transaction.**

an account number, name, short name, account type and balance. Account information can be modified, but before an account can be deleted, the balance on the account must be zero—the funds must be transferred to another account. This prevents the user from inadvertently creating an out of balance situation.

FMII-GL allows you to maintain and track a budget on each account.

At any time you can print a report showing the difference between amount budgeted and amount used. Report period can be by month, cumulative months, or yearly.

Transactions are entered by the standard account practice of double-entry bookkeeping. Each transaction involves the crediting of one account and the debiting of another. Again, the manual and sample demo accounts will assist you in understanding these principles. FMII-GL makes sure each transaction entered is in balance. If not, the transaction will not be accepted. FMII-GL allows for the possibility of transactions having multiple debit and credit entries.

If you wish to edit or review a transaction, FMII-GL has an excellent search function to help you locate it from amongst the 32,000 possible transactions. Searches are performed using a combination of criteria involving the transaction data. After finding the entry, you can change the transaction with two important restrictions: the system will not accept changes resulting in an out-of-balance status, and the number of parts in a multiple debit or credit entry must remain the same. Otherwise, you can delete the transaction and create a new one. After a delete, the system automatically updates the account.

A full range of reports is available with FMII-GL. General journal reports list all transactions which took place during a specific period of time. Account history will trace the activity of one or more accounts over a given period of time. Income statements tell you the net income or loss for a given period of time. Other reports tell you your financial position at any given time, sources of funds and how they were used, difference between an account's budgeted amount and actual amount used, and listings of the Chart of Accounts with respective balances. Most reports can be issued for a given point in time, a given period of time, and for an individual or series of accounts.

If you have a CGA or EGA display board, an IBM PS/2, or Hercules graphic card, you can plot active account balances by month and graphically display them on screen. To output the results you would need an EPSON 100 percent compatible printer.

FMII-GL is an excellent program for advanced personal or small business financial management. The elaborate demo files and the thorough education reference manual, make it possible for the novice to get as much use out of this fine program as an expert. It is unfortunate that the user is asked to purchase the other modules (accounts payable, accounts receivable, payroll, and, most unfortunately, account reconciliation) before trying them. However, FMII-GL is $40, which includes voice customer support, notification of updates, and a quarterly newsletter. If you hope to expand beyond the GL program, you should note that while you are under no obligation to register FMII-GL, the cost of the Accounts Receivable

AUG-8-89
6:58pm

YOUR PERSONAL FINANCES
HOME Demo Accounts
CHART OF ACCOUNTS

PAGE 2

ACT#	ACCOUNT NAME	SHORT	TYPE	BEGIN BAL
1400	Computer	IBMpc	A	0.00
1420	Stereo equipment	Stere	A	0.00
1440	TV sets	TV	A	0.00
1489	Total Electronic Assets	Elect	A	
1500	Books	Books	A	0.00
1600	Clothes	Cloth	A	0.00
1700	Jewlry	Jewlr	A	0.00
1900	Misc Other Assets	Misc	A	0.00
1989	Total Other Assets	Other	A	
1999	Total Fixed Assets	Fixed	A	
2000	House morgage	Mortg	L	65,000.00
2050	Bank loan	Bank	L	0.00
2100	Car loan #1	CarL1	L	8,000.00
2110	Car loan #2	CarL2	L	5,000.00
2189	Long Term Debt	Long	L	
2500	Master card	MC-In	L	0.00
2510	Visa card	VI-In	L	0.00
2889	Total Charge Card Debt	Charg	L	

PRESS ANY KEY TO CONTINUE

Figure 5.10: A partial Chart of Accounts. FMII-GL can maintain close to 2,000 accounts in each of several books with the user deciding the level of detail.

($30), Accounts Payable ($30), Payroll ($35), and Finance Utility ($20) modules, is a steep price to pay for sight unseen software. The Account Reconciliation module is $15 and is fully covered in the manual, and so may well be worth the gamble.

Program: Finance Manager II—General Ledger Ver. 1.2 © 1986, 1987, 1988
Author: N/A
Company: Hooper International
Address: P.O. Box 62219, Colorado Springs, Colorado 80962
Category: Financial Programs
Registration Fee: $40 (Add $3 shipping and handling; Colorado residents add sales tax)

General Evaluation: Finance Manager II—General Ledger Ver. 1.2

	Excellent	*Very Good*	*Good*	*Average*	*Poor*
Ease of Use		***			
Ease of Learning		***			
Documentation	***				
Utility	***				
Overall Rating	***				

6: Utility Programs

Introduction

If there is an area within the sphere of public domain or shareware software that can be designated as most vital, and perhaps most important, it is that of utility programs. These are, generally speaking, small programs designed to do a very specific job. Their purpose may be to show a real time clock in the upper righthand corner of any program's screen (CLOCK.COM), to encrypt sensitive data to keep it from prying eyes, making it available for use only by those who know the proper password (ENCRYPT.COM and DECRYPT.COM), or to print a calendar for a selected year on-screen (CAL.COM and THREECAL.COM). While none of these small programs may be of extraordinary importance, they, and other small gems from the thousands of available utilities, form a vital resource for any computer user. Perhaps most importantly, there are few commercial counterparts to the utility programs, since it is commercially unfeasible for software developers to market small, task-specific programs.

Not all utility programs are small and of limited use, however. Some, like the various versions of Norton's Utilities and Mace Utilities from commercial programmers Peter Norton and Paul Mace, have become invaluable tools for experienced computerists. They offer such priceless capabilities as recovering data from otherwise unusable disks, "unerasing" files which have been mistakenly deleted, defragmenting hard disks or floppies for greater efficiency, diagnosing hard-disk (or floppy disk) problems while they can still be repaired, sorting files in a disk by various criteria and even recovering data from a disk which has been accidentally reformatted. Most serious users would no more be without these programs—or others like them—than a skydiver would attempt to jump from an airplane without a parachute. Fortunately, there are also several programs in the public domain and shareware areas that perform some of the functions of the above software packages and work very much like them. For users who do not know anything about file recovery software or who have never heard of Paul Mace or Peter Norton, these programs are a must.

Disk Utilities

The new computer user seldom thinks about the way in which files are organized on a hard disk of floppy disk, let alone the problems that may arise when such seemingly inscrutable and exotic things as file allocation tables or low-level formats begin to go awry. As soon as one begins to feel comfortable with the computer and becomes familiar with DOS (the disk operating system, the system's software that controls all input, output and processing operations of the computer and without which an IBM-compatible computer cannot work), however, the operating system's limitations become clear, as does its iconoclastic command structure which is in many cases anything but easy to remember or use.

Fortunately, there is help available in dealing with DOS and in overcoming some of its limitations. There are programs which act as DOS shells and allow for some DOS commands to be performed through pull-down menus. The best of these programs also help with routine file maintenance, such as copying and deleting files, creating and moving between subdirectories and sorting files on a disk. Advanced features such as hiding files or changing file attributes are also supported.

Other programs also help in such matters as creating hidden subdirectories, retrieving accidentally deleted files and making sensitive data files unreadable to anyone not possessing the appropriate password. Still others will assist both new and experienced users by creating menu systems to easily access programs in hard disks or floppies through a pull-down menu system. All of these programs are quite useful and either free or an unbeatable bargain.

Disk Commander™ Version 1.10

Disk Commander is the type of program which one seldom thinks about until it is needed. The program is a disk manager which allows for some useful operations to be performed on hard disks or floppies. Among these are the ability to recover accidentally erased files, sorting disk directories and files in accordance to various criteria, defragmenting files for more efficient disk use, and performing some preventive maintenance and repairs on the underlying structure of either floppy disks or hard disks.

Perhaps the greatest benefit of the program is its ability to diagnose and automatically correct minor problems in the structure of a disk before they can become major ones rendering a whole disk or part thereof unusable. The program checks the integrity of the File Allocation Table, boot tracks and each individual file and sector in the disk. Where potential

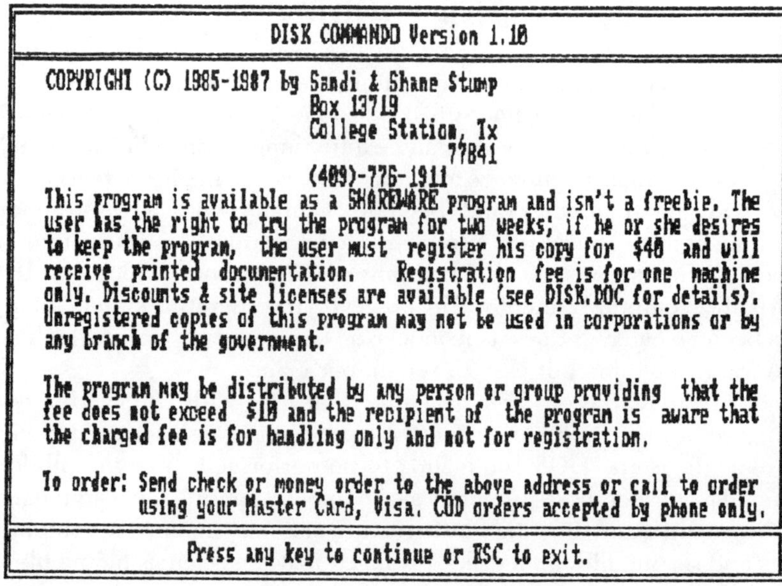

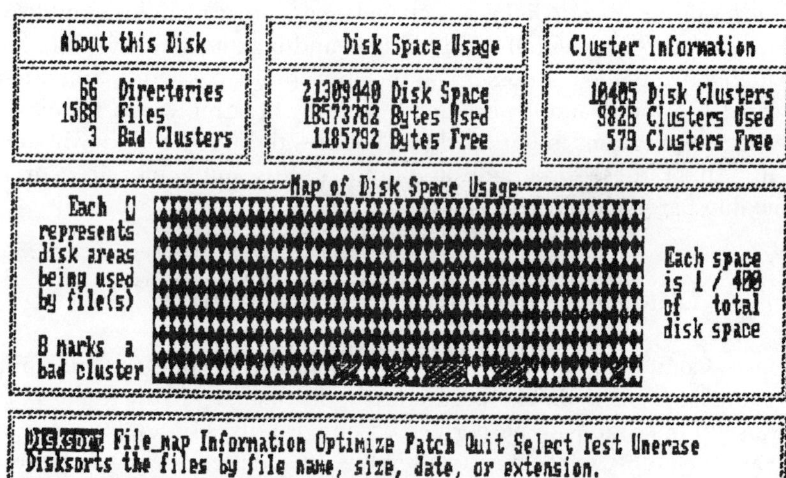

Top: **Figure 6.1: Opening screen and copyright notice for Disk Commander Ver. 1.0.** ***Bottom:*** **Figure 6.2: Main menu for Disk Commander Ver. 1.0.**

problems are encountered, they are corrected, if their correction is possible; even if a problem is discovered which cannot be fixed, the program reports the problem to the user, who can then take additional steps in order to prevent the loss of valuable data in the disk.

The program can also defragment files and thereby improve a disk's

[Checking Disk Boot Record, Fat Tables, and Root Directory]

Sector Range	Range Description	Condition
0 - 0	Boot Record	Good!
1 - 10	Fat Table 1	Good!
11 - 18	Fat Table 2	Good!
19 - 32	Directory	Good!

Boot Sector, FAT Tables, and Root Directory OK!

Checking Unused Data Clusters

Number of files	00229
Number of clusters on disk	02847
Number of existing bad clusters	00036
Number of new bad clusters	00000
Number of files to be repaired	00000
File at	00001
Cluster at	00417

Press <ESC> to Abort

Figure 6.3: Disk Test feature of Disk Commander Ver. 1.0. The program checks both disks and files for problems and fixes them where possible.

efficiency. As data are added and deleted from a floppy disk or a hard disk, DOS constantly reallocates the tracks and sectors where information for any given file is stored; hence, it is possible for a single file to be scattered about in many small fragments throughout a floppy disk. The more a disk is accessed and the file retrieved and resaved the likelier that the file will be fragmented, and that a problem will occur. Disk Commander makes it possible to store information in existing files in contiguous file clusters. This also improves disk access time, making programs and files load faster.

Another feature of Disk Commander is its ability to sort disk files by file name, file extension, size or the date they were created; in each case, files may be sorted in ascending or descending order. This feature will be welcomed by users with hard disks or who keep a substantial number of files on floppies. Viewing directories which are sorted with one of the noted options makes finding files simpler. The sorting process takes only seconds to perform.

Disk Commander also allows for the recovery of accidentally erased files. The program is especially useful when used with a hard disk, since it supports subdirectories and will graphically show when a subdirectory contains erased files. File recovery is both simple and automatic, and takes only a few seconds. The program lists the number of erased files in a selected

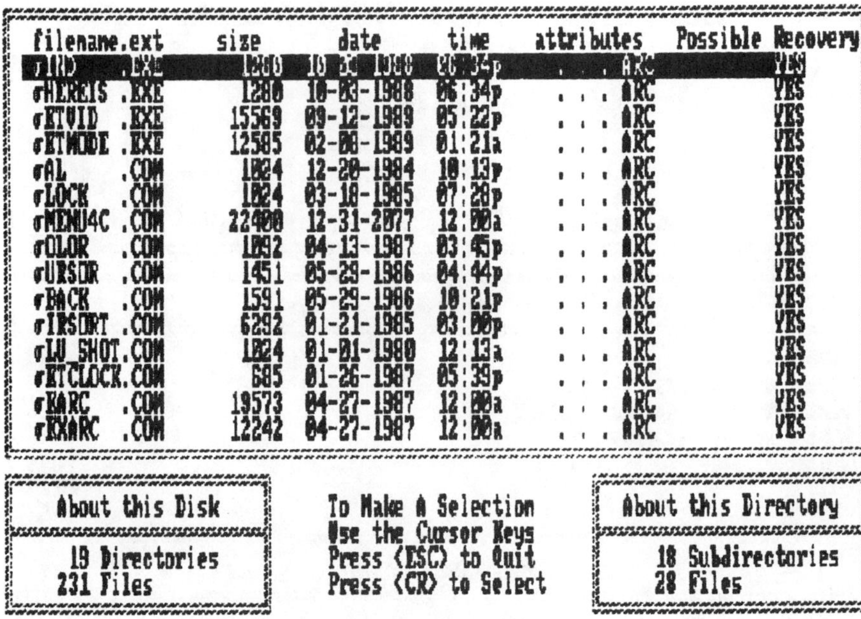

Figure 6.4: Unerase option of Disk Commander allows for files which have been mistakenly erased to be retrieved. The program advises which erased files are good candidates for recovery. Once a user selects a file by highlighting it, she need only supply the first letter of the filename; the program automatically searches for the lost data and revitalizes the file.

drive or directory and also reports which of these are recoverable. As a rule, every file accidentally erased is fully recoverable, provided that a user immediately uses a program like Disk Commander. Waiting to recover files at a later time makes it less likely that a given file can be recovered. As new files are created, they may be placed in a disk space previously occupied by the erased file; when this happens, the erased file is no longer recoverable.

The program can report on the technical specifications of a user's computer system and on any selected disk. Using this feature, the program will report on, among other things, the amount of Random Access Memory it finds, the number and type of output ports, and the speed of the system being used relative to the IBM PC's clock rate of 4.77 Megahertz.

The distribution copy of the program comes with only a three-page "documentation" file which is by no means complete. The program is so intuitive, however, that the lack of documentation is almost irrelevant. Printed documentation is available upon payment of the $40 registration fee.

Program: Disk Commander Ver. 1.10 © 1985–1987
Author: Sandy and Shane Stump
Address: Box 13719, College Station, TX 77841
Category: Disk Management Utility
Registration Fee: $40

General Evaluation: Disk Commander Ver. 1.10

	Excellent	*Very Good*	*Good*	*Average*	*Poor*
Ease of Use	***				
Ease of Learning	***				
Documentation					***
Utility		***			
Overall Rating	***				

Totaldir™ Version 1.1

Totaldir, which is short for Total Directory Display Utility, is a utility program which is designed to greatly enhance the DOS Directory (DIR) command. The DOS command gives users some flexibility in searching for files on a disk and in displaying the contents, or directories, of disks in general. Its limitations, however, are soon apparent to even the casual user. Among other limitations, the DOS command does not allow a user to scroll back and forth to view large directories. Directories cannot be easily sorted by file name, extension, size, or date (they can through DOS, but it is not a matter to be undertaken by the neophyte). Totaldir addresses these concerns and many others, and offers a wonderful enhancement to one of the most used DOS commands.

Among the program's powerful features are the ability to view the size of subdirectories within a disk, sort directories by any combination of size, date, time, filename or extension, or file attribute, the capability of scrolling up and down long directory listings and the ability to display hidden system files and file attributes, as well as change the latter. The program also offers the ability to add comments to file names which may be viewed in a directory listing. These comments can be changed at will, and are most useful in explaining what otherwise cryptic filenames stand for.

Totaldir is relatively easy to use and contains an on-line help feature, as well as pull-down menus for most of its options. The package is well conceived and implemented. For users who have grown to accept (though not *like*) the inevitable limitations of the DOS DIR command, the program will bring welcomed flexibility. One should not take the program's name too literally, for this is far more than a mere replacement for the DIR command.

```
Enter Command: █ Help Filename Attrib Data sorT Edit Quit BCDMNOFRUWXY
Copyright (C) 1988 Logical Business Systems  Press "W" for Shareware Message █

Directory Listing for : D:\*.*
IBMBIO    COM            22100 A  SHR We 18 Mar 87  12:00p
IBMDOS    COM            30159 A  SHR Tu 17 Mar 87  12:00p
DATA          (Dir) 1907876  D        We 22 Mar 89   7:10p
DOS           (Dir)  563282  D        Sa 11 Mar 89   7:03p
PZ            (Dir)  383998  D        We  5 Apr 89   8:00p
WS5           (Dir) 4578539  D        Su 12 Mar 89  10:36a
SLSOPT    $$$            24576 A   HR Sa 15 Apr 89   5:16p
AUTOEXEC  BAT              128 A      Tu  1 Jan 80  12:01a
B         BAT              128 A      Tu  1 Jan 80   2:06a
BACKUP    BAT              128 A      We 12 Apr 89   8:45p
MSS       BAT              128 A      Fr 19 May 89   5:42p
PZ        BAT               14 A      Fr 21 Apr 89   5:34p
Q         BAT                6 A      We 22 Mar 89   7:32p
SORT      BAT               12 A      Mo 20 Mar 89   8:24p
COMMAND   COM            25307 A      Tu 17 Mar 87  12:00p
PARK      COM              403 A      Sa 20 Feb 88  12:00a
SYSDAT    BAT                0 A      Fr 30 Jun 89   7:24p
HDPARK    EXE             7500 A      Mo 23 Feb 87   9:09p
ANSI      SYS             1678 A      Th 23 Mar 89   4:49p
```

Figure 6.5: Actual display of directory listing using Totaldir. Notice that there is more information on the screen than would be available with DOS, including the actual size in bytes taken up by each individual directory. The program allows one to scroll up and down through the directory listing, viewing all files on a disk at one time by directory without having to perform tedious directory searches using path statements. A wealth of options is available through pull-down menus.

In fact, the program brings together a wealth of features which can be found either in other programs or as stand-alone utilities (e.g., the ability to sort files, change file attributes and add comments to filenames). This nicely packages them all in one place and makes them easily available. The program also offers enhancements not found in most other utilities which can perform similar tasks; for example, many other utilities offer a sort capability, but few offer one which allows the sorting by file attributes. There are numerous other signs that this is a quality program that become apparent the more one uses it.

The distribution copy of the program comes with a 22-page printable manual which is well written and covers all the intricate commands and options for the program in language which is easy to understand. Useful examples of how the program can be used are given throughout. A printed copy of the manual, as well as the newest version of the program, is available for the $15 registration fee. For those who wish to register their program but do not need the printed manual, a $10 registration fee will still bring the newest copy of the program. This is indeed a small price to ask for a program which is as well designed and useful as this one.

```
              TOTALDIR SHAREWARE MESSAGE

 COPYRIGHT 1988, Logical Business Systems

 You may copy and distribute evaluation copies of this software
 free of charge if you distribute unaltered copies together
 with the accompanying TOTALDIR.DOC documentation file.
 If this software is of benefit to you and you use it frequently,
 send $15.00 registration fee to:

     Logical Business Systems
     346 N Walnut Street
     Fayetteville, AR 72701

 With yer registration fee, you will receive a new copy of the
 current version together with a printed manual and will be
 placed on our mailing list for notification of updates and new
 releases. Registration with new disk, but no manual is $10.00.

 Future enhancements include:  Copy, Delete, Move, Execute;
 Set Attributes, Date, Time; Faster execution; Smaller size.

Press any key to continue . . .
```

Figure 6.6: Copyright notice and shareware information screen for Totaldir. Unlike most other shareware programs, this screen does not automatically come up every time the program is invoked, but must actually be called up by a user wishing to see it. This soft-sell approach and the program's low registration fee leave users with no excuse not to register their copies if they decide to regularly use the program.

Program: Totaldir Ver. 1.1 © 1988
Company: Logical Business Systems
Address: 346 N Walnut Street, Fayetteville, AR 72701
Category: Disk Management Utility
Registration Fee: $15 for printed manual and latest version
$10 for latest version (no manual)

General Evaluation: Totaldir Ver. 1.1

	Excellent	*Very Good*	*Good*	*Average*	*Poor*
Ease of Use		***			
Ease of Learning		***			
Documentation	***				
Utility	***				
Overall Rating	***				

DOSamatic
NOT a Registered Copy....SN03001

If you find this program useful, you can register as a user and obtain the very latest version of the program and the user manual by sending a check or money order for $39.00 (suggested contribution) to :

Marin Pacific Software
1001 Bridgeway, Suite 514
Sausalito, CA 94965

Please enclose your name and address, along with any comments or suggestions which you may have. Registered users receive a 10% commission on copies registered with their number. Please give copies of this program to other users to evaluate, but DO NOT distribute it for any charge or fee. Please include the name and serial number above when writing to us. Site licenses are available for corporate users requiring multiple copies.
CompuServe users may contact Steve Mykytyn at userid 72447,2372.

Use of DOSamatic is at your own risk, and subject to the license agreement printed in the DOSamatic User Guide.

Copyright 1985 Steve Mykytyn

Press any key to start DOSamatic

Figure 6.7: Opening screen and copyright notice for DOSamatic.

DOSamatic™ Version 2.03

DOSamatic is a disk management program which offers various enhancements over DOS in managing disk files. The program offers a user interface which is easy to use, providing users with the ability to perform many DOS tasks (and others outside of the normal DOS functions) by using pull-down menus.

Among the program's many uses, it provides a simple way to view files in any subdirectory, and to scroll up and down any directory listing. It also allows for the creation and deletion of files, and the creation, removal and changing of subdirectories. It can also print text files, without having to exit to DOS or remember the corresponding DOS commands or their syntax. Files in directories may also be sorted by various criteria, and file attributes may be changed for any file; this means that hidden files may be viewed, and sensitive files may be toggled as hidden and read-only, to keep them from being seen by casual users or accidentally erased. This is a feature which DOSamatic shares with many other good disk management utility programs, including others reviewed herein.

The program allows users to browse through ASCII text files, or peek into binary files effortlessly. Advanced DOS features such as the Debug or Edlin programs can also be accessed through DOSamatic's pull-down

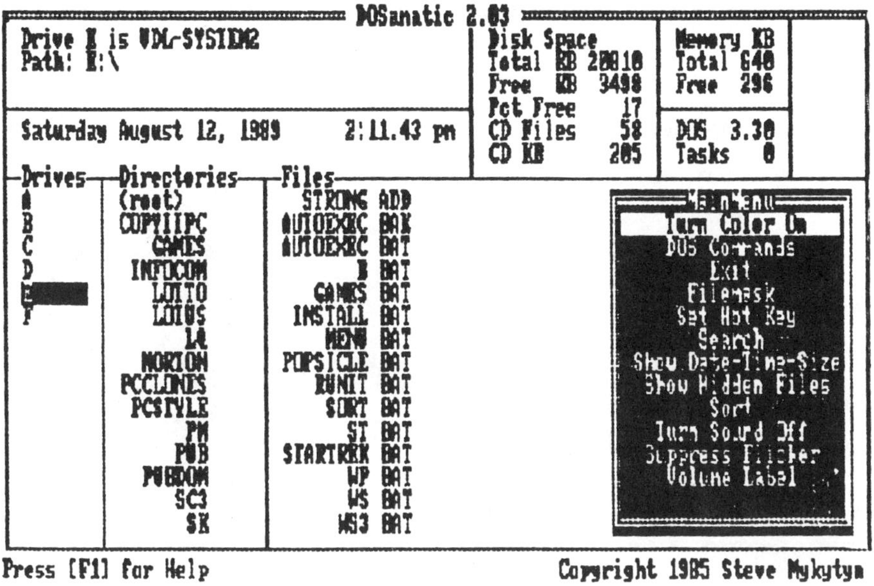

Figure 6.8: Main menu for DOSamatic. The program makes many of the most common functions of DOS easily accessible to users through a user-friendly pull-down menu system.

menus. Volume labels can easily be added to disks or changed if they already exist—another enhancement over DOS.

One of the more interesting features of DOSamatic is its ability to run more than one program at once. Although a computer running the Intel 80286 or 80386 microprocessors is needed for true multi-tasking capabilities—preferably running the OS/2 or Unix operating systems—this program is capable of emulating a multi-tasking environment on a plain IBM PC/XT or clone, providing sufficient memory exists to support multiple programs (preferably 640KB). The program allows for free RAM to be allocated for up to seven different programs to run at any given time, and to toggle between any of them, so that up to seven programs can be available and "running" at any given time; whenever a program is toggled "on," all others are suspended. Only one program can run at any one time, but the others are kept loaded and ready to resume working from whatever point they left off whenever they are called up.

While neither DOSamatic, nor other programs which work similarly to it, is a necessity for anyone running a computer, they can certainly be of enormous assistance, particularly for users who do not feel intimately comfortable working at the DOS command level. Even for advanced users, DOS shells like DOSamatic can be very helpful in performing routine file maintenance and functions outside the limits of DOS.

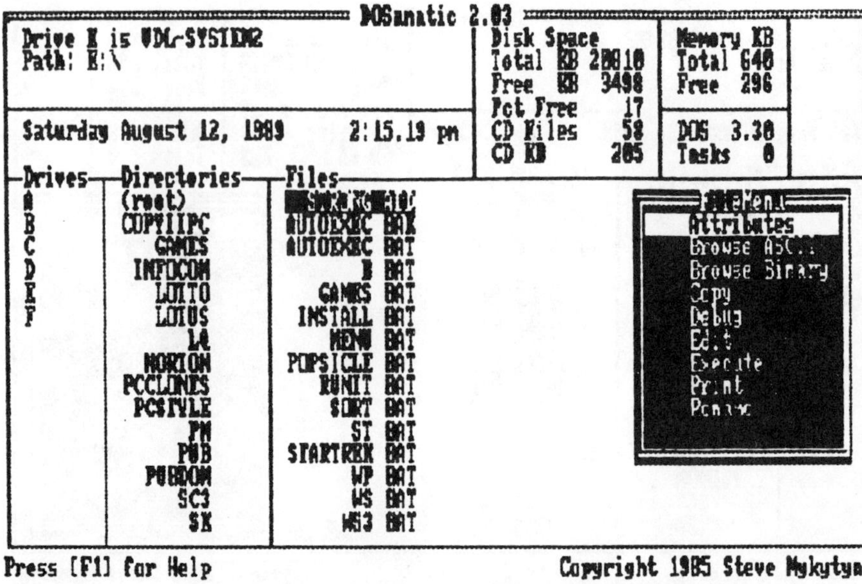

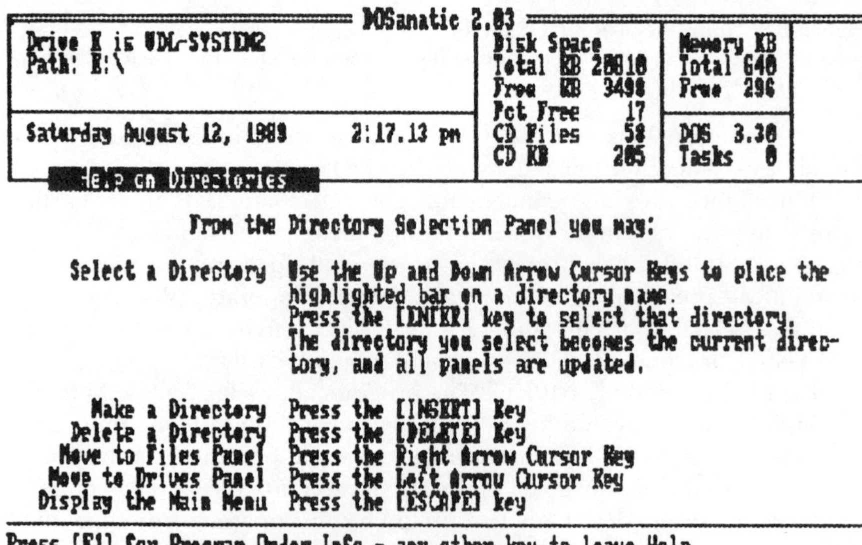

Top: Figure 6.9: File menu for DOSamatic. The program makes sorting files, changing file attributes, printing or typing programs onto the screen, as well as running Edlin (or any other editor) and Debug, a simple point-and-shoot operation. The program brings welcomed enhancements to many DOS features. Note that important information, such as the version of DOS being used, the amount of free RAM available for running programs and the number of tasks (programs) available to the computer at a given time are all displayed on screen. *Bottom:* Figure 6.10: Assistance is always a keystroke away through DOSamatic's context-sensitive help screens.

Program: DOSamatic Ver. 2.03 © 1985
Author: N/A
Company: Marin Pacific Software
Address: 1001 Bridgeway, Suite 514, Sausalito, CA 94965
Category: Disk Management Utility
Registration Fee: $39 (includes latest update and user's guide)
A 10% commission is given to registered users who distribute the program to other users who go on to register their copies at the full $39 fee.

General Evaluation: DOSamatic Ver. 2.03

	Excellent	*Very Good*	*Good*	*Average*	*Poor*
Ease of Use	***				
Ease of Learning	***				
Documentation		***			
Utility	***				
Overall Rating	***				

Directory Master™ Version 2.3

Directory Master is another disk management utility program whose main purpose is to help users copy and delete files, as well as perform other file management chores. Like other DOS shell or file management programs reviewed herein, this program enhances the ability of DOS to perform routine file maintenance, and offers capabilities not readily available through DOS.

Directory Master allows for easy scanning of disk subdirectories for files without the need to perform tedious directory searches with complicated path statements. The program is also quite useful in organizing files between floppies, within hard disks, or in any combination of floppies and hard disks. Like most programs of its type, Directory Master permits the copying or erasing of multiple files in a single operation. For example, if one wishes to copy all word processing files from a data diskette which contains word processing, database and spreadsheet data files, the relevant files can be highlighted on screen and then all highlighted (or "flagged") files can be copied onto a separate diskette or directory. Although DOS allows a similar operation through the use of wildcards, such operations are only possible where all related files have been given related names; for example, all files beginning with the characters L-E-T can be copied between disks or directories by DOS by issuing the command: COPY LET*.* [target drive] [target directory]. In this way, files whose names begin with LET

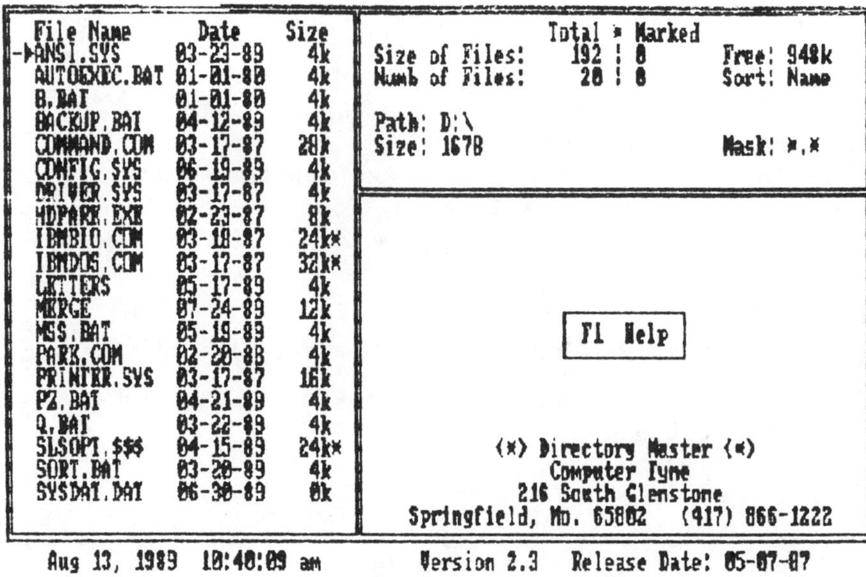

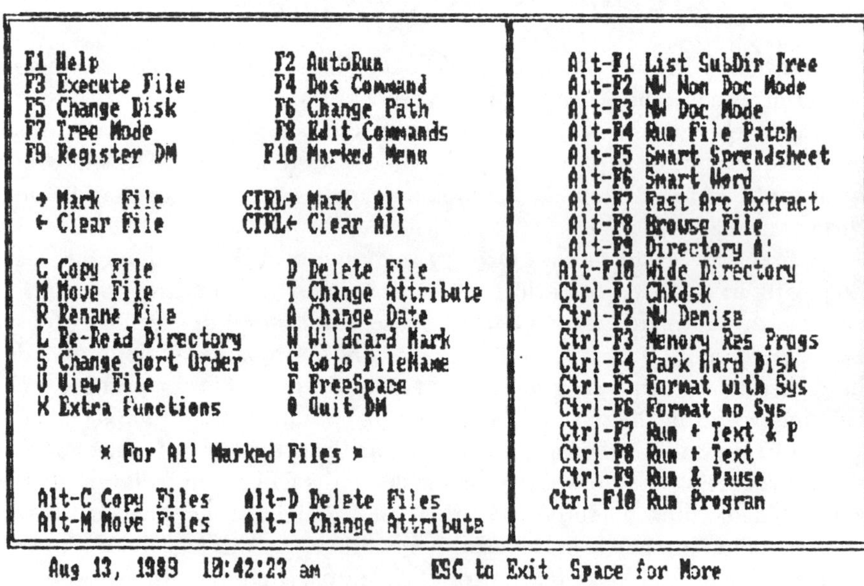

Top: Figure 6.11: Opening screen for Directory Master. _Bottom:_ Figure 6.12: Main help screen for Directory Master. All features are easily accessible by selecting the proper function key. The help screen works like an optional pull-down menu which one calls upon whenever needed by pressing the F1 key.

Copyright 1987, by Computer Tyme Inc. All rights reserved. This is a user supported shareware product. We encourage you to pass it along to others. For a registration fee of $60, you will receive a disk containing the latest DM, with your own registered serial number, a manual, and other software goodies. We think that after using it, you will see that DM is worth $60. Update disks are available for $25. Missouri residents add 5.725% sales tax. A $15 finders fee is paid to you for each user who registers using your serial number. A second level fee of $5 is paid for each user who your users get to register. We also pay up to $75 for suggestions we use, or bugs we fix. If you are in a position to widely distribute DM, or know someone who can, it could be somewhat profitable. Commercial distributors contact the author for special arrangements or site licensing. Written permission required.

To register, use the Print Registration Form command. This is necessary to pay the finders fee to the last registered users. Please fill out the registration form completely. We appreciate your comments. Thank you for supporting DM.

(*) Authors: Marc Perkel and Rufus M. McCluer Jr. (*)

Serial Number:
Computer Tyme IBBS: (417) 866-1665 * 14/631 or (417) 237-2111 * 14/633

Aug 13, 1989 11:58:33 am ESC to Exit Space for More

Figure 6.13: Copyright notice screen for Directory Master. Unlike most other shareware programs, this screen containing the shareware notice does not appear every time the program is invoked, but must be called up if one wishes to view it by accessing the third help screen. This is a nice convenience feature while one evaluates the program and a laudable "soft-sell" approach.

(such as LETTER, LETTER.889, LETBOBBY.AUG, etc.) would all be copied at once. But any word processing files which do not begin with the common L-E-T would not be copied, and separate copy commands would have to be issued for them—a tedious and time-consuming process. Directory Master greatly simplifies this process by allowing any group of files to be copied or deleted in a single operation, regardless of whether they share common elements in their file names or extensions.

The program's capabilities are not limited to easy file copying and deleting. Files can also be renamed, sorted, and their attributes changed (e.g., hidden files can be made visible, and read-only files can be modified, while otherwise visible files can be made invisible and protected from accidental erasure or change). Other DOS commands can also be run directly from the program by selecting them from a pull-down menu. These include the FORMAT and CHKDSK commands. In addition, total size of subdirectories in bytes is reported, a useful feature. The contents of ASCII files can also be viewed directly through the program in an enhanced version of the DOS TYPE command. Programs can also be selected and run using the "point and shoot" pull-down menu system. The program also offers the ability to program macro definitions into function keys for predefined tasks to be automatically performed; up to ten function keys may be programmed and later accessed.

The program comes with a 35-page printable manual which is well written and helpful. The manual covers the main features of the program and reviews some DOS concepts and commands which all users would do well to learn. At its $60 registration fee, the program is clearly the most expensive in its class without offering any great innovation or advantage over its competitors. A commission is offered to registered users who distribute the program to others who in turn register those copies; a generous $15 commission is given for first-generation registration and a $5 commission for every second-generation registration. Hence, users who widely distribute their programs may well get back *more* than they originally paid for their registered copy. They could make a nice profit. The program is certainly worth exploring as with all "try before you buy" shareware offerings. There is no obligation to register one's copy unless one uses it regularly after a reasonable evaluation period (the author states in the disk-based manual that anyone using the program for more than a week or two should send in the registration fee). The registration fee includes a printed manual and updates as they become available.

Program: Directory Master Ver. 2.3 © 1987
Author: Mark Perkel and Rufus M. McCluer, Jr.
Company: Computer Tyme, Inc.
Address: 216 South Glenstone, Springfield, MO 65802
Category: Disk Management Utility
Registration Fee: $60 (includes printed manual and future updates) Commissions given for future registrants ($15 for first-generation and $5 for second-generation)

General Evaluation: Directory Master Ver. 2.3

	Excellent	*Very Good*	*Good*	*Average*	*Poor*
Ease of Use	***				
Ease of Learning		***			
Documentation	***				
Utility	***				
Overall Rating	***				

Sorted Directory Listing™ Version 2.6

SDIR26 (Sorted Directory Listing) is a directory sorting utility which has been released into the public domain. It is meant as a direct replacement for the DOS DIR command and adds some useful features to that most used of all DOS commands.

SDIR26 lists a disk directory which contains from four to six columns of file listings. In addition, the command contains several switches that may be used with it for greater flexibility. These include the ability to list hidden files, pause the scrolling when the screen is full, and give output which is either unsorted, or has been sorted by file size, date, time or extension.

The program is not as powerful as full file managers, but is much more powerful than the DOS DIR command. And, best of all, it is in the public domain, so that it is absolutely free. Although documentation accompanying it is limited to a very small file (8 lines of information) listing the various switches available with the program, the program is easy to use despite the poor documentation. It should be noted that most utility programs in the public domain are released with either very limited documentation or none at all; but that is part of their allure, since there is much fun (and learning) to be gleaned for ferreting out these small gems.

Program: Sorted Directory Listing Ver. 2.6 (SDIR26)
Author: John F. Ratti
Category: Disk Management Utility
Registration Fee: None (Public Domain)

General Evaluation: Sorted Directory Listing Ver. 2.6

	Excellent	*Very Good*	*Good*	*Average*	*Poor*
Ease of Use	***				
Ease of Learning	***				
Documentation					***
Utility			***		
Overall Rating			***		

General Utilities

Utility programs are too numerous and varied so as to be easily categorized. While certain types of programs fit neatly into a given category, such as "disk utilities" or "printer utilities," most others do not. Many are so specific so as to be of use to only a small number of people (e.g., there are utilities of use only to engineers, attorneys or other professionals, as well as utilities which work with specific hardware which only a few people have, such as an obsolete printer or terminal). None of these will be explored here. Many programs which do not fit neatly into a given software niche are quite useful; we've assembled a sampling of useful utility programs—by no means an exhaustive one, since the vast number of excellent utility programs could fill several volumes such as this one by themselves—which are representative of what is available in the public domain and through the shareware form of software distribution. While none of these programs may be of tremendous importance of itself, each is quite useful and works well. Together, they are representative of a veritable cornucopia of terrific programs.

Clock™

Utility programs need not be grandiose in order to be noteworthy—only useful. A good example is the Clock program from GoldenSoft Software. This small utility program places a clock on the upper righthand corner of the screen, so that the proper time can be displayed from within most any program. By placing this program in the autoexec.bat, the program can automatically be loaded every time the computer is booted up. Since the clock is displayed in a portion of the screen which is seldom used for displaying information, it is unobtrusive.

The program is started simply by typing CLOCK and pressing the ENTER key at the system prompt. Provided that the system time has been accurately set either automatically through a clock calendar card or manually by a user through the DOS TIME command, the program will display the proper time (including AM and PM designations). The clock also includes an alarm function which beeps a pleasant 5-second alarm at any preset time. The clock is also easy to disable if it interferes with a given program's display; to do so, one merely types in CLOCK - (CLOCK followed by a hypen or minus sign) and presses the ENTER key.

While neither this program nor the many other utilities in the public domain that work like it is of enormous consequence in the scheme of things, it is a nice program which most users will find helpful. We tested this program with dozens of applications programs, including word processors, database management programs, desk-top publishers, spreadsheets and games, and have found it to work well with most of them. (An exception is games from Infocom, which will not configure properly if the program is loaded when the games are first installed.)

Program: Clock
Author: Unknown
Company: GoldenSoft Software
Address: N/A
Category: General Utility Programs
Registration Fee: None (Public Domain)

General Evaluation: Clock

	Excellent	*Very Good*	*Good*	*Average*	*Poor*
Ease of Use	***				
Ease of Learning	***				
Documentation				***	
Utility			***		
Overall Rating			***		

CMENU4™

The operating system for the IBM PC and its work-alikes is, to say the least, somewhat spartan. Users must memorize a large number of commands for routine file maintenance such as deleting, copying or formatting disks. In addition, every application program has its own sometimes rather arcane name needed to call up the program. To exacerbate matters, add a hard disk or two with their mysterious directory trees, and the potential for accessing thousands of programs and files, and you have the perfect recipe for chaos. This is particularly the case in an office setting, where a wide variety of programs may be used at any given terminal, with people at each terminal who may know the program they normally use, but understand very little about the way computers work in general. Fortunately, there are several programs which permit the setting up of a menu system to assist users with running different programs without the need to ever exit to the operating system or be confronted with the ominous C: prompt. Among these, CMENU4 offers excellent flexibility, ease of use, ease of learning and value. Even for experienced users who do not shy from working at the DOS level, CMENU4 can offer greater ease of use and time savings.

CMENU4 allows the programs on a hard disk (or floppy disk, if one wishes to set it up for such an environment) to be accessed through a pull-down menu system. Assume a user has a hard disk with WordStar and LOTUS 1-2-3, each in its own subdirectory (WS and LOTUS respectively). Working at the DOS level (C: prompt), a user would normally enter the following command to enter WordStar: CD/WS [Enter], WS [ENTER]. The program would then load and run. After exiting the program, should he wish to enter LOTUS 1-2-3, he would have to issue the following command at the C prompt: CD/LOTUS [RETURN], 123 [RETURN]. While this is not particularly onerous, a user would have to remember every program on his hard disk and the path to the subdirectory where it was placed. It would be much simpler if each program could be automatically executed simply by selecting it from a pull-down menu and pressing [ENTER]. This is exactly what CMENU4 accomplishes. The more programs one has (and the more

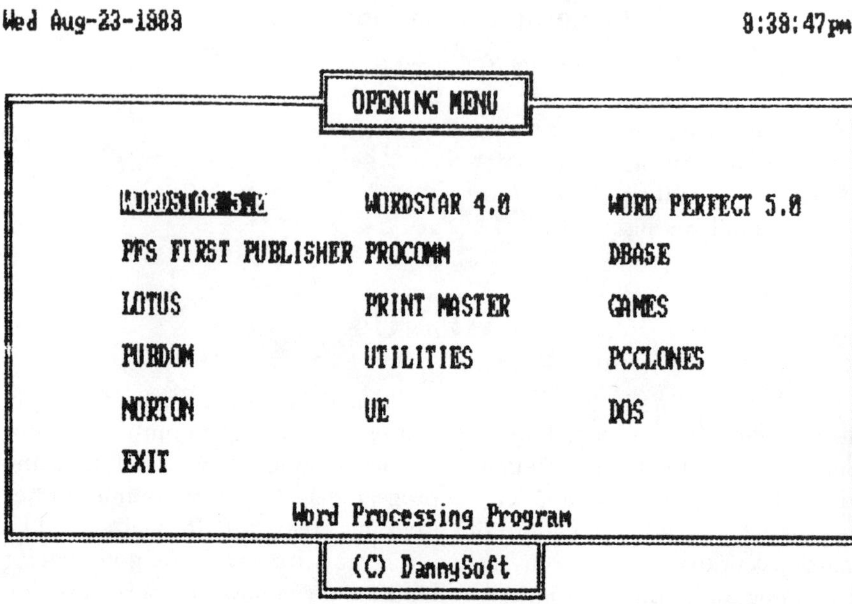

Figure 6.14: Opening menu and main screen for CMENU4. A one-line description of the highlighted program is available at the bottom of the screen. A program can be automatically run by highlighting it by moving the cursor over it with the cursor control keys and then striking the ENTER key. The program then automatically loads and executes. Exiting a program gets one back to the main menu screen where another program can be selected. Access can be limited to any or all programs through password protection for enhanced security in a multi-user environment.

complicated the path in the hard disk's tree structure to get to it), the greater the potential usefulness of this program. Likewise, the less experience a user has, the more she will benefit from having CMENU4 available.

In addition to permitting a score or more programs to be automatically run from a menu system, CMENU4 also makes it possible to automate DOS functions. It permits a submenu to be created containing, for example, the most used DOS commands which can then be automatically executed by selecting them from a pull-down menu. Using this option, often used commands such as FORMAT, DISKCOPY, and CHKDSK, as well as their variations (e.g., FORMAT A:, FORMAT A:/S, FORMAT A:/S/V) can easily be programmed for point-and-shoot execution. As an additional benefit for less experienced users, a description of what each command does can also be seen on screen as each command is highlighted. A sample DOS submenu is included with the evaluation copy of the program.

CMENU4 includes a separate program, NEWMENU6 which facilitates

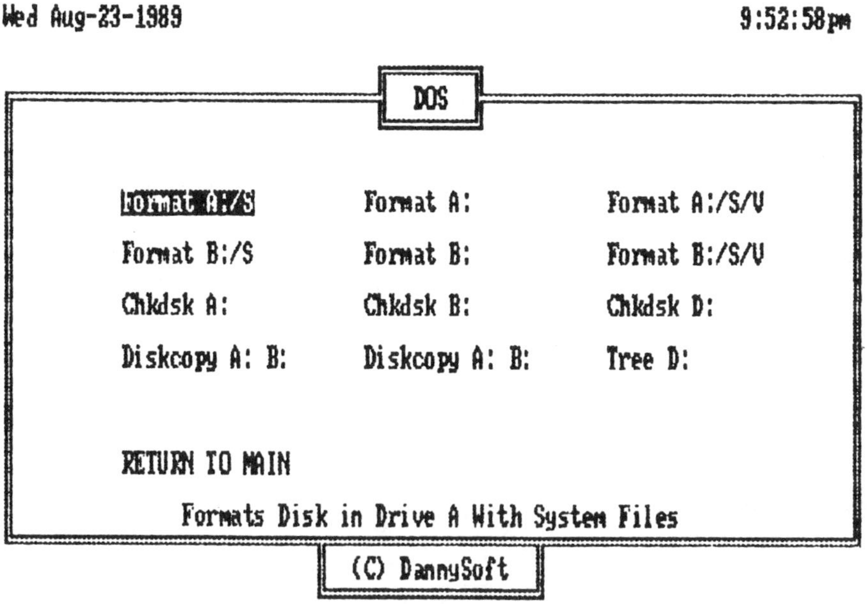

Figure 6.15: Sample submenu containing selected DOS commands which may be executed in the same way that any other program can be run: highlighting it and pressing ENTER. Note that a brief description of each DOS command may be viewed at the bottom of the screen as each command is highlighted—a very useful feature for computer users who are not familiar with DOS commands.

the creation of custom menus and submenus tailored to a particular user's needs. The program helps the user to develop his menu system by answering questions on-screen. Password protection is also available as an option for users who wish to restrict access to their systems or to any program in it. Multiple passwords are supported (e.g., one password to gain access to the system, and a different password for each program which can be accessed through the pull-down menus). While the password protection is by no means very sophisticated and can easily be defeated by an experienced user, it is nevertheless a useful feature in a multi-user situation—especially when most users are not likely to be highly sophisticated.

The evaluation copy of the program comes with a 16-page disk-based manual which covers the program's major features. At its $15 registration price, this program is a tremendous value. While its features can be largely emulated through the DOS batch file capability, the latter is generally not recommended for the novice computerist; furthermore, simple batch files will never look as nice while running. (CMENU4 uses batch files, but in the background, while the screen display is enhanced and useful information made available to the user.)

Program: CMENU4 © 1977, 1986
Author: Daniel B. Doman
Company: DannySoft
Address: 132 East 45th Street, Apt. 5G, New York, NY 10017
Category: General Utility Programs
Registration Fee: $15 suggested contribution
Registration entitles a user to assistance and information on updates.

General Evaluation: CMENU4

	Excellent	*Very Good*	*Good*	*Average*	*Poor*
Ease of Use	***				
Ease of Learning		***			
Documentation				***	
Utility		***			
Overall Rating		***			

Encrypt/Decrypt™ Version 1.1

Encrypt and Decrypt are sister programs from SoftLogic Solutions which make it possible to lock data files with a password, making them unreadable to anyone who does not know the password.

In today's office environment where numerous people may have access to a single computer, it is important to be able to lock out sensitive documents from prying eyes. The same is true for sensitive information in database or spreadsheet programs. One may also wish to prevent others from gaining unauthorized access to applications software. With the Encrypt command, any file may be successfully locked, whether it is composed of data or a program.

Using the programs couldn't be easier—which is fortunate, since they are not generally distributed with instructions. One merely types in Encrypt followed by a carriage return; the program then prompts the user for the name of the file to be encrypted, as well as a password. To unlock a file, the Decrypt command is used in much the same way: Decrypt is entered, and then the program prompts the user for the name of the program to be decrypted, as well as the password with which it was originally encrypted. Needless to say, it is important to remember the password with which one encrypts files; otherwise, it is very easy to be locked out of one's own files.

The programs support the use of wildcards both for file encryption and decryption, so that it is possible to encrypt and decrypt an entire disk or subdirectory at once, so long as the same password is acceptable for all files. For example, all files on drive B (both data and programs) can be locked by issuing the following command: Encrypt B:*.* [ENTER]. The program will then prompt the user to provide a password, and every file will then be locked out with the password given.

For anyone concerned about data security, this program is a must.

Program: Encrypt/Decrypt Ver. 1.1 © 1985
Author: N/A
Company: SoftLogic Solutions, Inc.
Address: Manchester, NH
Category: General Utility Programs
Registration Fee: None (Public Domain)

General Evaluation: Encrypt/Decrypt Ver. 1.1

	Excellent	*Very Good*	*Good*	*Average*	*Poor*
Ease of Use	***				
Ease of Learning	***				
Documentation					***
Utility	***				
Overall Rating	***				

FLU_SHOT™

Most anyone who is even remotely interested in computers and has read about them with the last year will have read or heard something about computer viruses. These are programs which are introduced into a host computer by a computer programmer through a variety of means and with wide ranging results. These can be as banal as a "Merry Christmas" message which pops up in all "infected" computers on Christmas day, to a Trojan Horse program which destroys all of a user's disks upon a certain event (e.g., at a predetermined date, upon a set number of times that the program is run, etc.). The effect of such Trojan Horses or viruses, however they are termed, are potentially dangerous.

The way that a virus is introduced to a computer system is simple: a user may log-on to a bulletin board or other on-line reference source which has been "infected" and the program may be transferred as the user downloads information from the electronic bulletin board; or a user may get a copy of a perfectly legitimate public domain, shareware or commercial software package from a friend or any other distribution source which has been infected. Since a virus may remain dormant and seemingly harmless in one's hard disk or floppy disk for months or years before becoming active, the program containing the virus can unwittingly be spread by innocent users. The only way to ensure that one's system will not be infected is to use only software which is shrink wrapped and factory fresh, and never to engage in telecommunications. And never accept data or program files from anyone else.

While it is impossible to get 100 percent protection against all viruses, there is at least one public domain program which offers some measure of protection against any virus which works by changing a disk's COMMAND.COM system file. The program, FLU_SHOT, works by warning users of any attempt to write to the COMMAND.COM file, and gives the user the option of allowing the attempt or aborting it if it is a suspect operation.

FLU_SHOT is simple to use: it is either called up manually by typing FLU_SHOT at the system prompt, or it can be made a part of the computer's autoexec.bat file. When the program loads, a short copyright message appears and the program then works in the background as a TSR (Terminate and Stay Resident) program. It works in a completely transparent manner so that one soon forgets it is part of the autoexec.bat and is always present. But when it encounters an attempt to write to the COMMAND.COM file, it beeps loudly and repeatedly for several seconds, advising the user that an attempt is being made to write to the COMMAND.COM file, and giving him the opportunity of allowing the attempt to continue or aborting the program. The program is noticeable whenever a disk is formatted with the system files, since the program's warning is engendered when the attempt is made to transfer the system files, which includes the COMMAND.COM file, to the new disk. At that point, simply answer "Y" to the prompt asking if the attempt to write to the file should be allowed. Rather than an annoyance, this occasional interruption serves as a pleasant reminder that the program is working in the background and protecting the system files.

FLU_SHOT comes with a disk-based brief document file which outlines the purpose of the program and explains how to set it up. In the file, the program's author Ross M. Greenberg asks users who spot a virus with this program to send him a copy of the file containing it via modem to his bulletin board RamNet BBS (212) 889-6438 so that "it may be dissected and a proper vaccine developed."

For the average user, chances are that a virus will never be encountered. But in the event it is, this program could prove invaluable in the time savings of replacing a hard disk full of information (especially if, as most users, you don't back up your hard disks as often as you should). The program works very much like an insurance policy: you don't need to think about it very much until you need it, at which time it's good to know it will be there.

Program: FLU_SHOT © 1987
Author: Ross M. Greenberg
Company: N/A
Address: N/A
Category: General Utility Programs
Registration Fee: None (Public Domain)

General Evaluation: FLU_SHOT

	Excellent	*Very Good*	*Good*	*Average*	*Poor*
Ease of Use	***				
Ease of Learning	***				
Documentation				***	
Utility		***			
Overall Rating		***			

Multi Spooler Version 2.0

When a file is sent to the printer from a word processing program, a database program, a spreadsheet program or any other applications program, the computer can be tied up until the file is finished printing. With many programs, the printing of a file results in a mandatory coffee break, since nothing further can be done with the system until the printing job is finished. This is, to say the least, annoying—particularly when the printing is being done on a *slow* printer, such as a true letter-quality daisy wheel printer. While the computer is capable of transferring data at a quick rate, it often must slow down to the rate at which a printer can accept the data. This causes a bottleneck which either shuts down the computer system or slows it down to a crawl.

Fortunately, help is available for the frustrated user. A print spooler program can be used to set aside a part of the computer's RAM (Random Access Memory) to store files to be printed, and then feed these to the printer at the rate it is capable of handling. The result can be a dramatic decrease in the amount of time a CPU must remain idle while printing, which translates into higher productivity and far less exasperation by users waiting for printing jobs to be completed.

For businesses who need to perform mass mailings or share printers between many terminals, print buffers are available; these perform a similar task to print spoolers, except that they contain their own memory (RAM) and do not tie up any computer's available RAM. While the cost of print buffers is relatively modest, starting at several hundred dollars a unit (with RAM sizes typically starting at 128K for the less expensive units), the average user or small business need not bear the extra expense to enjoy nearly the same decrease in CPU idle time, and its corresponding increase in productivity.

The Multi Spooler program gives a user the flexibility to set aside an amount of RAM best suited to her needs up to a maximum of 63K. It supports up to four printers (both serial or parallel, or any combination of the two) and can be loaded automatically by inclusion in the system's autoexec.bat file. After it is installed, the print spooler works transparently in the background and a user need not be concerned with it.

The program is distributed with a six-page printable instruction file on disk. The documentation is well written and quite informative, allowing even the novice user to quickly set up and use the program.

As has been noted, the effect of using a print spooler can be dramatic in terms of the time saved in waiting for a printing job to end before being able to use the computer. Even when using programs that may incorporate print spoolers, Multi Spooler can still be of use by allowing larger spoolers to be set up, and more than one printer to be controlled. It, as well as other programs like it in the public domain and in commercial software, can be a wonderful productivity tool. And you certainly can't beat its price.

Program: Multi Spooler Ver. 2.0 © 1986
Author: Rich Winkel
Company: N/A
Address: Columbia, MO
Category: General Utility Programs
Registration Fee: None (Public Domain)

General Evaluation: Multi Spooler Ver. 2.0

	Excellent	*Very Good*	*Good*	*Average*	*Poor*
Ease of Use	***				
Ease of Learning	***				
Documentation		***			
Utility	***				
Overall Rating	***				

PKX35A35™

PKX35A35 is a collection of utilities which make it possible to archive and unarchive program and data files in order to save disk space and time in the transmission of files over a modem.

These programs, and others like them, squeeze data and program files through various disk-packing techniques (e.g., removing all spaces between words and letters in a data file). Once a file has been "packed," it cannot be used as is, but must be "unpacked" through the use of another program (e.g., the spaces between words and letters must be added again).

By using the utilities which form part of PKX35A35, it is possible to obtain some very impressive size reduction in processed files. With data files from word processors, spreadsheets and database programs, size reductions of up to 90 percent are possible. With program files, size reduction is not generally as high, but is still significant. (In our tests, 10-50 percent reductions were recorded.)

For anyone who has a hard disk which is growing full, these utilities can be of incalculable worth. With them, it is possible to pack a directory containing seldom-used yet important data or even programs so that they take up only a fraction of their original size. The archiving process takes only minutes, even when very large or when multiple files are involved; likewise the unarchiving process is extremely simple.

As an example, we archived all of the files relating to this manuscript with the following results: 22 files were archived in well under a minute and packed into a single file taking up approximately 275,000 bytes on a disk. The original files, on the other hand, took up approximately 573,000 bytes. The approximate savings in disk space was 298,000 bytes, or approximately 52 percent. The percentage of reduction reported for each file ranged from 46 percent to 93 percent.

While file archiving can be a valuable disk management tool, it is of even greater importance when one sends or receives files over a modem. File transfers can be very slow over telephone lines, and the delay causes not just the inconvenience of lost time but considerable cost when long distance telephone charges are involved. By sending and receiving files in archived format, one can save a great deal of time and money. If we wished to transmit the files for our manuscript over modem at this point, the process would take several hours using a 1200 baud modem. By sending the archived files, the time required would be 52 percent less.

Archiving files is also useful when sharing software, such as the public domain and shareware programs reviewed herein. More information can be packed into a disk when files are archived, and the time to copy them onto a disk with the DOS COPY command is also reduced. For this reason, most distributors of public domain and shareware choose to archive files they distribute to computer users. (It is also the format in which almost every public domain and shareware program is found on bulletin boards, where users can directly download them into their systems.)

PKX35A35 is distributed in packed, self-extracting form. To unpack it and generate the usable program and document files, one need only type PKX35A35 at the system prompt. The program then automatically unpacks and creates the various files needed to run it. These include the program files PKXARC.COM (FAST! Archive Extracting Utility Ver. 3.5 used to unpack files), PKARC.COM (FAST! Archive Create/Update Utility Ver. 3.5 used to create archived files) and PKSFX.COM (Self-Extract Utility used to create executable, self-extracting program files).

The programs come with well-written document files on disk, one for each program and a general README.DOC file. The printable document files for PKARC.COM, PKXARC.COM and PKSFX.COM are 20 pages, 12 pages and one page in length, respectively, with the documentation for PKARC.COM and PKXARC.COM containing excellent tables of contents for easy reference. The documentation is comprehensive and well written, and the programs are well implemented, easy to learn and use, fast and excellent productivity tools. They are highly recommended.

Program: PKX35A35
Author: N/A
Company: PKWARE, Inc.
Address: 7032 Ardara Avenue, Glendale, WI 53209
Category: General Utility Programs
Registration Fee: $20 suggested contribution. Full registration fee, including next available updates, is $45. Volume discounts are offered, as are site licensing fees.

General Evaluation: PKX35A35

	Excellent	*Very Good*	*Good*	*Average*	*Poor*
Ease of Use	***				
Ease of Learning	***				
Documentation	***				
Utility	***				
Overall Rating	***				

CAL.COM and THREECAL.COM

CAL.COM and THREECAL.COM are examples of many small utility programs which perform a very specific, non-earth-shattering task, but can be quite useful. Both programs are very similar: CAL.COM prints a one-month calendar on screen either for the current month (if the computer's system date has been properly set) or for any month and year specified. The

```
E:\>CAL JAN 2000

        January 2000

Sun Mon Tue Wed Thu Fri Sat

                          1
  2   3   4   5   6   7   8
  9  10  11  12  13  14  15
 16  17  18  19  20  21  22
 23  24  25  26  27  28  29
 30  31

E:\>
```

Figure 6.16: CAL.COM used to display a calendar for the month of January 2000. As seen in this actual screen dump, the program displays the calendar in a small unenhanced format on the screen.

syntax is simple: to print a calendar for the month of January in the year 2000, one types CAL JAN 2000 at the system prompt, and the month is then printed on the screen. (It is then a simple matter to dump it onto a printer should one wish a hard copy.) THREECAL.COM works in a similar fashion, except that one gives the numerical value for the month, so that THREECAL 1 2000 will print out a three-month calendar on the screen for the months of December 1999, January 2000 and February 2000 (the target month alongside the months preceding and following it).

CAL.COM is distributed with a small, one-paragraph help file which assists in running the program. THREECAL.COM is not distributed with any documentation, although it can be found in several collections of Public Domain Utilities distributed through bulletin boards and shareware/public domain distributing sources.

We were not able to determine the origin of these programs, since they do not provide a Copyright notice when they are run and were not accompanied by documentation providing this information in the sources from which we acquired them. It is unfortunate, since we'd like to give their programmers credit. Both of these programs are representative of thousands of programs gracefully released into the public domain by programmers for the public's benefit.

Programs: CAL.COM and THREECAL.COM
Author: Unknown
Company: N/A
Address: N/A
Category: General Utility Programs
Registration Fee: None (Public Domain)

December, 1999

Su	Mo	Tu	We	Th	Fr	Sa
28	29	30	1	2	3	4
5	6	7	8	9	10	11
12	13	14	15	16	17	18
19	20	21	22	23	24	25
26	27	28	29	30	31	1
2	3	4	5	6	7	8

January, 2000

Su	Mo	Tu	We	Th	Fr	Sa
26	27	28	29	30	31	1
2	3	4	5	6	7	8
9	10	11	12	13	14	15
16	17	18	19	20	21	22
23	24	25	26	27	28	29
30	31	1	2	3	4	5

February, 2000

Su	Mo	Tu	We	Th	Fr	Sa
30	31	1	2	3	4	5
6	7	8	9	10	11	12
13	14	15	16	17	18	19
20	21	22	23	24	25	26
27	28	29	1	2	3	4
5	6	7	8	9	10	11

```
B:\>
```

Figure 6.17: THREECAL.COM used to display a calendar for the month of January 2000. The program sends a three-month calendar to the computer screen which is somewhat more appealing than the smaller, unadorned output of CAL.COM.

General Evaluation: CAL.COM and THREECAL.COM

	Excellent	*Very Good*	*Good*	*Average*	*Poor*
Ease of Use	***				
Ease of Learning	***				
Documentation					***
Utility			***		
Overall Rating			***		

WHEREIS.COM

Anyone who works with disk directories, whether in hard disks or floppies, sooner or later comes across the problem of finding a particular file which is "lost" somewhere in the subdirectory structure, safely out of sight and out of memory. The more complicated the directory tree, the more likely that one will forget where an important file lies. DOS does not provide an easy way to sweep through all of a disk's directory structure when looking for a file; the only option given by DOS is a repetitive DIRECTORY command for every single existing directory—a task that can become nearly overwhelming, particularly in view of the ever-increasing size of hard disks, and the accompanying ever-increasing complexity of the directory structure they necessitate.

Fortunately, help is available from a simple utility program in the public domain which allows for file searches of entire hard disks. For example: if I know I have a file called LETTER.MOM somewhere in one of my subdirectories, I can issue a single command that will search an entire disk at once and report where the file is. In this case, the command would be WHEREIS LETTER.MOM [RETURN]; my entire hard disk would then be searched and the program would return either a message to the effect that the file was not found, or, if found, the precise path leading to the file.

The program is distributed with a brief documentation file which teaches how to use the program and offers copyright information. The spartan documentation is typical of utility programs; but utility programs tend to be self-explanatory, so that they do not need voluminous documentation.

Program: WHEREIS © 1984
Author: John Socha (appeared in the January 1984 issue of the magazine *Softalk for the IBM Personal Computer*)
Company: N/A
Address: N/A
Category: General Utility Programs
Registration Fee: None (Public Domain)

General Evaluation: WHEREIS.COM

	Excellent	*Very Good*	*Good*	*Average*	*Poor*
Ease of Use	***				
Ease of Learning	***				
Documentation				***	
Utility			***		
Overall Rating			***		

XWORD™ Version 2.3

XWORD is a utility program which allows for conversion of file formats of many leading software packages into those of others, making possible the sharing of data between applications programs using different file formats to save data created by them.

The program is useful to anyone who might need to send or receive data files to another user with a different word processor. Let us take an example. The coauthors of this text are both using WordStar Ver. 5.0 to write

```
                              XWORD
                             Menu One

                         Format Converters

[W]ordStar              wordstar[2]000          [S]idekick

[A]scii                 reduce s[P]laces        [N]ultimate

[X]ywrite               wor[D]perfect           [?]=Help and Info

                          [I]=Invoice

          Press Space Bar To Change Menus or End to Exit

Source file format (or option): W
Target file format: A
Name of Source file (drive optional): D:\DATA\FICTION\PRICE.DRM
Name of target file: D:\DATA\FICTION\PRICE.ASC
```

```
                              XWORD
                             Menu Two

                      Logical and Bit Options

                  [A]ND               [O]R

                  [N]OT               [X]OR

                  RO[L]               RO[R]

                  r[E]place           [?]=Help and Info

          Press Space Bar to Change Menus or End to Exit

What Option:
```

Top: Figure 6.18: Main menu for XWORD Ver. 2.3. Using the program is a very simple process. The "bracketed" letter of the file format to be changed from is selected from the options menu, as well as the bracketed letter corresponding to the file format to be changed to. The filename of the file to be transformed is then given, along with its full path name, if applicable, and the same is done for the filename to be transferred to. The original file is, of course, left intact, and the program creates a new file with the selected file format and chosen filename. *Bottom:* Figure 6.19: Secondary menu for XWORD Ver. 2.3. The program is capable of performing logical search and replace operations, as well as manipulating the way that data is stored in a file as to make it illegible—a useful file encryption technique for protecting sensitive data.

the portions of the manuscript they are working on, so that file compatibility is not a problem. But if one decided to write with Word Perfect or Multi Mate, a problem would arise, since these word processors are not compatible unless one saves files under ASCII in each word processor—a procedure which limits the number of page formatting options one may use. Fortunately, both Word Perfect and WordStar include file transfer programs of their own, facilitating such exchanges. But what about a user who gets a file created by WordStar or Word Perfect and does not own these programs? In that case, a copy of XWORD can be invaluable.

XWORD supports a wide variety of programs, including WordStar, WordStar 2000, Side Kick (memo format), Multi Mate, Word Perfect and Xywrite II Plus. The program also provides a means for encrypting files, although it is not as easy to use as the Encrypt and Decrypt programs reviewed elsewhere herein.

In addition to changing formats from one word processor to another, XWORD also permits the replacing of special formatting or print control characters which may be lost during the translation process. Although no file transferring program can retain all of the special formatting characteristics of the original, and XWORD is no exception, such programs can be invaluable to anyone who needs to read and use files created by other word processing formats.

In evaluating the program, I converted two of my short story files from WordStar Ver. 5.0 and WordStar Ver. 4.0 to ASCII; the files contained approximately 40 kilobytes and 50 kilobytes of data, or approximately 6,300 and 7,800 words. The conversion process took less than five seconds in each case, which is far less than I had anticipated. The Release 4.0 file was perfect, while the Release 5.0 file needed some extraneous characters removed (print formatting commands which could not be translated). But even with the WordStar release 5.0 file, the extraneous characters could be removed through a simple search and replace operation, either through WordStar or XWORD itself in a matter of minutes. In no case was there any garbled text or "garbage" (illegible characters on the screen) in any part of the file.

XWORD's $20 registration price is quite reasonable for a program with its advanced features and ease of use. Free upgrades are available to registered users for a period of one year from the date of registration. After that, users may continue to receive periodic updates for an additional $8 per-year charge. (According to the shareware documentation on the distribution disk, future updates will include support for additional word processors, including VolksWriter and DCA, among others, as well as enhanced features.) The evaluation copy of the program includes an eight-page documentation file outlining the program's main features.

Program: XWORD Ver. 2.3 © 1986
Author: Ronald Gans
Company: N/A
Address: 250 West 55th Street #2-E, New York, NY 10019
Category: General Utility Programs
Registration Fee: $20 (New York residents add 8.25% sales tax)

General Evaluation: XWORD Ver. 2.3

	Excellent	*Very Good*	*Good*	*Average*	*Poor*
Ease of Use	***				
Ease of Learning		***			
Documentation				***	
Utility		***			
Overall Rating		***			

IBM Graphics Adapter Emulator for the Hercules Graphics Card (HGCIBM)™ Version 1.11

Until recently, buying a monitor for your computer system was a relatively simple matter. You had to choose between the IBM Color Graphics Adapter (or CGA) or the Hercules monochrome adapter. The former provided the advantages of color but at the expense of legibility when dealing with text; the latter provided the advantage of higher resolution for text, but offered only the dull choice of a green and black or amber and black display. The lower cost of monochrome monitors and the relatively high resolution relative to their color counterparts made them extremely popular. The only problem is that the majority of games are written to take advantage of the CGA card and do not work on monochrome monitors. Those opting for the lower price tag and the higher resolution of the Hercules card (and its clones) coupled to a monochrome monitor could not play games on their computers or take advantage of many drawing and graphics programs written for the CGA adapter.

Buying a monitor in the early 1990s is not as simple. The old standard CGA and Hercules cards are still available, although one reads much about the EGA, VGA and now Super VGA displays. The best of the new monitors and the display adapters needed to drive them can cost more than $2,000. But the old reliable Hercules cards and monochrome monitors can still be purchased for about $100; for a user on a budget, these displays are an exceptional bargain. Most entry-level systems are sold with

Hercules-compatible monochrome displays, something which is not surprising considering their price.

If a software package meant to be used with a CGA display is run on a Hercules-equipped system, the user may be warned through an on-screen message that the program can't run with the available display. More often than not, the computer simply hangs and needs to be reset. Fortunately, there are several programs both in the public domain and in the shareware area that allow a Hercules monitor to emulate a CGA display. Among the ones we have tried, HGCIBM is the best; in our tests, it has run every CGA program we have tested without a problem.

HGCIBM and similar CGA emulation software make the monochrome display work like a CGA display; the system is, in effect, fooled into thinking that a CGA display is present, and the software runs. A monochrome monitor cannot actually display more than one color, and it is not very good at dealing with shades or color intensity. But the important thing is that this wonderful utility makes it possible to run graphics-intensive games and drawing programs on systems which could not otherwise run them. (The effect is not unlike watching a color program on a black and white set, except that the display is yellowish or greenish in hue, as opposed to grayish.)

HGCIBM is capable of running in either full or half modes, depending on how it is toggled when it is initially run. In half mode, it displays graphics in CGA mode and text in normal (higher resolution) Hercules mode. In full mode, it displays both text and graphics in CGA-emulation mode.

HGCIBM is a memory resident (TSR) program; but it takes up only one kilobyte of memory which does not noticeably impact on a system's available RAM. The program is loaded once and stays resident until it is either unloaded or the computer is reset. (We did not come up with any significant conflicts running a variety of applications programs in monochrome mode with the program loaded in half-mode.)

Documentation for this program is scant, as is usually the case with utilities. But the program is such that detailed documentation is unnecessary. A small document file is included with the program giving instructions on its use, and if one types HGCIBM at the system prompt without any additional toggle (e.g., HGCIBM /F for full mode, HGCIBM /H for half mode and HGCIBM /U to remove the installed program from memory), several screens of information scroll by, prompting the operator to strike a key after reading each. These include additional information about the program, as well as a copyright notice and shareware notice, terms for use of the software and a request for contributions from users.

No emulation program will run every software package intended for the CGA adapter. But HGCIBM runs more packages than any other we have seen, while not unduly interfering with other resident programs or non–CGA programs when it is run in half mode. This is an excellent, must-have program for anyone with a Hercules display.

Program: HGCIBM Ver. 1.11 © 1986
Author: J. Gary Batson
Company: Athena Digital
Address: 145 Green Hills Road, Athens, GA 30605
Category: General Utility Programs
Registration Fee: A contribution of $6 to $9 is suggested.

General Evaluation: HGCIBM

	Excellent	*Very Good*	*Good*	*Average*	*Poor*
Ease of Use	***				
Ease of Learning	***				
Documentation				***	
Utility	***				
Overall Rating	***				

Printer Utilities

Although a computer without a printer can still be a very useful tool (provided one has adequate software available), no computer system is complete without at least an inexpensive printer. Perhaps in the not too distant future paper will be replaced by magnetic media, such as floppy and hard disks, Write Once and Read Many Times (WORM) drives, erasable CD drives, and other innovative magnetic, digital or silicon-based mass storage media. And while it is possible to send files via modem or floppy disk from one location to another (an ever-growing number of publishers, for example, accept manuscripts for evaluation in electronic form, and much business is conducted today via computer networks and other telecommunications media), paper is still the primary medium for information exchange, and is likely to remain so for some years to come.

There are basically five types of printers available today, each with its own benefits and liabilities: 1) true letter quality or daisy-wheel printers which work similarly to typewriters; 2) impact dot matrix printers which form characters by means of small needle-like rods which are projected from a printhead and strike a nylon ribbon, making an impression on the page which form letters, numbers and other characters through a mosaic-like series of dots; 3) thermal-transfer printers which form characters on specially treated paper by warming up different parts of a ceramic printhead, or by melting a special ribbon onto plain paper; 4) ink-jet printers which spray a fine network of dots onto a page in order to create characters or graphics; and 5) laser printers which work on technology closely paralleling that of plain-paper copiers. With the general exception of true letter-quality printers which are for the most part incapable of general enhancement (they print a limited type of characters, just like a standard typewriter), all other types have had programs developed to enhance their power and flexibility, mainly in their ability to print graphics and to enhance the way characters are printed on a page.

Of the noted types of printers, dot matrix printers are by far the most widely used today for two main reasons: they are among the least expensive and they are quite flexible in their ability to print graphics and different typefaces or fonts at a reasonable speed. Of these, the Epson and IBM brands of printers have come to be the most widely accepted, leading most manufacturers to offer printers which emulate the way they work. For this reason, we examined several sample programs which will work on most Epson and IBM printers and their compatibles. These are only representative of hundreds of additional programs which are similar and will work with other printers (e.g., Diablo and Okidata). There are also myriad programs for the enhancement of printing functions for laser printers, in particular the Hewlett Packard Laser Jet I and II printers and their workalikes. What even the most inexpensive printer can be capable of by utilizing one of the following programs can be amazing.

Altpage[PD] Version 1.0

Altpage is a helpful program available which can reduce a printer's hunger for paper by as much as 50 percent by allowing documents to be printed on both sides of the page. Altpage automatically formats most data files to be printed on both sides of the page. The program does this by first splitting up programs to be printed into two separate files, each containing either odd-numbered pages or even-numbered pages. To print on both sides of the page, the file with the odd-numbered pages is printed first (page 1 is followed by page 3, which is followed by page 5, and so on). The paper is then ejected from the printer and reversed so that page number 2 can be printed on the back of page number 1. All even-numbered pages are then printed in order where it belongs. The net result is that long files are printed on both sides of the paper.

Altpage includes a three-page document file which fully explains how to use the program. If the name of the program is typed at the system prompt without further parameters, a brief help file is printed instructing the user how to run the program. Using the program is relatively simple:

one types in the name of the program followed by the name of the document file to be converted for printing on both sides of the page and then the name for the files to contain the odd and even page text files. As an example, to convert a file called MYFILE for printing through the use of Altpage, one would type at the system prompt: ALTPAGE MYFILE MYFILE.ODD MYFILE.EVN. MYFILE.ODD would contain the odd-numbered pages and MYFILE.EVN the even-numbered pages to later be printed separately. The actual conversion process takes only minutes, even for large files. (A file of 100 pages will convert in under three minutes.)

The program is not very useful for small files taking up 10 pages or less; most users will find it is not worth the extra trouble of running the program and reversing the paper to save 10 pages of paper. But with long document files—the kind that anyone exploring public domain and shareware programs will definitely end up printing on a regular basis—this neat utility noticeably reduces the cost of paper, while cutting down on its waste and saving some trees in the bargain. Some advanced word processors such as WordStar Ver. 5.0 support this function directly, but most do not. For users whose present (or prospective) word processor does not permit printing on both sides of the page, this utility is well worth having.

Program: Altpage Ver. 1.0 © 1985
Author: Eric Ewanco
Company: (SYSOP, Fido 130/920)
Address: 7633 Beckwood Drive, Fort Worth, TX 76112-6051
Category: Printer Utility Programs
Registration Fee: None. Unspecified donation requested by the author.

General Evaluation: Altpage Ver. 1.0

	Excellent	*Very Good*	*Good*	*Average*	*Poor*
Ease of Use			***		
Ease of Learning		***			
Documentation		***			
Utility			***		
Overall Rating			***		

Epson Print Control™ Version 1.5

There are a wide variety of programs in the public domain and user supported software categories which allow a user to change the default printing style of a printer, as well as various other printing attributes. These programs generally give greater flexibility to printers which may only be

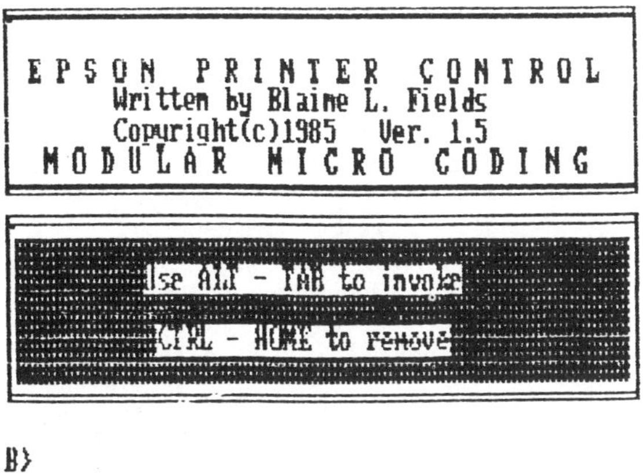

Figure 6.20: Acknowledgment message from Epson Printer Control Ver. 1.5. This small screen pops up on the upper-left of the display screen when the program is first loaded in its TSR memory-resident mode. The program is then invoked from most any application by depressing the ALT-TAB key combination.

capable of printing in one style, and offer different fonts which can give a printed document a different (and often better) look.

One of the easiest programs to use is Epson Print Control. The program can be made to work both in memory resident mode as a terminate and stay resident (TSR) program, or loaded from disk as needed. For users who have the approximately 42 kilobytes of free RAM which the program requires for memory resident operation, the program, once loaded, is always two keystrokes away and can be called up by striking the TAB and ALT keys simultaneously. (For users who have limited memory in their systems, a version of the program is included in the evaluation version of the program which makes Epson Print Control work as a stand-alone program; to use the program in this mode, one types EPSHELL2 at the system prompt, as opposed to typing EPSHELL1 for the memory-resident mode.) Once invoked, a main menu screen opens up from which a user may select various attributes to change prior to printing a given file. These include selecting from three type fonts—pica, elite, and italics, as well as five font sizes—compressed (17 characters per inch), expanded (five characters per inch), expanded-elite (six characters per inch), expanded-compressed (eight characters per inch) and proportional print. In addition, the program allows for the setting of lines per inch from a submenu system, as well as settings for other formatting options, such as margins and tabs. This gives the program some of the features found only on true document formatting programs. All functions are quite easy to use.

Unfortunately, the program is supplied without documentation. The one document file in the distribution diskette merely states the names of the two program files supplied with the program, and the name and address

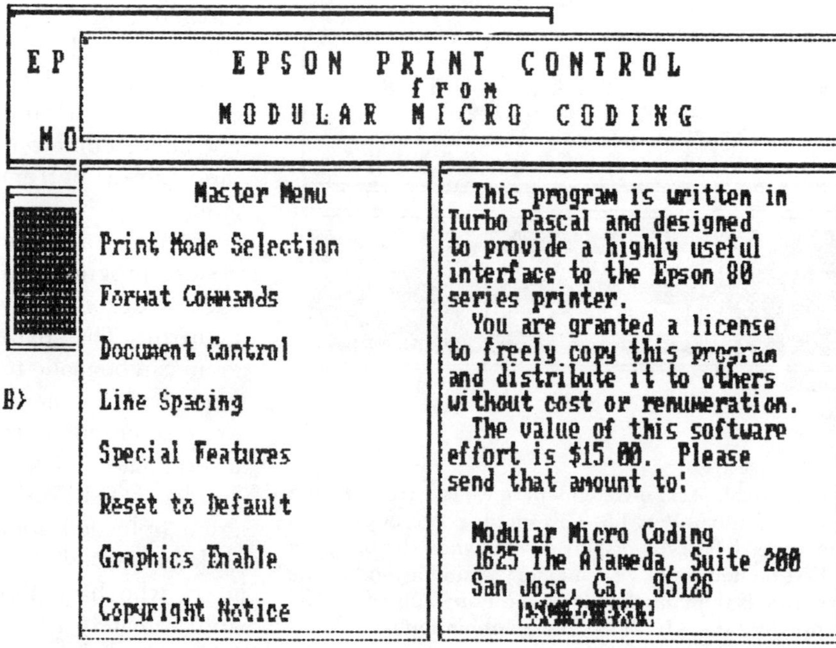

Figure 6.21: Main menu for Epson Printer Control Ver. 1.5. This actual screen dump also shows the program's copyright notice. Any option in the program is accessed by simply pressing the first letter of the command. To view the copyright screen shown here, one must type the letter C for Copyright. The program is easy to use and self-explanatory, which is fortunate since there is no documentation provided with it.

of the program's developer, Modular Micro Coding. But the program is so simple to use with its menu system that this is not a fatal flaw. A little bit of experimentation with the program's options is all that's needed in order to successfully utilize the program's features.

For a user of the latest releases of WordStar, Word Perfect and some of the other leading professional word processing packages, Epson Print Control will have little appeal, since these programs already contain excellent document formatting and font programs. But for users of word processors with less sophisticated print enhancement and formatting features, which include the vast majority of the commercial and user-supported programs, this is an excellent program which can give even the most modest dot matrix printer new-found flexibility, and enhance the appearance of any document.

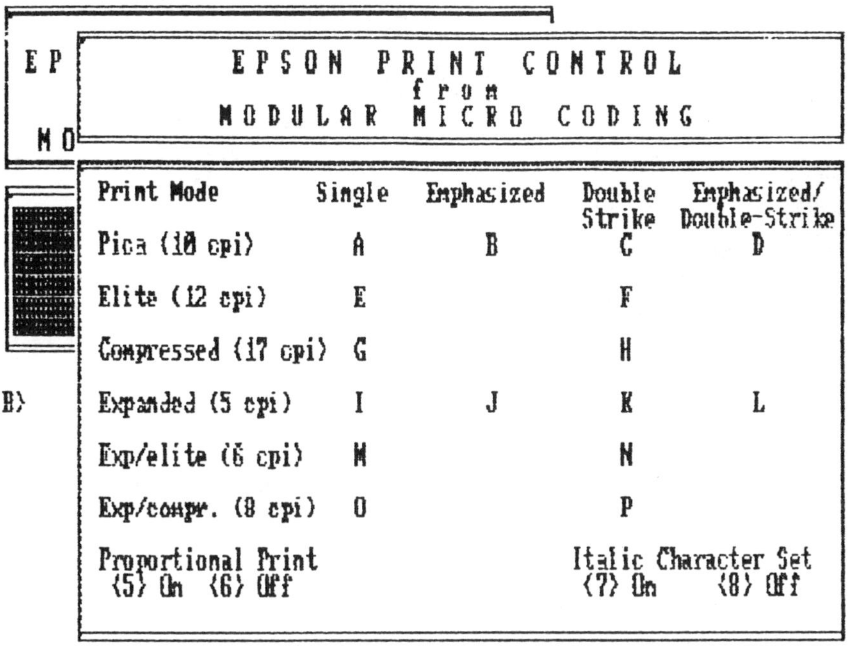

Figure 6.22: By selecting P for Print Control from the main menu, one gains access to the program's generous print enhancement options. These will offer even the least expensive Epson-compatible printer a wide range of print styles which can greatly enhance any printed document.

Program: Epson Print Control Ver. 1.5 © 1985
Company: Modular Micro Coding
Address: 1625 The Alameda, Suite 200, San Jose, CA 95126
Category: Printer Utility Programs
Registration Fee: $15

General Evaluation: Epson Print Control Ver. 1.5

	Excellent	*Very Good*	*Good*	*Average*	*Poor*
Ease of Use		***			
Ease of Learning			***		
Documentation					***
Utility	***				
Overall Rating		***			

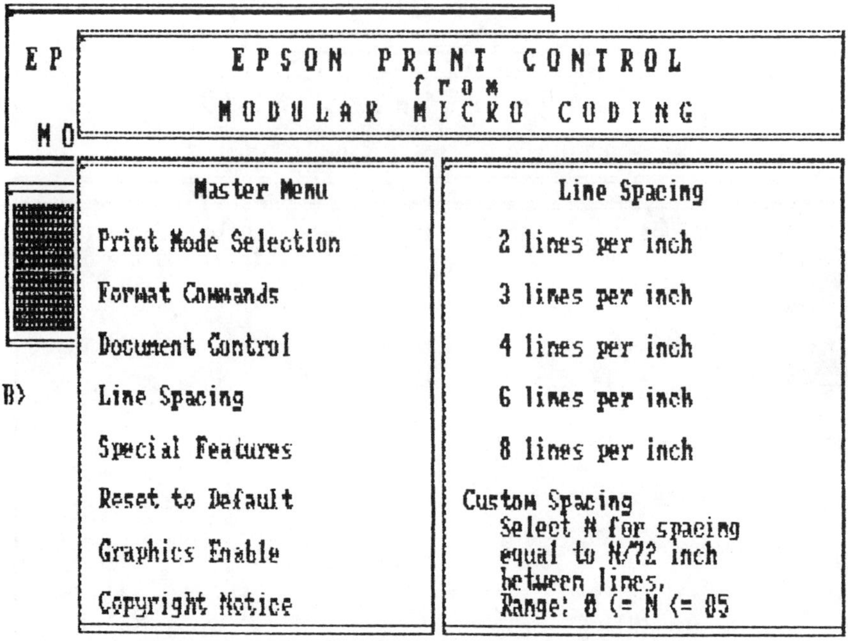

Figure 6.23: Epson Print Control offers a user a simple interface for documents. By selecting option L for Line Spacing, a user can easily set the number of lines per inch which will be output in the printed document. While line settings, along with some other features provided by the program can be set through most word processing programs, the commands to do so are not always easy to remember. Some users will also prefer to format their documents after they are finished, just prior to printing; Epson Print Control offers that flexibility.

LQ™ Version 2.26

For a person desiring the maximum amount of flexibility in font selection and in control over the printed output of any document, LQ is the incontestable choice. No other program in its class or price range comes close to offering the sheer number of available fonts (19) in conjunction with the ability to generate and incorporate graphics. The program even includes a subprogram to assist with the creation of letterheads (which may also incorporate company logos or any other self-generated graphics image). The results are close to typeset quality print.

LQ may be used in a variety of ways to produce high quality printed output from a number of printers, including Epson, IBM, Star Micronics and C-Itoh printers. (The program can also be configured to work with most any other dot matrix printer, although users will have to do a considerable

```
        LQ (tm)
Letter quality from dot matrix printers.

LQ Version 2.26.  Revised on 18-Oct-87.  Registration #2373
(C) Copyright 1985 by Mark Harris, Granny's Old-Fashioned Software (tm).
All Rights Reserved.

LQ works with Epson-compatible and most other dot matrix printers; see the
documentation for configuration details.

LQ is a 'Shareware' product.  You may distribute copies of the full LQ disk,
but don't give out modified versions or copies of the printed manual.  If you
find LQ useful, you are encouraged to buy a registered copy.

Your registration fee of $35 will provide the following benefits:
  1. A current version of LQ with printed manual,
  2. a mail-in card for a future version of LQ,
  3. a $10 commission each time someone registers from one of your copies,
  4. telephone support for your technical questions.

Phone (MC/VISA) or mail orders accepted.  NC orders add 4.5%.
Granny's Old-Fashioned Software, Rt 4, Box 216, Boone, NC 28607  (704) 264-6906

Press Esc to cancel, any other key to begin...
```

```
    BIGPRINT

(c) 1986 by Mark Harris, 4/11/86

This program lets you print posters using any of the LQ character sets.

Name of character set? (Default = ROMAN.SET)

Is your printer Epson-compatible? y

Enter string:

This text will be printed on a large banner using LARGE print in the Roman Font!
```

Top: **Figure 6.24: Opening screen and copyright notice for LQ Ver. 2.26. When loaded in its default resident mode, the program remains in the background and may be called up at any time to change the default fonts used in printing. It works transparently with most any word processing program and can also be used to print preexisting ASCII data files without the need of a word processor.** *Bottom:* **Figure 6.25: LQ comes with a variety of additional programs which greatly enhance its utility. A banner-generating program is pictured here; the program prints out W-I-D-E banners in any of LQ's resident fonts and outputs messages in continuous pinfeed paper at approximately four characters per sheet of standard 8.5″ × 11″ paper. A letterhead-generating program is also included, making LQ a marvelously flexible (and useful) package.**

COURIER2

!"#$%&'()*+,-./0123456789:;<=>?@ABCDEFGHIJKLMNO
PQRSTUVWXYZ[\]^_`abcdefghijklmnopqrstuvwxyz{|}~

GREEK

!"#$%&'()*+,-./0123456789:;<=>;@ΑΒΓΔΕΦΓΗΙΘΚΛΜΝΟ
ΠΞΡΣΤΥ ΩΧΨΖ[\]^_'αβγδεøγηιθκλμνοπΞρστυςωχψζ{¦}~

HELV2

!"#$%&'()*+,-./0123456789:;<=>?@ABCDEFGHIJKLMNO
PQRSTUVWXYZ[\]^_`abcdefghijklmnopqrstuvwxyz{|}~

HELVITAL

!"#$%&'()+,-./0123456789:;<=>?@ABCDEFGHIJKLMNO*
PQRSTUVWXYZ[\]^_`abcdefghijklmnopqrstuvwxyz{|}~

MAIN

!"#$%&'()*+,-./0123456789:;<=>?@ABCDEFGHIJKLMNO
PQRSTUVWXYZ[\]^_'abcdefghijklmnopqrstuvwxyz{¦}~

PALATINO

!"#$%&'()+,-./0123456789:;<=>?@ABCDEFGHIJKLMNO*
PQRSTUVWXYZ[\]^_'abcdefghijklmnopqrstuvwxyz{|}~

ROMAN

!"#$%&'()*+,-./0123456789:;<=>?@ABCDEFGHIJKLMNO
PQRSTUVWXYZ[\]^_'abcdefghijklmnopqrstuvwxyz{¦}~

SANSITAL

!"#$%&'()+,-./0123456789:;<=>?@ABCDEFGHIJKLMNO*
PQRSTUVWXYZ[\]^_'abcdefghijklmnopqrstuvwxyz{¦}~

SANSSER2

!"#$%&'()*+,-./0123456789:;<=>?@ABCDEFGHIJKLMNO
PQRSTUVWXYZ[\]^_'abcdefghijklmnopqrstuvwxyz{¦}~

HOLLOW

!"#$%&'()*+,-./0123456789:;<=>?@ABCDEFGHIJKLMNO
PQRSTUVWXYZ[\]^_'abcdefghijklmnopqrstuvwxyz{|}~

COMPUTER

!"#$%&'()*+,-./0123456789:;<=>?@ABCDEFGHIJKLMNO
PQRSTUVWXYZ[\]^_'abcdefghijklmnopqrstuvwxyz{¦}~

amount of work in order to configure the program to work with printers that are neither listed nor compatible with one of the listed printers.) The program is also capable of running in memory-resident mode for users who have the requisite 100 kilobytes of available RAM, or called up as needed from the system prompt for users with limited RAM.

LQ can be either extremely simple to use, or moderately complicated, depending on what one wishes to accomplish with the program. If one simply desires to switch a printer's default printing mode for one of the 19 included letter-quality fonts, the program is simple to use: one need only press the program's "hot keys"—the LEFT SHIFT and RIGHT SHIFT keys pressed simultaneously—and select one of the four default fonts by number. After that point, anything printed from most any word processing program will be output with the new font. At the system prompt, one need only type LQ followed by the font style desired (e.g., LQ Cl'COURIER' [RETURN] will load the COURIER font as the default).

It is also possible to enhance existing text by changing both fonts and type sizes at any point in the document, producing different styles of print within the same printed document. The procedure required to achieve this result is somewhat more complicated, but well within the ability of the average computer user to perform. It should be noted here that even novice users can quickly learn even most of the program's advanced features, due in no small part to the program's excellent included 41-page documentation file which is clearly written, well organized and offers understandable, helpful information on all of the program's main features.

Anyone who has ever attempted to undertake the task of programming a new font for a printer is painfully aware of the painstaking, time consuming and, for most of us, infuriating nature of the task. The sheer number of fonts which have been programmed for LQ is an amazing accomplishment. The program offers truly exceptional print on even the latest expensive dot matrix printers available. Consequently, the $35 registration fee for the program is most reasonable. And users who register their programs will receive the following additional benefits: a disk with the latest copy of the program (which should include additional fonts); a mail-in card for a free future upgrade; and a $10 commission any time a new user registers a copy of the program given to him by the registered user.

Opposite: **Figure 6.26: An actual printout of some of the available fonts with LQ. The printout here is from a Panasonic KX-P10911 (Epson and IBM compatible). This program has been tested on a number of Epson-compatible printers in the $150 to $400 range with similar results. The program even makes it possible for users to define their own fonts, a process which is not difficult, but is time consuming and requires no small amount of patience.**

Program: LQ Ver. 2.26 © 1985, 1986
Author: Mark Harris
Company: Granny's Old Fashioned Software
Address: Route 4, Box 216, Boone, NC 28607
Category: Disk Utility Programs
Registration Fee: $35 (Includes latest version of program, free future upgrade, $10 commission for users who register copies with registrant's serial number, and free phone technical support.)

General Evaluation: LQ Ver. 2.26

	Excellent	*Very Good*	*Good*	*Average*	*Poor*
Ease of Use		***			
Ease of Learning			***		
Documentation	***				
Utility	***				
Overall Rating		***			

Public Domain SideWays[PD]

Anyone who works with spreadsheet programs using large files knows how difficult it can be to print files which may have hundreds of columns. The average printer with a 10″ carriage (by far the most common for home use, and often found in small business as well) can only print 80 columns of text in normal mode, and 136 columns in expanded mode (this is all that can be accommodated in a standard, 8″ wide sheet of paper). Even wide-carriage printers fare only slightly better, since they can print a maximum of 140 characters on a 14″-wide sheet of paper in standard (pica) mode, or 238 characters in compressed mode. But a spreadsheet of even modest size quite often goes well beyond 200 characters in width. This leads to printing contortions—and wasted time—as portions of the spreadsheet must be printed separately on standard size paper and then either pasted together in an effort at reconstructing it as near its original form as possible, or viewed in the smaller fragments as printed.

Fortunately there is help in getting around the width limits of most any printing job. Public Domain SideWays, a program developed by Donovan Kuhn and released into the public domain in 1985, allows for the printing of files with a maximum of 1,024 columns per line and 48 lines per page—more than adequate for most applications. The program, and others like it available through normal commercial developers, allows any ASCII file (which can optionally be generated by most word processor or spreadsheet programs) to be printed sideways on the paper. The fact that files are printed sideways allows most standard printers—even those with the small 10″ carriages—to print spreadsheets or text files which are approximately 750 percent wider than those normally produced in compressed format, and a full 1280 percent wider than those produced by these printers in normal print mode. These results can be obtained with standard-size paper on most any existing printer (10″, 12″ or 15″ carriage). Although the program is primarily of use for people who work with large spreadsheets, the program can also be used with word processing files. Although the need to produce extra-wide documents may not arise as often in a word processing situation, there are instances where extra width in printing may be welcomed. Almost everyone who works extensively with word processing—particularly in a business setting—will eventually need to print a document of greater width than is supported by her printer. In such a case, Public Domain SideWays may be the best available option.

While the program may not be as complete as some of its commercial counterparts (e.g., it does not offer wide ranging printer support, multiple fonts or a host of other niceties found in its flashier commercial brethren), it is a nifty, functional program which will work fine in most applications requiring wide printing. And, while others may claim greater options and flexibility, none can claim a better value.

Program: Public Domain SideWays © 1985
Author: Donavon Kuhn
Company: N/A
Address: N/A
Category: Printer Utility Programs
Registration Fee: None (released into the public domain in 1985)

General Evaluation: Public Domain SideWays © 1985

	Excellent	*Very Good*	*Good*	*Average*	*Poor*
Ease of Use		***			
Ease of Learning	***				
Documentation				***	
Utility		***			
Overall Rating		***			

Baker's Dozen™

It is impossible to consider any area of user-supported software without coming across Jim Button, owner of ButtonWare and one of the original founders of the shareware concept. Button is universally acknowledged as a

```
Exit with X or Esc - AltB=Save screen

            The Baker's Dozen

 A | Bttncalc mini-spreadsheet
 B | Look at Calendar
 C | Locate a file
 D | Find a text string in a file
 E | Compare two text files
 F | Sort a file
 G | Print a file at 90 degrees
 H | Capture printer output to disk
 I | Take a Snapshot of the screen
 J | Disk Utility
 K | Remove a subdirectory
 L | Keyboard information
 M | Swap COM1 and COM2
 N | Swap LPT1 and LPT2
 O | Go to DOS temporarily
 X | Exit the Baker's Dozen

  Select with letter or ↑↓ and Enter
```

```
               MISCELLANEOUS FUNCTIONS

x,y=(value)    n,r=(integer)

ABS(x)         ABS(14.5)         = 14.5    ABS(-14.5)         = 14.5
CEIL(x)        CEIL(2.1)         =  3.0    CEIL(-1.2)         = -1.0
COMB(n,r)      COMB(3,2)         =  3.0
EXP(x)         EXP(1)            =    e
FACT(n)        FACT(3)           =  6.0
FIX(x)         FIX(2.1)          =  2.0    FIX(-1.6)          = -1.0
FLOOR(x)       FLOOR(2.9)        =  2.0    FLOOR(-2.1)        = -3.0
LOG(x)         LOG(e)            =  1.0
LOG10(x)       LOG10(100)        =  2.0
MAX2(x,y)      MAX2(5,3)         =  5.0
MIN2(x,y)      MIN2(5,3)         =  3.0
MOD(x,n)       MOD(20.7,3)       =  2.7
PERM(n,r)      PERM(3,2)         =  6.0
REMAINDER(x)   REMAINDER(3.4)    =  0.4    REMAINDER(-3.4)    = -0.4
ROUND(x,n)     ROUND(27,-1)      = 30.0    ROUND(7.45,1)      =  7.5
SGN(x)         SGN(5)            =  1.0    SGN(-5)            = -1.0
SQRT(x)        SQRT(4)           =  2.0
```

Top: Figure 6.27: Menu system for Baker's Dozen. To select any one of the 14 separate programs that make up this admirable package, one need only highlight the chosen program by means of the cursor keys and strike the "Enter" key. Upon exiting a program, the user is returned to the menu screen to make a new selection. _Bottom:_ Figure 6.28: Button-Calc, includes useful on-screen help screens. This screen covers some of the advanced functions supported by the spreadsheet.

October 1989						
Su	Mo	Tu	We	Th	Fr	Sa
1	2	3	4	5	6	7
8	9	10	11	12	13	14
15	16	17	18	19	20	21
22	23	24	25	26	27	28
29	30	31				

```
My Calendar

 2 Child Health Day
 9 Leif Ericsson Day
 9 Columbus Day
15 Poetry Day
24 United Nations Day
31 Halloween
```

```
Press ←→ to change month
Press ↓↑ to change years

The Year of the Snake
The Jewish Year: 5750

                    Copyright 1987 by WyndhamWare and ButtonWare
```

```
GKEY                          Copyright 1987 by WyndhamWare
                              Copyright 1987 by ButtonWare

   OPTIONS:

Press H for: Hexadecimal ASCII character table
      D for: Decimal     ASCII character table
      K for: Keyboard values sent to PC processor
      S for: Scan code and character values

Press Esc to Quit
```

Top: Figure 6.29: Baker's Dozen includes a useful calendar function that generates monthly calendars onto a computer screen for any selected month. Recurring holidays are highlighted on screen and annotated for quick reference. *Bottom:* Figure 6.30: Baker's Dozen includes a handy on-screen reference guide to hexadecimal and decimal ASCII characters—a useful aid to programming printers to output special characters.

Figure 6.31: Baker's Dozen allows the viewing of the complete ASCII and extended-ASCII character sets on screen at any time (likewise the complete decimal ASCII and extended-ASCII character sets).

top-notch programmer, and his software offerings in most every applications category have won high praise from critics and users alike.

It is not surprising to find high quality programs from Jim Button in the utilities area. With Baker's Dozen, Button has brought together a wonderfully useful collection of various small programs and tied them together with a nice pull-down menu user interface. While the programs are meant to be used separately, the built-in menu system is a useful enhancement, especially for less experienced users.

Baker's Dozen consists of 14 independent programs with widely varying uses. Among these is an excellent one-page full-featured spreadsheet (ButtonCalc) which is simple itself to use and supports a surprisingly large number of mathematical and statistical functions. A calendar program (Calendar.COM) is also included; this program displays a calendar on the screen for any year and month, allowing for easy scrolling to any month or year by use of the cursor control keys. A full-featured disk utility program that is capable of, among other things, assisting in recovering damaged file allocation tables and accidentally-erased files (DISKUTIL.EXE) is also included. There are also utilities to help in locating files on a disk (LOCATE.EXE), print files at 90-degree angles for outputting extra-wide spreadsheets or word processing files onto standard 80-column printers (P90.EXE), sort files with a variety of options (PC_SORT.EXE), remove all children and files of a parent subdirectory in a single step (RDIR.EXE), save a graphics screen onto disk for later printing or inclusion into graphics programs (SNAPSHOT.EXE) and several additional useful printer and screen utilities. An eight-page brief documentation file is also included in the evaluation copy of the program.

Baker's Dozen, like most other software offerings from Jim Button, is a terrific, useful applications software package. Taken together, these programs are a wonderful bargain and, coupled with their user-friendly interface, a package that even a novice can fully utilize.

Program: Baker's Dozen © 1987
Author: Jim Button
Company: ButtonWare
Address: P.O. Box 5786, Bellevue, WA 98006
Category: General Utility Programs
Registration Fee: $59.95 (quantity discounts available)

General Evaluation: Baker's Dozen

	Excellent	*Very Good*	*Good*	*Average*	*Poor*
Ease of Use	***				
Ease of Learning		***			
Documentation		***			
Utility	***				
Overall Rating	***				

7: Games

Introduction

Of all available applications software, perhaps none has been more important to the development of general computer literacy than computer games. Many computer users were first introduced to computers through video games. Whether through a dedicated game system or true "home computers" like the low-end systems from Atari or Commodore, most users' first contact with computers has probably been in zapping alien nasties or rescuing fair maidens from the clutches of some horrendous meanie. For most users, particularly younger ones, the experience was a positive one; most importantly, the computer could be seen as a non-threatening entity worthy of further exploration, as opposed to some intimidating, demonic object.

Although games may be an excellent icebreaker for new computer users, their appeal to most users will continue regardless of their level of computer expertise. Graphics-oriented action games are by no means the only types of games available either in the public domain/user supported areas or in traditional commercial software. There are excellent chess, checkers, and other board games to choose from, along with adventure games and interactive fiction to keep almost anyone enthralled for weeks or months. You can relive famous historic battles and pit your strategy against that of famous generals, or trek across the galaxy at the helm of a starship. You can "spin the wheel" for cash and prizes as you compete with friends (and the computer) to solve word puzzles, or you can play trivial games with your friends or against the computer. If you prefer classic games such as Monopoly or Scrabble, you will find them here.

And, of course, you can always shoot the slimy aliens from planet Zoombamboom or gobble dots while being chased by familiar ghosts around a maze. There is literally something for everyone, and the following will, due to space limitations, regretfully only offer a brief glimpse at some of the enormous quantity of entertaining, high quality games available both in the public domain and as user-supported programs. The field is well worth exploring.

Adventure Games

Adventure games were among the first to be created for computers. The grandfather of them all, Colossal Cave, was developed by Willie Crowther for use in a mainframe computer. Although the sophistication of these games has been greatly enhanced through parsers (command-language interpreters) that can understand complex sentences and boast vocabularies of thousands of words, the original Adventure is just as playable and enjoyable today as it was two decades ago.

Adventure games are a mixture of fantasy role-playing games and interactive novels, where one either becomes the hero, or assists him as he takes part in a quest for treasure, wisdom or whatever. An imaginary locale is created for the game-player which can be as richly varied as the author's imagination. There are adventure games which are set in Arthurian England, in the present, or in some far-off galaxy in the future. What binds them together is that the hero or heroine, with a player's able (or, more often than not, inept) assistance must surpass a series of obstacles and solve myriad logical puzzles in order to complete her quest. (To rescue the king, recover lost treasure, find a powerful magical amulet, or simply escape with one's life are all possible—and not necessarily mutually exclusive—objects of a quest.) In trying to resolve the problems that the hero is faced with, one must often visit at least hundreds of different locations, pick up, carry, examine and use various artifacts, and make thousands of moves. The possibilities are only limited by the program developer's imagination, and successfully completing a given adventure can easily take weeks or months.

A well constructed adventure game is often addictive. A challenging adventure game can engross the unsuspecting adventurer for several hours per day for weeks on end. And when the final thrill of victory is experienced and the world is saved, or the king rescued or one returns home with countless treasures, there is always another adventure game to be tried.

A final word about adventure games. While it is perhaps true that many computer games will appeal most to children or teens—particularly in the arcade game genre—this is not the case with adventure games. Their appeal is universal. They may be enjoyed by precocious, patient, ten-year-olds as well as octogenarians who enjoy an intellectual challenge. Their target audience is generally the young-adult and adult computer user.

Whatever your age, if you have not yet experienced the thrill of an adventure game, you are in for a treat. And the sample games reviewed herein are a good place to begin what may well become a lifelong quest—for enjoyment.

```
ADVINT - Copyright (c) 1986, by David Betz
Welcome to the sample adventure.
This appears to be the livingroom. There is a hallway to the north and a closet
to the west.
:GO WEST
This is the livingroom closet. The livingroom is through a doorway to the east.
There is a small silver key here.
:TAKE THE SMALL SILVER KEY
small silver key taken.
:GO EAST
You are in the livingroom
:GO NORTH
You are in a long narrow hallway. There is a door to the east into a small dark
room. There are also exits on both the north and south ends of the hall.
:GO EAST
You are in a small storage room with many empty shelves. The only exit is a
door to the west. There is a rusty key here.
:TAKE THE RUSTY KEY
rusty key taken.
:GO WEST
You are in the hallway.
:LOOK
You are in a long narrow hallway. There is a door to the east into a small dark
room. There are also exits on both the north and south ends of the hall.
```

ADVSYS - 1986

ADVSYS is an adventure writing system developed by David Betz. The program is of great value to anyone who wishes to write text adventures. But it is also of importance to players who are not interested in developing their own adventures, since it can be used to play adventures created by others, many of which can be found in the public domain.

ADVSYS comes with a complete sample adventure which is rather simple in nature but helps to illustrate how the program operates. Other more challenging adventures have been created by various individuals using this program and may be found as public domain or shareware offerings; a copy of ADVSYS is needed in order to run any adventure created with it.

Any adventure game needs a means of interfacing with a player—of giving her information about the game as it progresses and processing her commands as she issues them. This important function is handled by a game's parser. Generally speaking, the more powerful the parser, the easier it is to play the game, and the more enjoyable the experience. The parser utilized by ADVSYS is a sophisticated one, making a game created with the program capable of utilizing multiple commands per line (e.g., take the blue book and the red pencil) in plain English, as opposed to the more limiting traditional interface which only accommodated two-word sentences containing only one subject and one verb (e.g., take book). The program also permits for easy expansion of the vocabulary it can recognize, so that a thoughtful program developer can create an adventure game which is capable of recognizing thousands of different words.

ADVSYS is distributed with a 17-page manual on disk which is informative and easy to understand. It should be noted here that the creation of an adventure game, even with an excellent program such as ADVSYS, should not be undertaken lightly by a beginner. An adventure which will be worthy of being played will take a considerable amount of time to construct. Having some previous exposure to programming in any language, although not strictly necessary, will be helpful to anyone undertaking the task. With that caveat in mind, ADVSYS is a program well worth exploring both by adventure enthusiasts as well as by anyone interested in finding out how interactive games work. With a little imagination, it is easy to create games which are entertaining and even educational thanks to the generosity

***Opposite:* Figure 7.1: Actual screen display from the sample game included with ADVSYS. The program does not display graphics, as is true of most adventure games. A player gives instructions to the computer at the ready prompt, which for this game is the colon. The parser then interprets your instructions and communicates the result of your command. The game's parser is a sophisticated one, capable of understanding complex sentences and multiple commands on one line.**

of ADVSYS's developer, David Betz, who has made the program available to the general public free of charge for unrestricted, *non commercial* use.

Program: ADVSYS © 1986
Author: David Betz
Address: N/A
Category: Adventure Games
Graphics Display: Works with Hercules—compatible monochrome or CGA displays.
Registration Fee: None (Public Domain)

General Evaluation: ADVSYS

	Excellent	*Very Good*	*Good*	*Average*	*Poor*	*N/A*
Holds User's Interest	***					
Ease of Learning			***			
Level of Challenge	***					
Level of Recreation	***					
Documentation			***			
Graphics Quality						***
Graphics Variety						***
General Evaluation		***				

DND™

The Dungeons & Dragons series of role-playing games have built up a sizable following over the years, with thousands of fans of all ages getting together to play their favorite game on a regular basis.

Precisely why Dungeons & Dragons players are so devoted to their favorite game is not easy to say. Perhaps it is the ability that the game provides for someone to take on a new persona—to become, say, a warrior, a cleric, a magician or a thief—and to live out some heroic fantasy within the safe confines of one's own living room. At any rate, the game offers great diversion and the opportunity for some perfectly safe escapism.

DND is not played like the original role-playing game which inspired it, but it retains much of its namesake's flavor. There is none of the rolling of dice to build a character's various attributes and experience level, nor can the game be played between many people and controlled by one Dungeon Master. The computer acts as Dungeon Master, providing the player with different playable scenarios, keeping score and retaining a list of existing characters with their relevant attributes and experience levels.

User-Supported Software

If you use and find this program of value,
your $25 contribution will be appreciated.

R O Software
2000 Cross Bend
Plano, TX 75023

You are encouraged to copy this program as described below.

Users of this program are granted a limited license to
make copies of this program for use by others on a private
non-commercial basis. This limited license does not include:

1. Distributing this program in connection with any other product.
2. Making the program available for any consideration or 'copy fee'.
3. Distributing the program in modified form.

Copyright (C) 1984, 1986 R.O.Software

Figure 7.2: Opening screen and copyright notice for DND.

The computer game is a single-player game, although any number of characters may be saved on disk and played at any time.

To begin the game, one must select to either run an existing character or create a new one. If the latter option is chosen, a character is given a name along with a "secret name," so that only its creator may play that character in the future, and his attributes are selected. A character may be a fighter, a magician or a cleric. The character type determines its particular characteristics, such as strength, charisma, constitution, intelligence, and dexterity. A character's type also determines what general strengths and weaknesses it will possess; a fighter, for example, is generally strong, a good fighter and heals well when wounded, while clerics and magicians are better at casting spells, are more intelligent and better at negotiating with the enemy (or seeking assistance from various gods or the spirit world).

Once a character is chosen, a store of supplies is visited from which the player must decide what armament, clothing and sundry supplies should be purchased for the character with the limited amount of gold available to him to start. Once equipped, the character is transported to one of five possible dungeons, each with a score of levels to be explored, an endless supply of fiends to be conquered and untold lost treasures to be regained, ranging from vast riches to weapons abandoned by luckless heroes whose quests met a premature end.

DND offers a wealth of options and locations so that tiring of the game is a process which may take years; consequently, playability is rated as

```
Name     Victor Lopez      [Fighter]
Dungeon The Cavern

Level           9   Magic weapon +12 STR 18        IIIIIIIIIIIIIIIIIIII
Exp        393337   Magic armor  +30 INT 17        I         $
Gold        51429   Magic shield +11 WIS 12        I         X
Hit Pts        81   Magic ring   +20 CON 18        I
                    Elven boots  +10 DEX 18        I       IIIIIIIIIIII
Wand   15 15 16 13  Elven cloak  +20 CHA  7        I
                                                   I
                                                   I
                                                   I
                                                   I

Move>East
You have discovered a chest.
Press (CR) to open it or (DEL) to ignore it.
The chest contains a pile of gems.
Press (CR) to pick it up or (DEL) to ignore it.
```

excellent. There are sufficient options and variety to the game so that learning all of its available features may take a player months—even assuming that the disk-based manual is read and available help screens explored. Yet the game is intuitive enough so that a new player with little or no experience with adventure games may begin playing the game almost immediately. The game combines elements of a classic text-based adventure game with those of board games and graphics-based games. Graphics screens are available, although they are relatively crude by design; they serve only to plot out the heroes' movement throughout the mazes, as well as indicating the existence of danger, treasure and other useful topographical information. The game was not intended as an arcade-style program, and anyone who expects graphics displaying glorious battles in gory detail will be sorely disappointed. This is a game of imagination intended primarily for adults, and its strengths run far deeper than the superficial appeal of superior graphics; the program is very well constructed, full of game-enhancing features and will provide countless hours of wonderful entertainment.

Program: DND © 1984, 1986
Company: R.O. Software
Address: 2800 Cross Bend, Plano, TX 75023
Category: Adventure Games
Graphics Display: Works with Hercules-compatible monochrome or CGA displays.
Registration Fee: None (A contribution of $15 is suggested, however.)

General Evaluation: DND™

	Excellent	*Very Good*	*Good*	*Average*	*Poor*	*N/A*
Holds User's Interest	***					
Ease of Learning			***			
Level of Challenge	***					
Level of Recreation	***					
Documentation			***			
Graphics Quality					***	
Graphics Variety				***		
General Evaluation	***					

Opposite: **Figure 7.3: Actual playing screen from DND. A spartan graphics display is offered on the right side of the screen useful only for tracking the basic movements of the character on the screen. Most of the screen's display is reserved for displaying important information relevant to the game, including information on a character's current status (upper-lefthand corner of the screen), while information relating to the current move appears on the lower-lefthand of the screen. On-screen help is available at all times.**

```
Welcome to ADVENTURE!

Original development by Willie Crowther.

Major features added by Don Woods.

Conversion to BDS C by J. R. Jaeger

Unix standardization by Jerry D. Pohl.

Would you like instructions?

>YES

Somewhere nearby is Colossal Cave, where others have
found fortunes in treasure and gold, though it is rumored
that some who enter are never seen again. Magic is said
to work in the cave. I will be your eyes and hands. Direct
me with commands of 1 or 2 words. I should warn you that I
look at only the first five letters of each word, so you'll
have to enter "Northeast" as "ne" to distinguish it from
"North". (Should you get stuck, type "help" for some
general hints).
```

Figure 7.4: Opening screen from Adventure showing preliminary help message.

Adventure^PD

Adventure was the first full-fledged computer adventure game. It was first developed using a mainframe computer, and was subsequently adapted for use by a wide variety of computers and various operating systems. The game has inspired a veritable flood of adventure games and interactive fictions by a host of software companies; the latter have come to surpass their older progenitor and can boast better, more "intelligent" parsers able to comprehend multiple commands containing large vocabularies. Some of the

```
There are some keys on the ground here.
There is a shiny brass lamp nearby.
There is tasty food here.
There is a bottle of water here.
>TAKE KEYS
ok.
>TAKE WATER
ok.
>TAKE LAMP
ok.
>EAT FOOD
Thank you. It was delicious!
>GO WEST
You are standing at the end of a road before a small brick
building. Around you is a forest. A small stream flows out
of the building and down a gully.
>ENTER BUILDING
bad grammar...
>GO BUILDING
You're inside building.
>EXAMINE
Sorry, but I am not allowed to give more detail. I will
repeat the long description of your location.
You are inside a building, a well house for a large spring.
>
```

Figure 7.5: Sample playing screen from Adventure.

newer games can even produce exquisite graphics displays to accompany the text and significantly add to the overall playing experience. Despite all the enhancements found in the newer games, the original Adventure with its relatively limited vocabulary and the ability to deal only with two-word commands can still deliver many hours of pure playing pleasure.

As the game opens, the player is prompted as to whether she wishes to read the instructions. If she answers "yes," a brief one-paragraph help file is displayed on the screen (see Figure 7.4), after which the opening scene of the game is displayed. From that moment on, a player must give instructions to the character in the game which will do what is commanded, provided he can understand the player's instructions. (He is not particularly bright, as is usually the case with epic heroes; but with a little bit of patience, he'll eventually understand what you want him to do, and do it—if it is within his power.) With the player's assistance, the game character will explore hundreds of different locales, meet interesting characters, discover wonderful treasure (as well as useless junk which you'll have him carry along "just in case he'll need it later") and probably die young. Adventure, as well as most of its successors in the same vein, is quite generous with punishment for even relatively slight oversights, and our poor heroic alter-egos in the game are more often than not dispatched quickly. Fortunately, they can easily be revived; and Adventure, along with all worthwhile adventure or interactive fiction programs, allows for the saving of one's place at any point in the game—a useful feature when one finally gives in to the natural need for sleep after an Adventure session.

For anyone not familiar with adventure games, Adventure is a *must-have* program, if only to see what all the fuss is about. Although the game was not specifically developed for children, a patient, precocious youngster may well both enjoy the game and do quite well with it. In fact, unlike most video games or arcade-style shoot-em-ups which can only improve hand-eye coordination, a good adventure game can actually help a young player develop (or hone) analytical, and problem-solving skills, while promoting (and rewarding) clear thinking and ingenuity in general. Furthermore, young and old players alike will practice their typing skills extensively in order to play any adventure or interactive fiction game and, if they are new to computers, will be introduced to the wonders of this great tool in a painless, enjoyable way.

Program: Adventure
Author: Original Development: Willie Crowther
Additional Features: Don Woods
Conversion to C language: J.R. Jaeger
Unix Standardization: Jerry D. Pohl
Company: N/A
Address: N/A
Category: Adventure Games
Graphics Display: Works with Hercules-compatible monochrome or CGA displays.
Registration Fee: None (Public Domain)

General Evaluation: Adventure

	Excellent	*Very Good*	*Good*	*Average*	*Poor*	*N/A*
Holds User's Interest	***					
Ease of Learning		***				
Level of Challenge	***					
Level of Recreation	***					
Documentation			***			
Graphics Quality						***
Graphics Variety						***
General Evaluation	***					

Hack™ Version 1.0.1

Hack is an adventure in the Dungeons & Dragons tradition which offers a wide variety of playing options and rough graphics to assist any willing adventurer in successfully fulfilling his quest for the Amulet

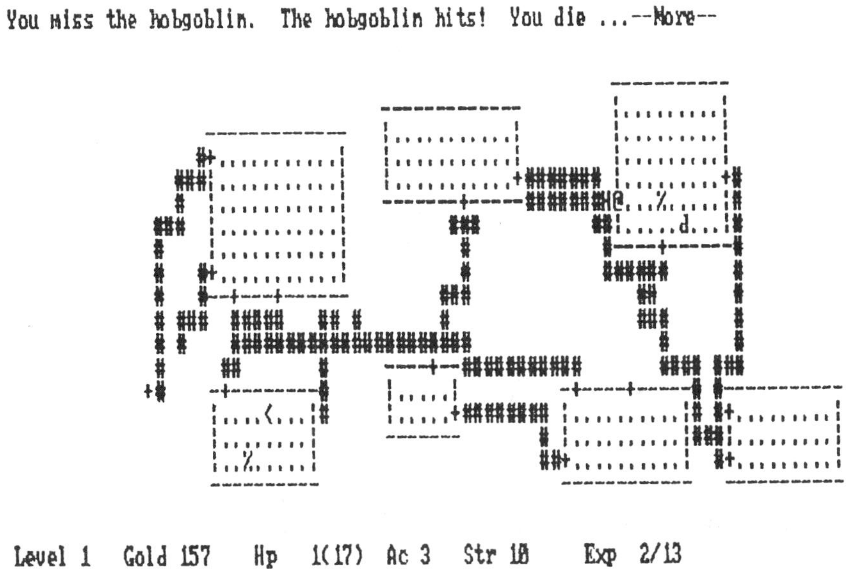

Figure 7.6: Sample playing screen from Hack. The graphics of rooms and various important objects may seem somewhat crude, but they are quite important to the game and very useful when one gets used to reading them. In general, the darker areas formed by the "#" character are passageways. Rooms are clearly outlined. Some important characters are assigned letters (e.g., monsters), while other items are assigned various symbols. In the sample screen, "%" denotes food (dead monsters are sometimes edible), while "<" denotes a staircase leading to the previous level. There are dozens of other symbols for weapons, scrolls, and sundry items. Fortunately, each is listed and explained in the included documentation files and in available on-line help screens.

of Yandor, purportedly hidden somewhere on the 20th level of the dungeon.

Hack, like DND and other games based on the Dungeons and Dragons role-playing game, allows a player to select a character from several available types (knight, fighter, tourist, speleologist, caveman or wizard). The character is then transported onto the first level of a dungeon containing 20 levels. While engaged in his quest, the hero will be confronted with all sorts of perils and come across a wide variety of artifacts. Magic, as is the custom, works in the dungeon, and perils (as well as assistance) can come from the spiritual, as well as physical, world. Unlike most other games of this kind, our hero is accompanied by a small dog as a faithful companion and sidekick. The latter can be quite useful in fighting monsters alongside

Figure 7.7: Novices to this game die often, but at the newly-initiated may take some comfort in the knowledge that their remains will not be left lying about the dungeon for some hungry monster to devour. Free funeral services are generously offered.

the hero; but it must be fed on a regular basis, or it will die. (Fortunately, it isn't a fussy eater; most any dead monster will do quite nicely as an entree.) Unfortunately, the animal isn't too bright; I managed to kill it repeatedly in my first tentative tries at this game by walking over it when it got in my way. After awhile, I learned to issue the "wait" command before moving if it was in my path, and it always got out of the way if I told my hero to wait enough times.

On the positive side, the game offers a wealth of playing options which can keep a player interested (as well as busy learning) for quite some time. The dungeon has been well planned and well stocked with a fair amount of perils and treasures, but not so many as to make it cumbersome on the player; one can explore without constantly running into a treasure to pick up (or ignore) or an adversary to dispatch (or evade)—something which cannot be said of DND reviewed elsewhere in this volume.

On the negative side of the equation, Hack can be a difficult game to learn to play. Unlike most other games in its class, one cannot play Hack without *carefully* reading the instructions or constantly referring to the help screen. There are simply too many commands to learn, none of which are easy to remember. For example, in order to move "up" on the screen (or "north"), one must press the "k" key, while south, east and west are "j," "l" and "h" respectively. These keys are neither phonetic for the functions they perform, nor are they found in the usual diamond pattern for such cursor movements (e.g., the famous WordStar CTRL-E, CTRL-X, CTRL-S and CTRL-D sequence for the up, down, left and right keys respectively). Other

```
Goodbye Knight victor...

You died on dungeon level 1 with 204 points,
and 157 pieces of gold, after 498 moves.
You were level 2 with a maximum of 17 hit points when you died.

You made the top ten list!

Number Points  Name                                              Hp [max]
  1     270   Victor-F escaped the dungeon [max level 1].        14 [14]
  2     204   victor-K was killed on level 1 by a hobgoblin.      - [17]
  3     145 Nick Danger-K quit on dungeon level 1.                ? [12]
  4      87    Fuzzy-W was killed on level 1 by a kobold.         - [15]
  5      50 Nick Danger-K escaped the dungeon [max level 1].     12 [12]


B>
```

Figure 7.8: After the inevitable comes to pass, defeated heroes and heroines may find solace in that their best efforts will be memorialized in a permanent Hall of Fame for all the world to marvel (or snicker) at.

commands are likewise as seemingly illogical (e.g., an "a" is typed to unlock a door and a "q" to drink a potion). To make matters worse, lower case and upper case letters are assigned different functions. In a word, learning enough commands to move around and explore the dungeon while giving the hero even the slightest chance of staying alive for more than 20 moves or so requires a bit of preparation. You will need to spend at least half an hour learning to perform the fundamental movements for the game, as well as manipulating such vital assets as the hero's weapons and simply learning to "read" the graphics screens.

In fairness to the game, most complicated software packages require a considerable amount of learning time; this is also true of board games. This is perhaps among the worst packages for a user new to adventuring to try, since he is likely to be confused and become frustrated. But for someone with some previous experience with adventure games (public domain, user-supported or commercial ones), Hack can be a wonderful source of diversion for many hours. It is certainly worth exploring.

Program: Hack Ver. 1.0.1

Author: Unknown (developed at the Stichting Mathematisch Centrum in Amsterdam). Converted to MS/DOS from the UNIX original operating system by Don Kneller.

Note: The address given below for the remittance of contributions is that of Don Kneller. The effort required to port the program from Unix to MS/DOS is considerable, and fans of the program who would like to see future enhancements should support this program as well as all of their favorite user supported programs.

Company: N/A (Don Kneller)
Address: 2 Panoramic Way #204, Berkeley, CA 94704
Category: Adventure Games
Graphics Display: Works with Hercules-compatible monochrome or CGA displays.
Registration Fee: None (An unspecified contribution is, however, requested.)

General Evaluation: Hack Ver. 1.0.1

	Excellent	*Very Good*	*Good*	*Average*	*Poor*	*N/A*
Holds User's Interest	***					
Ease of Learning					***	
Level of Challenge	***					
Level of Recreation	***					
Documentation			***			
Graphics Quality				***		
Graphics Variety				***		
General Evaluation		***				

Marooned Again™

Marooned Again is an adventure game with a futuristic setting. You are stranded in an alien world, injured and dying. Fortunately, you were able to produce various clones of yourself which you can send out into the world to search for parts you will need to get you back home aboard an abandoned alien ship. These clones, or alter-egos, are not too smart, and can only understand two-word commands, such as "take rope" or "jump up." Their vocabulary is also quite limited, so that communicating with them is not always easy. With a bit of patience, however, it should be possible to successfully complete the quest by finding all of the necessary spare parts to repair the ship.

Despite the futuristic setting, this is a fairly standard adventure. The puzzles it provides are challenging and perhaps harder to solve than in the average adventure game. The game's parser, or command interpreter, is rather limited, yet adequate. Unfortunately, it does not support multiple commands or complex sentences. The game is, nevertheless, interesting and challenging. As with most adventure games, expect to die often before you get the hang of the way the universe functions in the adventure game.

This is an average skill level game perhaps best suited for adventurers with some previous experience. As with all adventure games, patience is a definite prerequisite, as well as creative thinking and the willingness to make a commitment of at least a couple of weeks (and perhaps even several months) of playing time. Finishing the game in less than 15 hours of playing time seems unlikely. (But this is true of every adventure game—at least every game worth playing.)

Program: Marooned Again © 1985
Author: Dennis Drew
Company: Computer Tutor
Address: P.O. Box 101, Joplin, MO 64802
Category: Adventure Games
Graphics Display: Works with Hercules-compatible monochrome or CGA displays.
Registration Fee: Donations requested. ("[W]hatever donation you feel is fair.") Donors become registered users and "may call in for help if you get stuck."

General Evaluation: Marooned Again

	Excellent	*Very Good*	*Good*	*Average*	*Poor*	*N/A*
Holds User's Interest			***			
Ease of Learning		***				
Level of Challenge		***				
Level of Recreation			***			
Documentation			***			
Graphics Quality						***
Graphics Variety						***
General Evaluation			***			

Arcade Games

Of all the types of games available for the personal computer, arcade games are undoubtedly the ones with which most readers will be familiar. These types of games are the ones advertised on television for a lot of systems, including the Atari, Nintendo, Coleco and a host of other dedicated game systems. Most of these games have in common an emphasis on fast-paced action in which the player is pitted against the computer or another player. Good eye-hand coordination and quick reflexes are important here, whether one is shooting down alien spaceships or trying to rescue a damsel in distress from a never-ending assortment of fiends. Unlike adventure games, arcade games do not require much thought or many hours to complete; the average game lasts only minutes, and graphics displays (the moving images that a computer is capable of producing) are emphasized over deductive reasoning or logical thinking. There are, of course, exceptions, and one should not make assumptions that all such games are relatively mindless. Even the least complicated of these games can provide wonderful entertainment value; and there is an inexplicable satisfaction in doing something intrinsically difficult, like shooting at a moving target and learning to do it well. Whether you are a child of eight or a grandmother of 80, many of these games are simply good fun. And if they won't help you become a better typist or think logically, neither will watching the average television show. At least with these, you will be working on a computer, something in and of itself useful for the new user.

Centipede™ Version 1.0

Centipede is a game patterned after the classic Centipede arcade game. It offers fast-paced shoot-em-up action for one or two players in three different levels of difficulty.

The basic premise of the game is a simple one: to shoot every piece of a centipede which is trying to make its way down the screen. Every time a piece of the centipede is shot, it turns into a barrier making it more difficult to later shoot at other pieces of the troublesome pest. The game ends when any part of the centipede touches the player's laser cannon at the bottom of the screen. Every time a centipede is completely destroyed by a player, a new one emerges at the top of the screen which is faster, and therefore harder to destroy, than its predecessor. An assortment of other dangerous creatures also appear on the screen from time to time which must also be shot or avoided.

The game provides enough levels of difficulty so as to be difficult to master. Play gets progressively more difficult within any of the three levels. A help screen is available to provide information as to how the game is played and all available options. The game may be played either with joysticks or by using the keyboard. The game's various levels of play and fast-paced action will provide many hours of entertainment.

Program: Centipede Ver. 1.0 © 1983
Author: R.J. Grafe

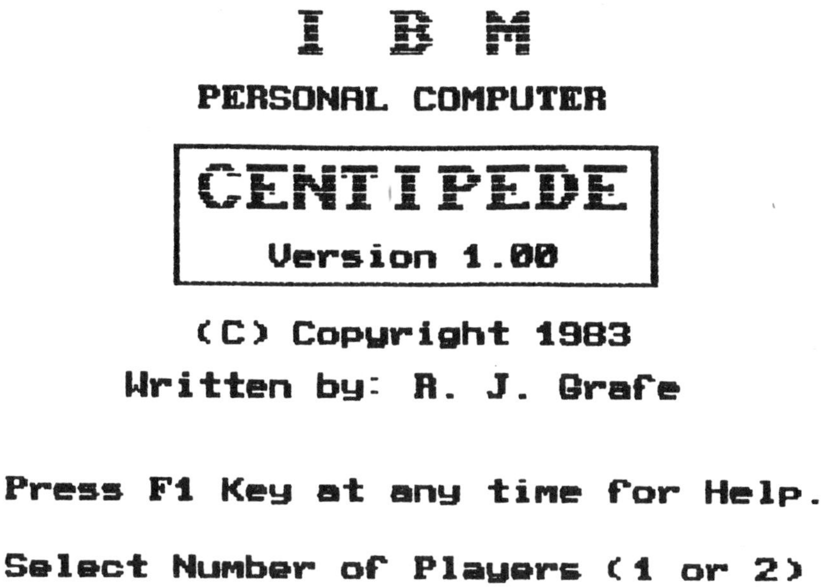

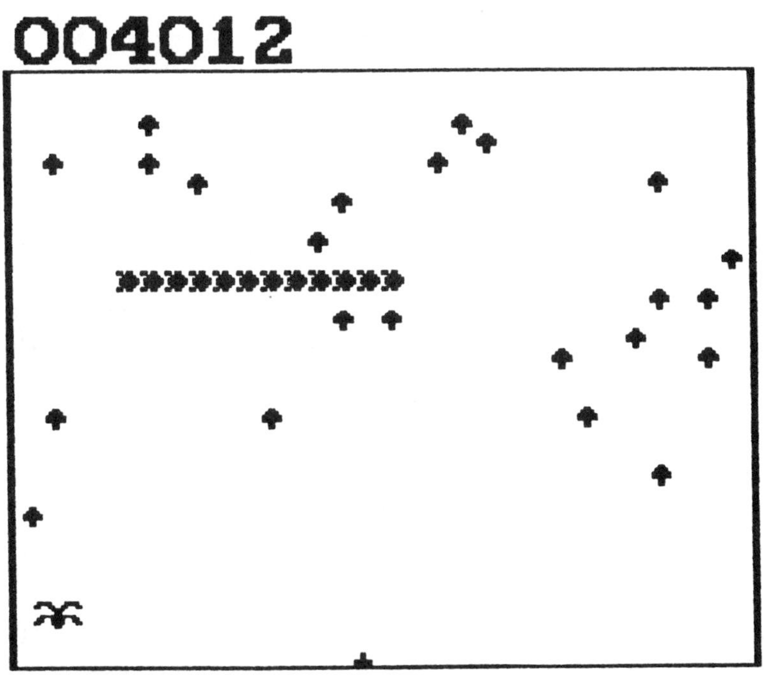

Top: Figure 7.9: Opening screen and copyright notice for Centipede. *Bottom:* Figure 7.10: Main playing screen for Centipede. The game offers fast-paced action and a variety of playing levels much like the arcade classic after which it is patterned.

Company: N/A
Address: N/A
Category: Arcade Games
Graphics Display: Requires Color Graphics Adaptor (CGA) display or CGA emulation software for use with Hercules monochrome display.
Registration Fee: None (Public Domain)

General Evaluation: Centipede Ver. 1.0

	Excellent	*Very Good*	*Good*	*Average*	*Poor*	*N/A*
Holds User's Interest		***				
Ease of Learning		***				
Level of Challenge	***					
Level of Recreation		***				
Documentation						***
Graphics Quality			***			
Graphics Variety				***		
General Evaluation		***				

Dragons™

Dragons is an arcade-style game which resembles the arcade classic Breakout. In this fantasy adaptation of the arcade original, a princess is captured by an evil emperor, Peter the Nerd. Emperor Nerd has imprisoned poor Princess Gwendolyn behind his nearly impenetrable fortress. The fair damsel's only hope is for some worthy commoner to rescue her by bouncing magical gold coins off a magical sword and into the thick palace walls. Every contact between the coin and the wall results in a brick being destroyed. When enough bricks are destroyed so that the coin can enter the castle itself, then the princess may be rescued. Every time the princess is rescued from one level, she is whisked away into another of eight possible castles by her captor, and our hero must continue to undefatigably bounce coins off his magic sword to attempt her rescue. Furthermore, while the player knocks out bricks with the bouncing coins, one of several of Emperor Nerd's minions will be busily adding new bricks throughout the screen.

After each level of play, when the coin breaks through to the inner castle, the player is promoted in rank from dwarf, to serf, and so on until the rank of king is achieved and the princess can then finally be rescued. After

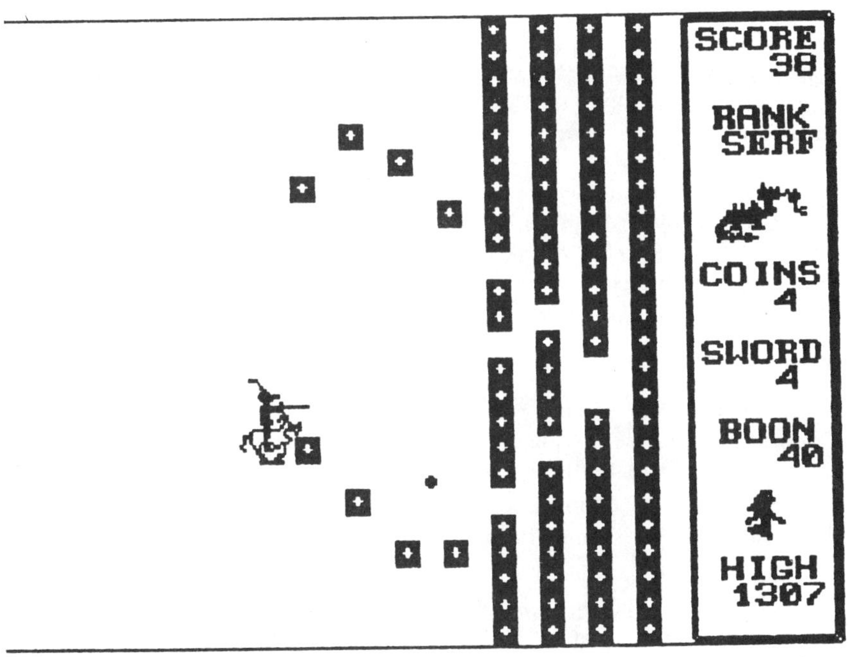

***Top:* Figure 7.11: Opening screen for Dragon. *Bottom:* Figure 7.12: First playing screen for Dragon. The game is evocative of the old arcade favorite Breakout and offers a wide variety of playing options and graphics screens so as to keep the game challenging even after many hours of play.**

several hours of play, I was only able to achieve the third level at my chosen degree of difficulty of 5 (1 is hardest and 9 is easiest). The nine available levels of difficulty make it difficult to master this game prior to many hours of play. Graphics for this game are also quite good and serve to further enhance the playing experience.

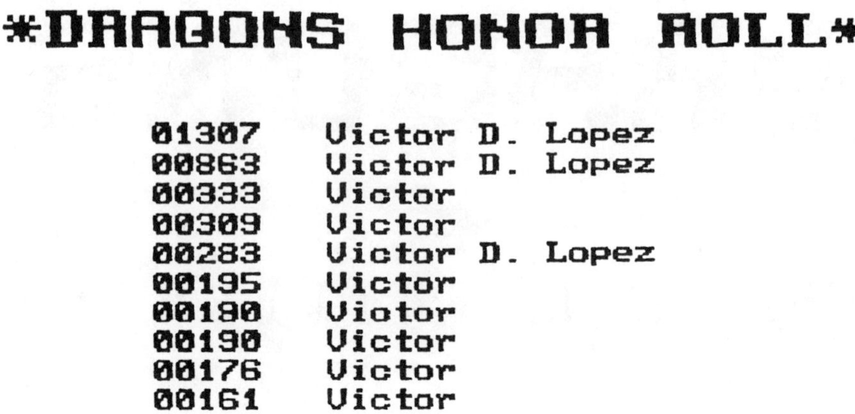

Figure 7.13: Dragon, like many of the arcade-style games reviewed herein, includes an "Honor Roll" of the top ten scores on disk. The scores are automatically updated at the end of every game.

Dragons is an interesting game which is easy to learn yet hard to master and should provide many hours of entertainment.

Program: Dragons © 1986
Author: F.A. Willshaw
Company: N/A
Address: N/A
Category: Arcade Games
Graphics Display: Requires Color Graphics Adaptor (CGA). Also works with a Hercules monochrome card and CGA emulation software.
Registration Fee: None (Public Domain)

General Evaluation: Dragons

	Excellent	*Very Good*	*Good*	*Average*	*Poor*	*N/A*
Holds User's Interest		***				
Ease of Learning	***					
Level of Challenge	***					
Level of Recreation		***				
Documentation		***				
Graphics Quality		***				
Graphics Variety			***			
General Evaluation		***				

Dueling Star Ships™ Version A

Dueling Star Ships is a superb space war simulation for two players. The game bears a strong resemblance to the large number of games based on the popular *Star Trek* television show. This game is far superior to most others of its kind in that it offers true interactive play for two players who pit their skills—and available hardware—against each other while battling in a universe created and controlled by the computer. The human factor makes playing this game a far richer experience both intellectually and in terms of sheer enjoyment; while it is always nice to beat the computer in a game, it is far more rewarding to test one's skill against a human opponent.

The premise of the game is a simple one: two equally equipped starships do battle against each other until one is beaten. There are no flashy graphics and there is no fast-paced action; war is a business which requires a great deal of preparation and strategy leading up to relatively ephemeral confrontations. Both starship captains must carefully select and arm their weapons from the available arsenal, as well as plot a course and set speed either towards their enemy or away. Minutes can go by while players busily code instructions to their ships' computers, while the ships move inexorably towards each other. When they are within range of their various weapons (and that range varies in accordance with the weapon used), these may be deployed and the damage they inflict is measured by each ship's computer. Both ships are capable of sustaining many waves of attack, provided the captain has allocated sufficient power to the deflector shields. Available weaponry includes phasers, photon torpedoes, mines and probes, each with a different capability to inflict damage and a different radius of effectiveness.

Strategy is all important here. The temperament of the opposing "captains" determines in great part the length and complexity of the battle, which may be fast and furious (lasting only minutes), long and cautious (lasting hours) or anywhere in between. All out attacks are possible with both ships slugging it out at close range, while more cautious approaches may also be taken with evasive maneuvers. Whatever approach is taken, the game is highly enjoyable both while it is in progress and after it has ended, as players exchange strategies and congratulate each other on the effective tactics they have used.

Program: Dueling Star Ships © 1984
Authors: Robert W. Dea and Vince J. D'Angelo
Company: N/A
Address: P.O. Box 968, Fremont, CA 94537
Category: Arcade Games

DUELING STARSHIPS (tm) Version A.00.00

DONATIONS

If you find this game to be of value, your donation to the Authors will be greatly appreciated. (Suggested donation is $15)
DO NOT SEND CASH

Checks should be made payable to: Robert W. Dea and Vince J. D'Angelo
and mailed to:

Robert W. Dea and Vince J. D'Angelo
Dueling Starships
P.O. Box 968
Fremont, CA 94537

Users are encourged to copy and share this game. In situations where a copy cannot be made from other users, a user may request a copy from the Authors for a fee of $6 (check made payable to Robert W. Dea and Vince J. D'Angelo

CONFIGURE SHIPS (Y/N): ?

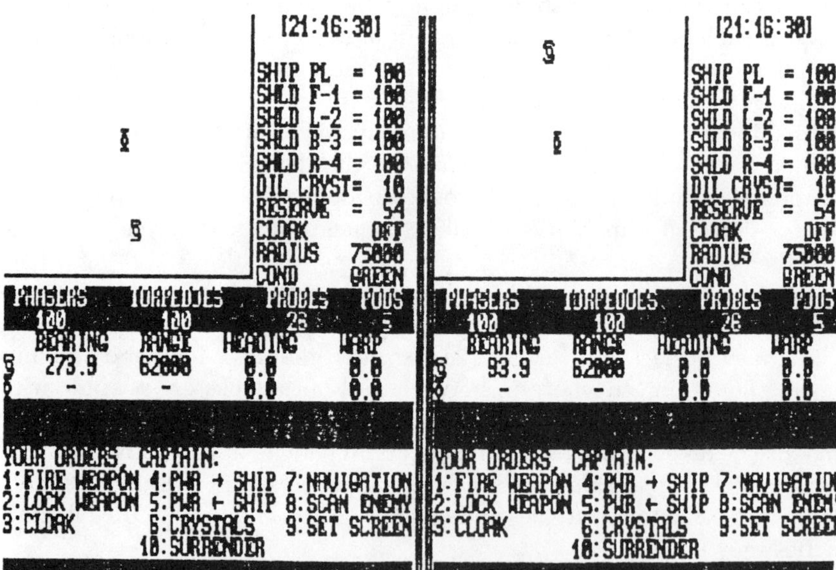

Top: **Figure 7.14: Dueling Star Ships opening screen and copyright notice. *Bottom:* Figure 7.15: Main screen for Dueling Star Ships. This program offers an excellent space battle simulation for two players. The screen is divided into two equal parts, making available a tactical display screen for each player. The game's real-time interactive action and wealth of options make for a truly engrossing playing experience.**

Graphics Display: Hercules Monochrome or Color Graphics Adaptor
Registration Fee: Donations requested (suggested donation: $15)

General Evaluation: Dueling Star Ships Ver. A

	Excellent	*Very Good*	*Good*	*Average*	*Poor*	*N/A*
Holds User's Interest	***					
Ease of Learning			***			
Level of Challenge	***					
Level of Recreation	***					
Documentation		***				
Graphics Quality					***[1]	
Graphics Variety					***[2]	
General Evaluation	***					

[1]Graphics screens are spartan, at best. But there is a *wealth* of relevant information provided on screen at all times.

[2]The screen remains substantially unchanged throughout the game, but this is not a criticism; the screen's main purpose is to provide tactical information, including the status of the ship and its various weapons and defensive systems.

Janitor Joe[PD]

Janitor Joe is a game which combines excellent graphics with fast-paced arcade action.

The game's hero, Joe, is a janitor in an automated space station in which robots have turned homicidal and are trying to kill him. His only hope of escape is to retrieve all of his keys from every room of the space station before being touched or shot by a robot. His only weapons are his speed, his ability to jump over objects, and his wits.

Playing the game is quite simple, but mastering it is not. There are five different levels, representing each of the five rooms which Joe must visit to retrieve his lost keys. Each room is represented by a different graphics screen presenting new (and more difficult) challenges for the player. The quantity and quality of the graphics screens is much better than average. The game also allows a player to choose from among five levels of difficulty, making it unlikely for anyone to tire of the game quickly, or master it prior to many hours of play.

For those who like fast, challenging action, this game will not be disappointing.

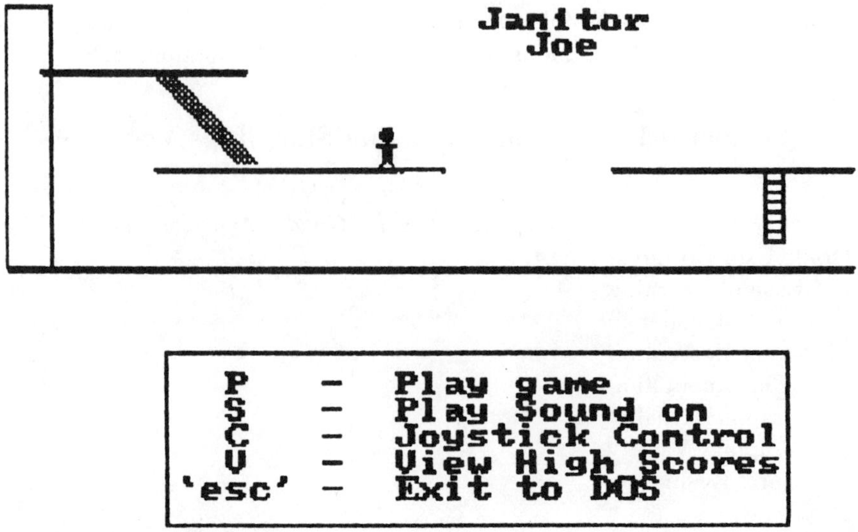

Top: **Figure 7.16: Opening screen and options menu for Janitor Joe.** ***Bottom:*** **Figure 7.17: One of five playing screens (second level) for Janitor Joe. Very good graphics and challenging action make this a good choice for fans of arcade-style games.**

Program: Janitor Joe © 1985
Author: Kevin Bales
Company: N/A
Address: 1250 Lindenwood Lane, Atlanta, GA 30319
Category: Arcade Games
Graphics Display: Requires Color Graphics Adapter or emulation software for a Hercules monochrome adapter.
Registration Fee: None (Public Domain)

General Evaluation: Janitor Joe

	Excellent	*Very Good*	*Good*	*Average*	*Poor*	*N/A*
Holds User's Interest		***				
Ease of Learning	***					
Level of Challenge	***					
Level of Recreation		***				
Documentation				***		
Graphics Quality		***				
Graphics Variety		***				
General Evaluation		***				

David's Kong[PD]

David's Kong is an arcade style game patterned after the famed Donkey Kong. While the game's graphics and general feel in no way rivals the original, it is interesting and challenging enough to keep a player busy for many hours.

The premise of the game is a simple one: a heroine has been abducted by an overgrown ape and is in need of rescuing. In order to get to her, a player must maneuver the would-be rescuer over precarious girders and ladders, while avoiding the flaming barrels of oil being cast down on him by the ape. If the player successfully reaches the girl, the ape throws down a barrel of oil in great anger, destroying part of the structure that must be traveled back down. The chivalrous hero must then climb down the girders and leap across missing sections of the same, while carrying his lady love. He must also leap over the flaming barrels which are both cast down by the hairy beast above and miraculously return from the ground below.

While the game breaks no new ground, it is a good clone of an arcade classic and will provide a good measure of challenge and entertainment with its five selectable levels of play.

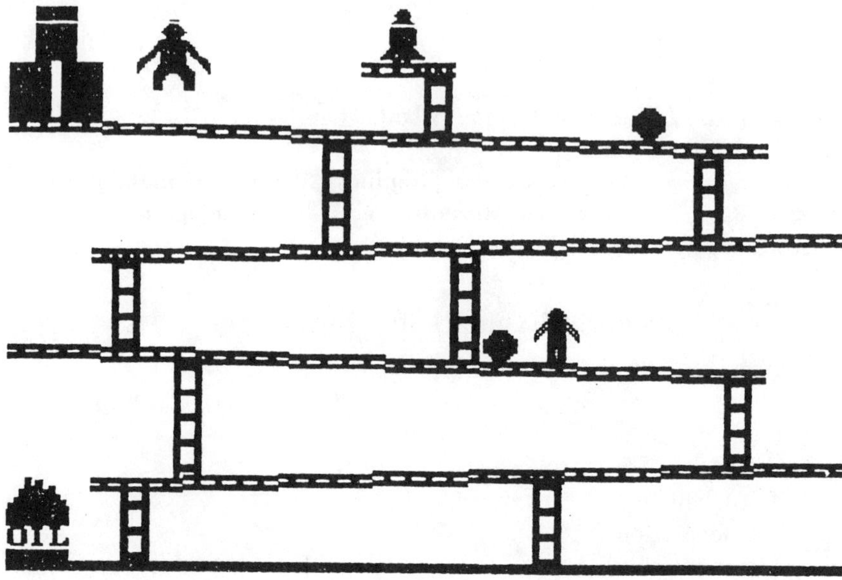

Top: **Figure 7.18: Main playing screen for David's Kong.** ***Bottom:*** **Figure 7.19: Second-level screen for David's Kong.**

Program: David's Kong
Author: N/A (One may presume his first name was David.)
Company: N/A
Address: N/A
Category: Arcade Game
Graphics Display: Color Graphics Adapter or CGA emulation software for Hercules monochrome display.
Registration Fee: None (Public Domain)

General Evaluation: David's Kong

	Excellent	*Very Good*	*Good*	*Average*	*Poor*	*N/A*
Holds User's Interest			***			
Ease of Learning		***				
Level of Challenge			***			
Level of Recreation			***			
Documentation				***1		
Graphics Quality			***			
Graphics Variety				***		
General Evaluation			***			

[1]Note: There is no separate documentation with this game (as is usual with public domain games and programs in general), but built-in help messages make the game self-explanatory.

Bert and the Snake[PD] Version 1.0b

Bert and the Snake is an entertaining game patterned after the arcade classic Qbert. In this game, the rather odd-looking hero, Bert, hops about the game screen from one box to the next trying to stay one hop ahead of the deadly snake which chases him—or the bouncing apple which seems equally fond of squashing Bert or his nemesis, the snake. The object of the game is for Bert to hop onto every square on the screen before being caught. After this is done—a feat which is not too difficult in the first few levels—the game advances one level and Bert must now successfully bounce onto each game square twice before getting caught. The third level requires each square to be jumped on three times. Since there is no documentation, it is impossible to tell if there is an upper limit on this progression. Squares change color every time they are stepped on so that one may keep track of how many times a given square has been stepped on. On the third level and

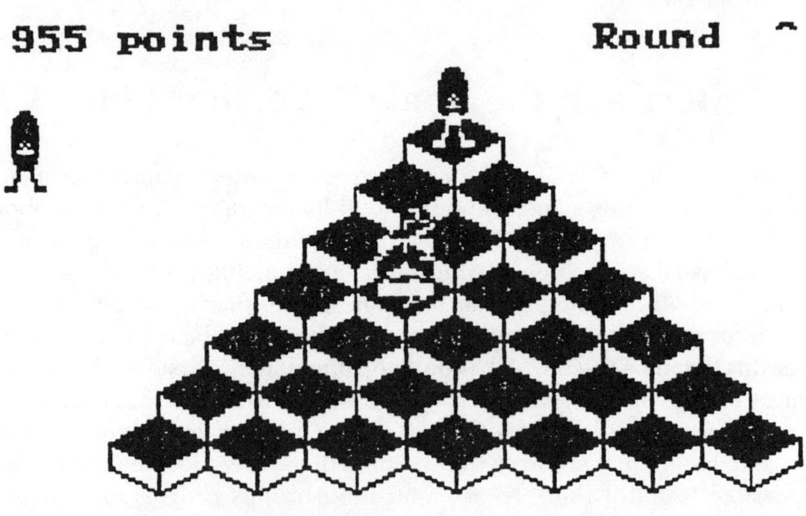

Top: Figure 7.20: Opening screen and copyright notice for Bert and the Snake.
Bottom: Figure 7.21: Third round playing screen for Bert and the Snake.

beyond, portions of a square light up in different colors each time they are stepped on, until the complete square is lit up in its final requisite color once it has been stepped on the maximum number of times.

The above may sound complicated, but the game is really quite simple to play, even though there are no on-screen help files or instructions on disk. While we believe the game may be most enjoyable for younger players, it is challenging enough to keep anyone busy for many hours without obtaining mastery over its play.

Program: Bert and the Snake Ver. 1.0b © 1983
Author: Bill Piazza
Company: N/A
Address: N/A
Category: Arcade Game
Graphics Display: Requires Color Graphics Adapter (CGA) or CGA emulation software when used with a Hercules monochrome graphics card.
Registration Fee: None (Public Domain)

General Evaluation: Bert and the Snake Ver. 1.0b

	Excellent	*Very Good*	*Good*	*Average*	*Poor*	*N/A*
Holds User's Interest			***			
Ease of Learning			***			
Level of Challenge			***			
Level of Recreation			***			
Documentation					***	
Graphics Quality			***			
Graphics Variety				***		
General Evaluation			***			

Sopwith[PD]

Sopwith is a game of air-to-air and air-to-ground combat combining good graphics and nonstop action. The game provides various options, including the ability to play against the computer, or simply to practice flying and shooting at and bombing ground-based targets. When playing against the computer, a player must fly his biplane and outfox the seemingly endless number of planes which the computer will send. A player should also try to bomb or shoot at enemy ground-based targets, including tanks, fuel depots and various buildings; unfortunately, the computer's planes will

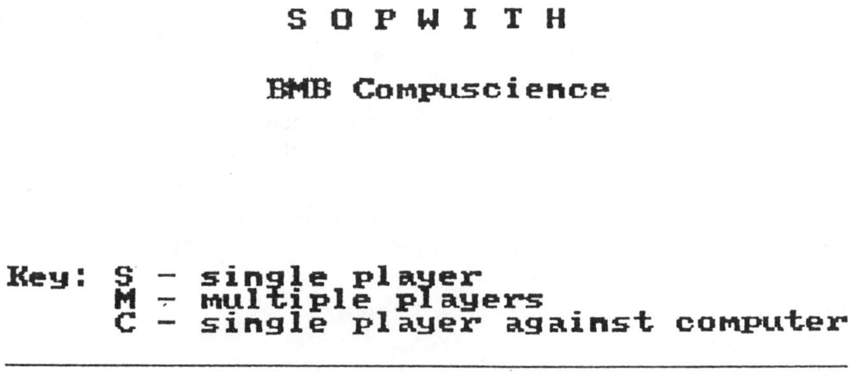

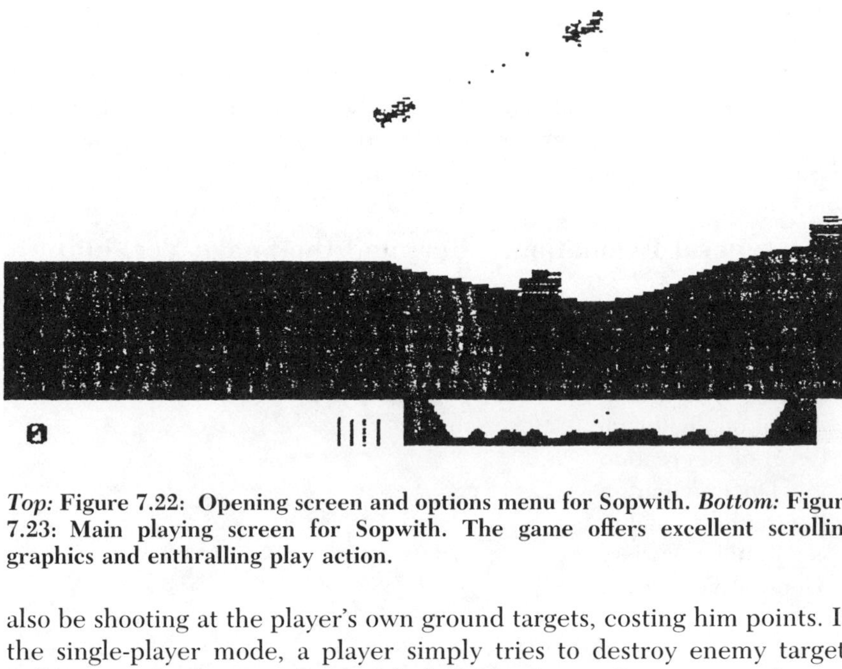

Top: **Figure 7.22: Opening screen and options menu for Sopwith.** ***Bottom:*** **Figure 7.23: Main playing screen for Sopwith. The game offers excellent scrolling graphics and enthralling play action.**

also be shooting at the player's own ground targets, costing him points. In the single-player mode, a player simply tries to destroy enemy targets (when in single player mode, the whole field is "enemy" territory, and points can be gained by blowing up all sorts of targets throughout the large playscape). The graphics screens scroll over a rather generous terrain, so that planes do not "bounce off" corners of the display, or continuously disappear from one end of the screen to reappear in another. The effect is much more pleasing as the screen scrolls to the right and left as the planes fly overhead, with the terrain below constantly changing.

The game is quite simple to learn, but difficult to master. Even in the single-player mode, where there are no enemy aircraft in the air, it is extremely difficult to blow up every single installation over the large map before all planes are destroyed; although ground-based units do not fire at the airplane, some of the buildings and other landmarks are situated where it is very difficult to get at them without crashing the plane (e.g., along hillsides and near the top of mountains). Sopwith is a very enjoyable game which offers solid entertainment.

Program: Sopwith © 1985
Author: N/A
Company: BMB Compuscience
Address: N/A
Category: Arcade Games
Graphics Display: Color Graphics Display required. Also works with Hercules monochrome displays if CGA emulation software is used.
Registration Fee: None (Public Domain)

General Evaluation: Sopwith

	Excellent	*Very Good*	*Good*	*Average*	*Poor*	*N/A*
Holds User's Interest	***					
Ease of Learning		***				
Level of Challenge		***				
Level of Recreation	***					
Documentation				***		
Graphics Quality	***					
Graphics Variety			***			
General Evaluation		***				

Space Commanders II PD

Fans of the classic arcade games will immediately recognize this as a slightly reworked Space Invaders clone. The game is faithful to the theme of the original, although not on as grandiose a scale. Commercial copies of similar software for the once popular Intellivision, Atari 5200 and Texas Instruments TI994A systems are not very different from this public domain version.

For fans of shoot-em-up, fast-paced arcade action, this game can provide hours of entertainment. It is an easy game to learn and, while not as challenging as the original, is still difficult to master. As the strange assortment of aliens slowly descend in unison down the screen and some are killed by the player's laser blasts, the pace quickens. When only a handful

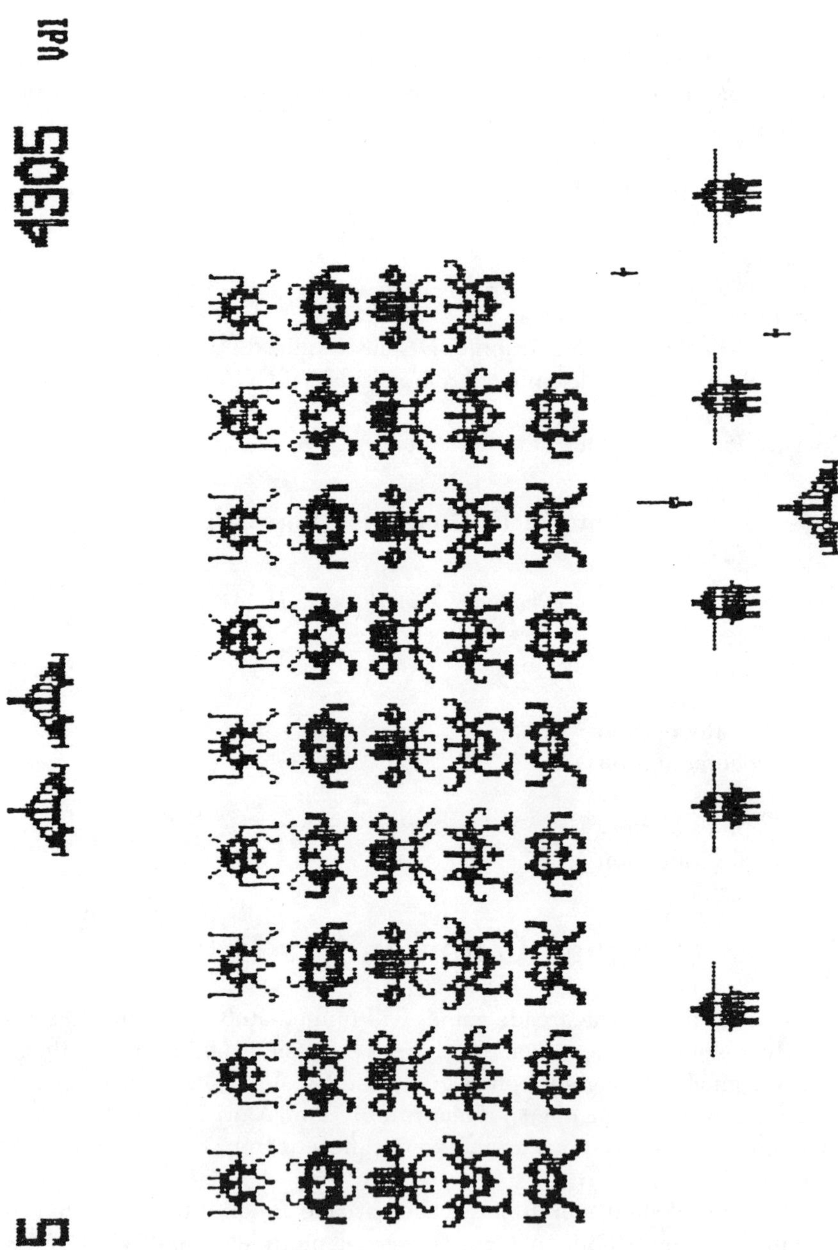
4305
UP1
5

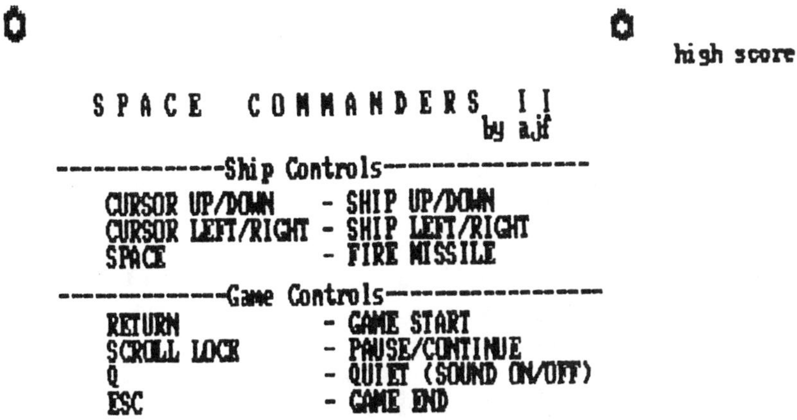

Figure 7.25: Space Commanders II opening screen.

remain on the screen, they advance at a frenzied pace so as to be very difficult to shoot. With a little practice, it is possible to stave off several waves of the never-ending alien hoard before any one of the unpleasant fellows can reach the bottom of the screen.

Program: Space Commanders II[PD]
Author: N/A (Initials are A.J.F.)
Company: N/A
Address: N/A
Category: Arcade Games
Graphics Display: Color Graphics Adapter or Hercules monochrome card with CGA emulation software.
Registration: Fee: None (Public Domain)

General Evaluation: Space Commanders II

	Excellent	*Very Good*	*Good*	*Average*	*Poor*	*N/A*
Holds User's Interest			***			
Ease of Learning		***				
Level of Challenge			***			
Level of Recreation			***			
Documentation						***
Graphics Quality			***			
Graphics Variety				***		
General Evaluation			***			

Opposite: **Figure 7.24: Main playing screen for Space Commanders II.**

STARGATE

In keyboard mode:	In joystick mode:
A - Up Z - Down ! - Stop vertical motion. < - Go left > - Go right Spc- Fire laser S - Smart bomb K - Hyperspace L - Inviso	The ship moves in the direction of the stick. Button A1 fires the laser. Button A2 fires a smart bomb. Pressing both activates the inviso cloaking shield.

Scroll lock - Quit   Esc - Pause

Press G to play in keyboard mode.

Press button A1 to play in joystick mode

Other commands:

F1 - Two player   F2 - Adjust joystick

F3 - Set difficulty   F4 - Reveal Secrets

Stargate^PD

Stargate is a popular arcade game by Atari, the computer and software giant who has released it, along with several other old arcade favorites, into the public domain.

The game-playing scenario of Stargate is a simple one: you are in command of a sophisticated, well-armed fighter and are the last line of defense against a dastardly enemy who is snatching away the citizens of your world. You are their only hope, as you strive to fight off wave after wave of assorted enemy ships, mines, smart-bombs and various other deadly hardware. As you fight against overwhelming odds, you can see your fellow citizens ensnared by the enemy and lifted up towards slavery. If you are good enough, you can snatch these poor innocents from the malevolent clasp of the enemy and bring them down to safety. The task is not an easy one, but one which may be accomplished with some courage—and much practice.

The game is quite absorbing, and will certainly please aficionados of adrenalin-pumping arcade games. There is no separate documentation provided with this game, but there are good on-screen instructions. This is certainly among the best "shoot-em-up" games, and will provide countless hours of solid entertainment.

Program: Stargate
Company: Atari, Inc.
Category: Arcade Games
Graphics Display: Color Graphics Adapter required (or Hercules monochrome card with CGA emulation)
Registration Fee: None (Public Domain)

General Evaluation: Stargate

	Excellent	*Very Good*	*Good*	*Average*	*Poor*	*N/A*
Holds User's Interest	***					
Ease of Learning			***			
Level of Challenge	***					
Level of Recreation	***					
Documentation						***
Graphics Quality	***					
Graphics Variety		***				
General Evaluation	***					

Opposite: **Figure 7.26: Setup screen for Stargate.**

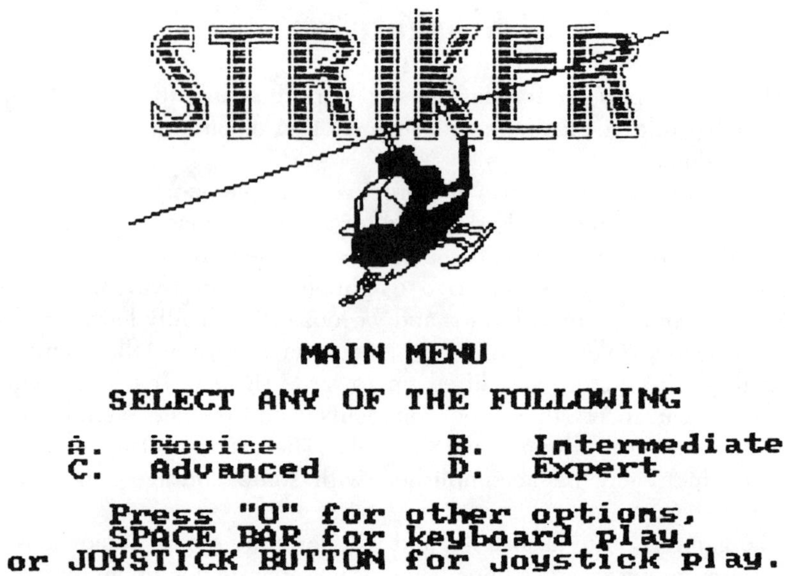

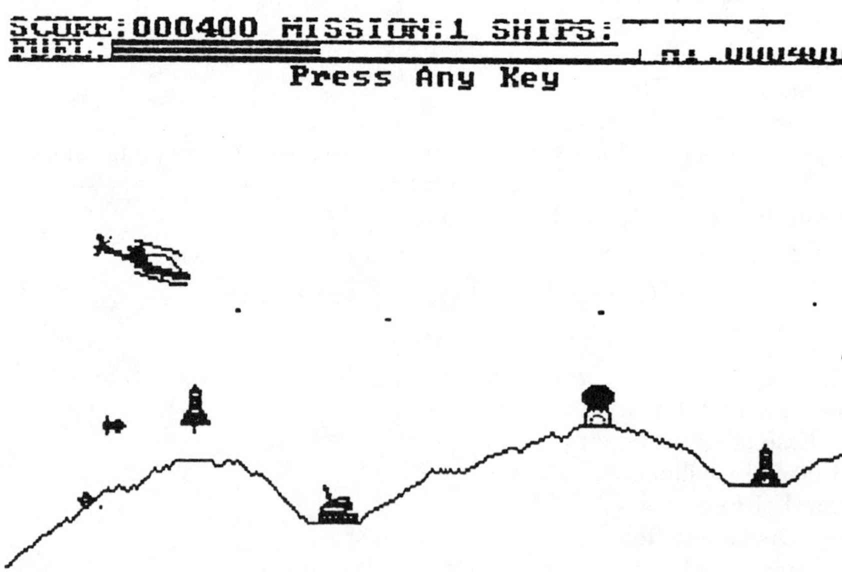

Top: **Figure 7.27: Main menu screen for Striker. This game combines superior graphics with a generous selection of difficulty levels from which to choose, making it a difficult game to master or tire of. *Bottom:* Figure 7.28: Sample playing screen from first-level mission in Striker.**

Striker™

Striker is an excellent arcade-style game which offers a wide range of playing levels and a multitude of different playing screens. The player becomes a helicopter pilot who must traverse dangerous terrain in order to accomplish one of five different missions. In order to successfully complete a mission, the player must fly through enemy territory and destroy both land-based and airborne weaponry seeking to destroy him. Once he arrives at his designated target, he must complete his mission by performing one of five different tasks: pick off spies from a building; drop off the spies into an embassy rooftop; pick up crates of sensitive cargo; rescue stranded people from a burning rooftop; or destroy an enemy missile factory. At all times he must maneuver his craft with skill and fight off an assortment of sophisticated enemy weapons deployed against him.

The game provides richly varied scenarios which help to keep it fresh and interesting, not to mention challenging, for a far longer period of time than most similar games. The game also offers four different levels of difficulty; the higher the level, the more diverse, numerous and dangerous the weapons that the enemy deploys. Even at the easiest level, the game provides plenty of challenging action even for experienced arcade game enthusiasts.

Another nice feature of Striker is that it comes with an excellent disk-based six-page documentation file written by the author. The documentation is clearly written and informative, and is further evidence of the thoughtfulness and care that has gone into this program's development.

Program: Striker © 1985
Author: Derek Williams
Company: N/A
Address: N/A
Category: Arcade Games
Graphics Display: Color Graphics Adapter required. The game will also run on a Hercules monochrome display if CGA emulation software is used.
Registration Fee: None (Public Domain)

General Evaluation: Striker

	Excellent	*Very Good*	*Good*	*Average*	*Poor*	*N/A*
Holds User's Interest	***					
Ease of Learning		***				
Level of Challenge	***					

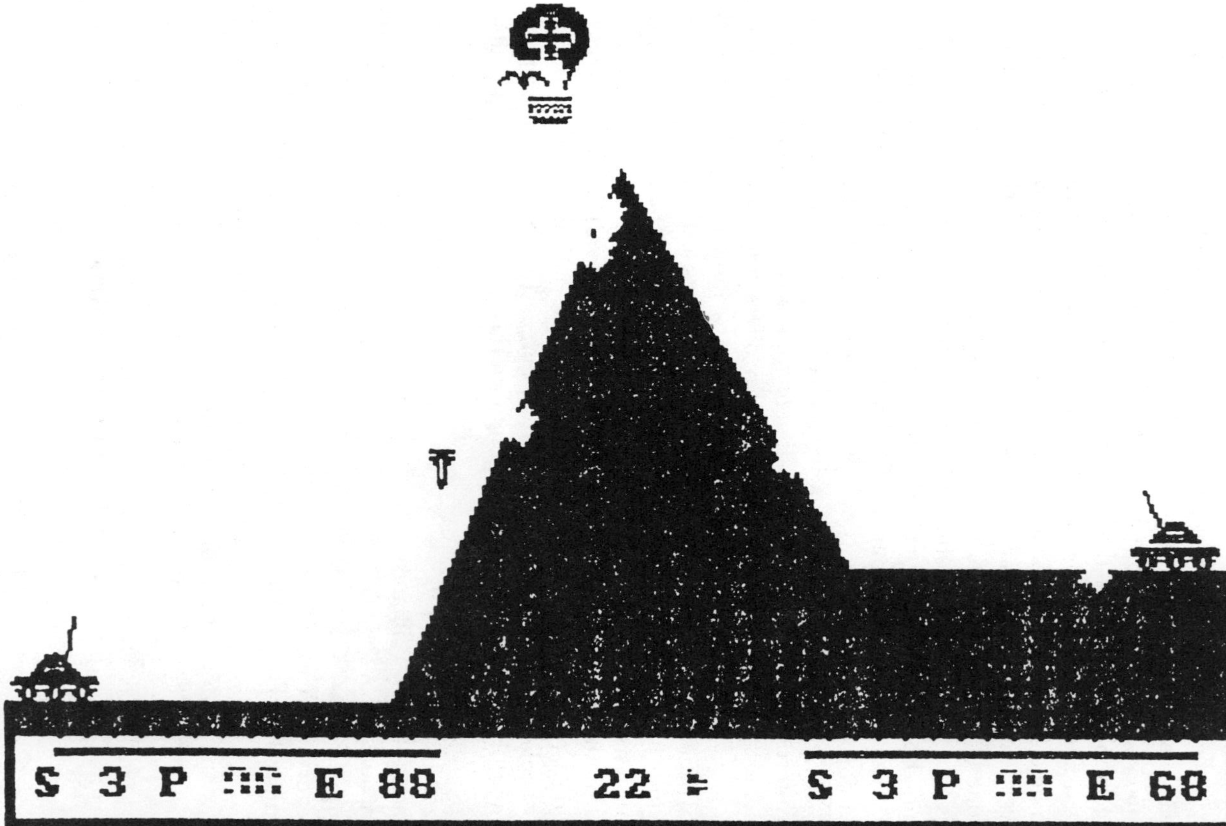
S 3 P E 88
22
S 3 P E 68

General Evaluation: Striker (cont.)

	Excellent	Very Good	Good	Average	Poor	N/A
Level of Recreation	***					
Documentation	***					
Graphics Quality	***					
Graphics Variety	***					
General Evaluation	***					

Tank Wars[PD]

One of the earliest arcade games involved warring tanks, in which two opponents squared off and tried to blow up the other. That idea has been reintroduced by Cody Snider into a new form, with greater challenge and more playing options. The result is a highly entertaining, well designed game which can be played either by two live opponents, or by a single player against the computer.

In Tank Wars a player is provided with a fully functioning tank and must try to blow up her opponent before he can do the same to her. Each player can control the movement of her tank, as well as the elevation of the gun turret and the force to be applied to the projectiles. If too little force is specified, the bombs fall short of their target, gouging out holes in the ground; too much force and the target is overshot. Of course, whenever a tank is moved, the elevation and force quotients must be readjusted.

Tank Wars provides players with several game options, including a hard and easy game option, as well as the option to play with or without wind as a factor. During play, one can also count on aerial support and hindrance by way of an airborne balloon and birds controlled by the computer. After each encounter, the terrain changes (see figure 7.29) in a random fashion so that it is difficult to anticipate optimum turret elevation or bomb energy quotients from one game to the next. The graphics screens offered are of high quality and ample variety. There is no separate documentation provided with this game, but on-screen help screens are available which are both comprehensive and quite easy to understand. The overall effect is a game which is both challenging and highly entertaining, as well as difficult to master, particularly when two human opponents play against each other.

***Opposite:* Figure 7.29: Sample playing screen for Tank Wars. Screens change at the end of every game to provide a different playing field. Games can last for hours, since scores are accumulated after each encounter; winning a few battles is no guarantee of winning the war.**

Program: Tank Wars © 1985
Author: Cody Snider
Company: N/A
Address: N/A
Category: Arcade Games
Graphics Display: Color Graphics Adapter required. Will also work with a Hercules monochrome card and CGA emulation software.
Registration Fee: None (Public Domain)

General Evaluation: Tank Wars

	Excellent	*Very Good*	*Good*	*Average*	*Poor*	*N/A*
Holds User's Interest		***				
Ease of Learning	***					
Level of Challenge		***				
Level of Recreation		***				
Documentation			***			
Graphics Quality		***				
Graphics Variety	***					
General Evaluation		***				

Board Games

When we think of computer games, images of fast-paced action and flashy graphics come to mind. But the computer has also embraced traditional game forms and made them its own. These include timeless classics, such as chess, as well as modern favorites. A large number of versions of these games can be found in the public domain and through the shareware or "try-before-you-buy" form of software distribution. Some of these may also be found in regular commercial offerings in a similarly large number of versions.

The IBM PC is an excellent game-playing machine, as well as a superior productivity tool. It is therefore no wonder that an enormous number of game packages are available for it in the public domain and as shareware offerings. It is not possible to mention them all here. What follows is merely a representative sampling of some of the fine games available at the lowest possible cost (often free). This is an area in which each reader is encouraged to sample for himself the luscious fruits graciously offered by a plethora of programmers.

Chess^{PD}

Chess has been played for countless centuries with little change. Masters of the game will be quick to call any computer chess program inadequate; after all, the computer can only carry out strict instructions given it by a programmer, and is incapable of creativity or true strategy. While it is true that a chess master will beat any computer program with *relative* ease, not so the rest of us who are not true students of the game. And even a master can be given a challenge by a good program which, though limited in its ability to strategize, is incapable of making errors and can look ahead five or more moves (something which is beyond the ability of all but the best chess players). The result is that a computer program of even limited complexity can beat any casual player with ease, and provide countless hours of challenging play even for expert players.

There are many chess programs available commercially as well as in the public domain and as shareware. Chess was selected for review not because it is one of the flashiest, but because it is one of the first and, while newer programs boast better graphics, its features are still hard to beat today.

Chess offers a wide range of options, including an impressive 24 levels of play. The computer is also programmable to play itself at any of the 24 levels; this function is particularly useful as a learning tool for less experienced players. The program can be used to set up and play specific playing situations so that chess problems or historic chess games can be recreated. It is even possible to have the computer make a move for a player who gets stuck in a difficult situation, another valuable option for those new to the game.

A very appealing feature of the game is that it offers such a variety of playing levels, making the game quite adaptable to one's present level of play, and allowing it to remain competitive as one's mastery of the game improves. There is no separate documentation with the program. However, an on-screen help file which lists all available options is available at any time by typing I for Instructions from the playing screen.

The program is an excellent starting point for players who are new to computer chess; it offers flexibility and variety in playing options which is hard to match, and has the additional benefit of working on most any IBM PC compatible computers, with CGA or Hercules monochrome displays and unexpanded memory. But anyone who is interested in the game is encouraged to sample the many additional programs available—especially if better graphics (including 3-dimensional graphics) are desired.

Program: Chess © 1980
Author: M.C. Rakaska (Adapted for the IBM PC by S.W. Huggins in 1981.)

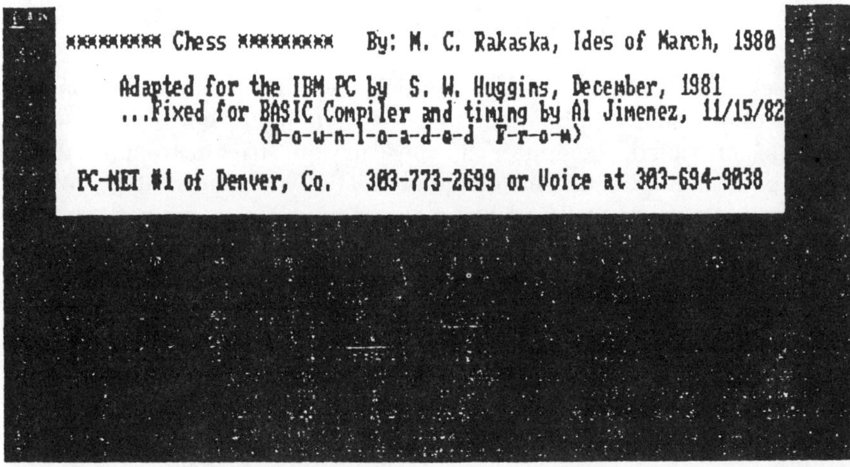

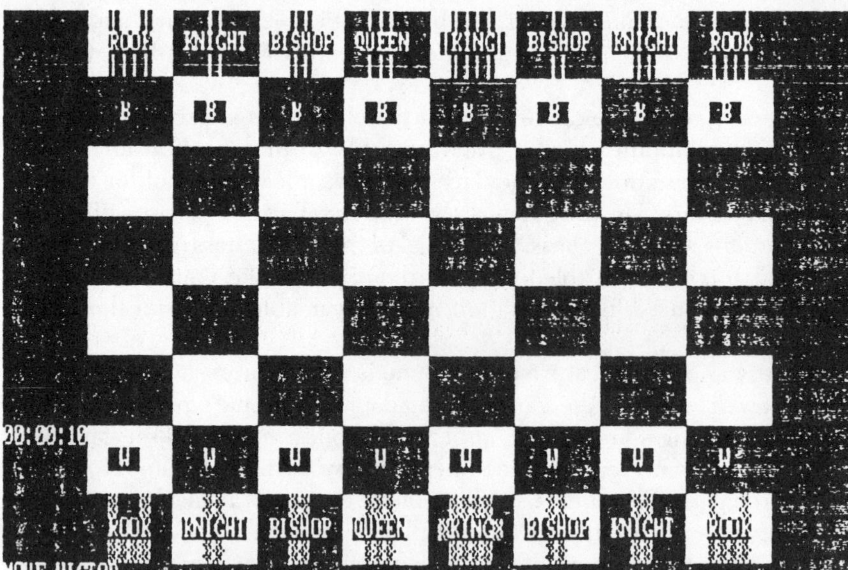

Top: **Figure 7.30: Opening screen and copyright notice for Chess.** ***Bottom:*** **Figure 7.31: Playing screen for Chess.**

Company: N/A
Address: N/A
Category: Board Games
Graphics Display: CGA or Hercules Monochrome displays
Registration Fee: None (Public Domain)

General Evaluation: Chess

	Excellent	*Very Good*	*Good*	*Average*	*Poor*	*N/A*
Holds User's Interest	***					
Ease of Learning			***			
Level of Challenge	***					
Level of Recreation	***					
Documentation				***		
Graphics Quality				***		
Graphics Variety						***
General Evaluation		***				

Monopolize™

The board game Monopoly needs no introduction. It is not surprising that this enormously popular game has been copied by a number of software developers. A number of games have attempted to replace the Monopoly playing board by integrating a graphics playing board as an integral part of the game. While some of these are quite good, we prefer to play the game on the familiar playing field, with real houses, hotels and deeds to make the playing experiences more realistic. This version of the famous game does not attempt to replace the normal playing board. Rather, the computer acts as a sort of "game master," rolling the dice and giving the player the opportunity to buy or pass up property he lands on. The computer keeps track of how much money a player has available at all times, and disburses payment (e.g., every time a player passes "Go") and automatically collects payments due (e.g., Income Tax and property assessments).

The main advantage of this game is that it allows a player to play against the computer. The playing board and property deeds must still be utilized. The computer becomes a built-in player when a human player is not available. Normal game rules are followed, with some minor exceptions (e.g., a limit of how much a player may owe the bank prior to losing is selected prior to game play, and there is no mortgaging of property).

Monopolize will provide countless hours of playing fun for players of all ages. It is a good enhancement to the classic board game, and not just copy of a great idea.

Program: Monopolize
Author: Frank R. Neal
Company: N/A
Address: 1358 Byron Avenue, Columbus, OH 43227

```
Monopoly........

If you like to play Monopoly but, are unable to find a partner then
your problems are solved. Welcome to Monopolize. In this Monopoly
game the computer is your opponent. Watch out though, for he is
not easily beaten.
This program is distributed under the 'FREEWARE' concept.
If you find this program enjoyable and find value in it then you
are urged to contribute to its author. A suggested sum is $15.
Registered users will receive update notices in the future along
with new release bulletins. For an additional $5 and a disk the
source code will be made available to registered users.
Feel free to pass along copies of this program to all of your friends.
This program may not be sold by anyone other than the author. User
groups are granted permission to charge up to $6 for distribution
charges. Send your cash, check, money order or gold to:

        Frank R. Neal
        1358 Byron Ave.
        Columbus, Oh   43227
        75206,1402

Your comments, suggestions or praise are welcomed.

                                        PRESS ENTER TO CONTINUE...
```

```
IT'S YOUR TURN,
YOU HAVE 10 SPACES FROM INCOME TAX
 TO VIRGINIA AVE..
DO YOU WISH TO BUY VIRGINIA AVE.?
IT COSTS $ 160 ?



THE ROLL IS A  5 AND A  5 FOR A TOTAL OF  10
```

Top: **Figure 7.32: Opening screen and copyright notice to Monopolize.** ***Bottom:*** **Figure 7.33: Playing screen for Monopolize. The game offers no graphics and makes no attempt to replace the classic Monopoly board or playing pieces; these must still be used to play this game. Rather, the computer becomes a substitute for a live player, and also helps by serving as banker, doling out money and keeping track of each player's cash totals throughout the game.**

Category: Board Games
Graphics Display: Color Graphics Adapter or Hercules compatible monochrome display.
Registration Fee: Contributions Solicited (Author suggests a $15 contribution.)

General Evaluation: Monopolize

	Excellent	*Very Good*	*Good*	*Average*	*Poor*	*N/A*
Holds User's Interest			***			
Ease of Learning		***				
Level of Challenge		***				
Level of Recreation			***			
Documentation				***		
Graphics Quality						***
Graphics Variety						***
General Evaluation			***			

Phrase Craze™ Version 1.05

Phrase Craze is a game which bears some resemblance to the famous television game show *Wheel of Fortune* (which is itself patterned after the timeless Hangman game). Up to four players can compete against each other, or a single player can practice the game by herself.

The idea of the game is to guess the meaning of a phrase by selecting letters which form a part of it. Before guessing a letter, the computer randomly selects the value that a properly-guessed consonant will represent for the player. Players may also buy vowels with cash accumulated from each accurately-guessed consonant. When enough letters are revealed on the board, players can venture a guess at the partially hidden phrase to end a round.

A nice feature of the game not found in other similar commercial or shareware versions is that famous quotations, book titles or other sources for the hidden clues are fully explained once correctly guessed. This gives the game an additional dimension and makes it into an educational experience, as well as plain fun. (See figure 7.35.) The phrases selected are interesting and challenging. The game also provides the option of adding additional phrases once the ones it contains are exhausted; this also enhances its educational value, as users search for appropriate phrases or book titles for which they must provide encapsulated explanations. It would be simple, for example, to tailor a version of the game to include vocabulary

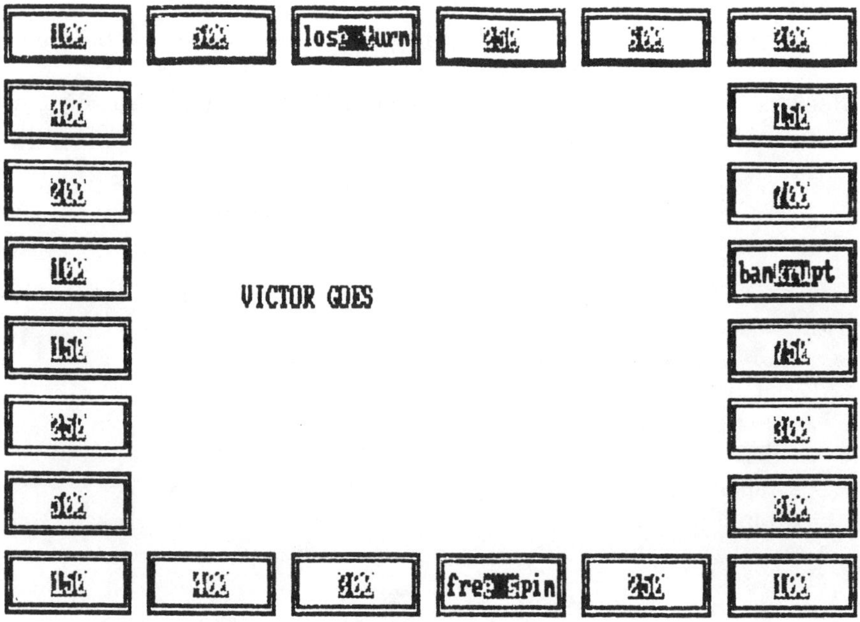

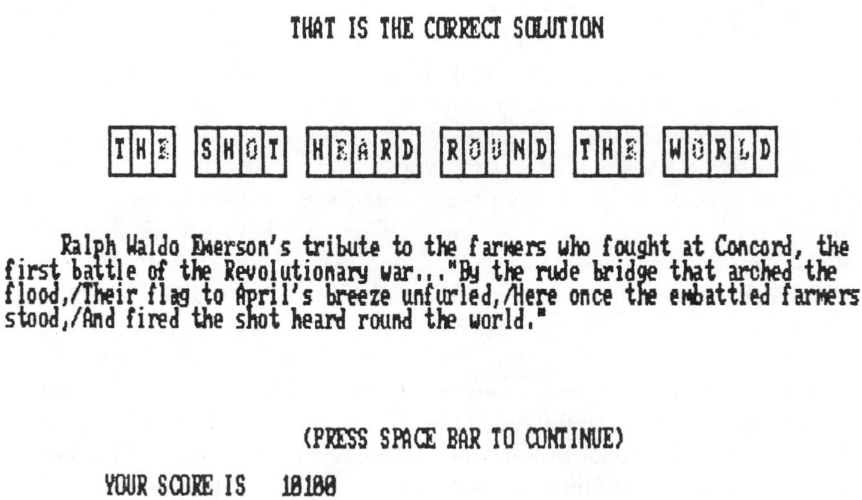

Top: **Figure 7.34: Simulated electronic wheel for Phrase Craze. Luck determines the value of each consonant one accurately guesses, but skill is needed in order to ultimately succeed at this entertaining and educational game.** ***Bottom:*** **Figure 7.35: Sample phrase used in Phrase Craze. Notice the explanation of the phrase that follows after the puzzle is successfully solved.**

words for a given grade level so that they can be painlessly practiced by a child as she plays the game.

The shareware version of the game is limited in the phrases it contains. Phrase Craze was included here because, although limited, it does contain sufficient phrases for a full, fair trial, and does provide the opportunity for users to add their own phrases. Upon registration, a version with a much larger phrase file will be sent to the user.

Program: Phrase Craze Ver. 1.05 © 1985, 1986
Author: N/A
Company: Excelsior Software, Inc.
Address: P.O. Box 226, New Milford, NJ 07646
Category: Board Game
Graphics Display: CGA or Hercules monochrome displays
Registration Fee: $30 for enhanced version with more than 500 phrases.

General Evaluation: Phrase Craze Ver. 1.05

	Excellent	*Very Good*	*Good*	*Average*	*Poor*	*N/A*
Holds User's Interest			***			
Ease of Learning		***				
Level of Challenge			***			
Level of Recreation			***			
Documentation		***				
Graphics Quality				***		
Graphics Variety						***
General Evaluation				***		

Scrabble™ Version 1.3

Scrabble is a computerized adaptation of the classic board game by the same name.

Scrabble supports up to four players and includes a dictionary file for validating words. Although the built-in dictionary is rather limited, players can easily add to it by acknowledging that a suspect word is in fact valid; hence, the dictionary expands automatically as the game is played.

The game sports a nice display—especially when played on a color system. The board game Scrabble is not needed in order to play this computer adaptation; a computer-generated board is available for players to place their "letters" on. But players who do not own the game or have not played it before will have problems playing this computer version. It is best

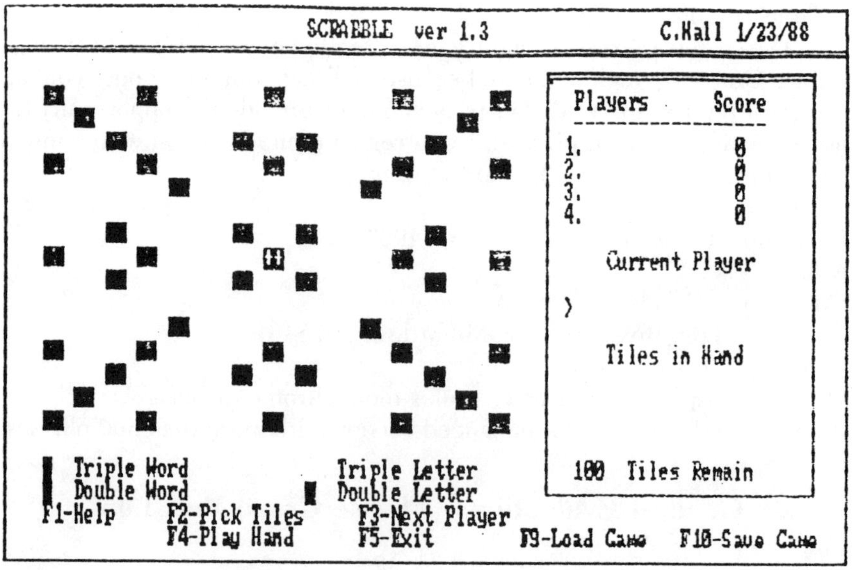

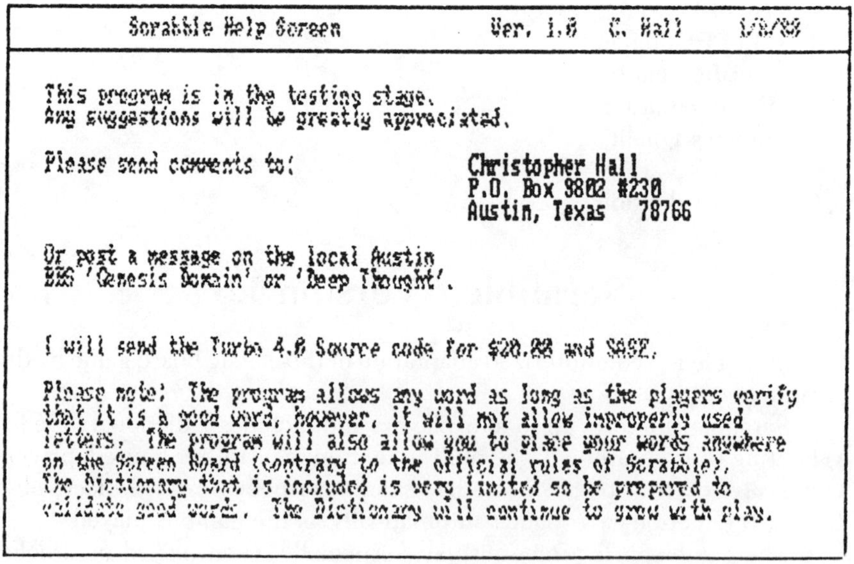

Top: **Figure 7.36: Main playing screen for Scrabble.** ***Bottom:*** **Figure 7.37: The one available help screen for Scrabble will not be of much use to players who do not own the original board game by the same name. Ownership of the board game is a prerequisite for playing this computerized version.**

for a player to acquire the board game and familiarize herself with the rules. The computer version is perhaps best used as an enhancement of the original, and not a replacement. The standard rules of Scrabble apply, with some modifications which are noted in the computer game's instructions.

The game is both fun and educational for both children and adults, and should provide hours of enjoyment for the whole family.

Program: Scrabble Ver. 1.3
Author: Christopher Hall
Company: N/A
Address: P.O. Box 9802, #230, Austin, TX 78766
Category: Board Game
Graphics Display: Color Graphics Adapter or Hercules monochrome display.
Registration Fee: N/A (Public Domain)

General Evaluation: Scrabble Ver. 1.3

	Excellent	*Very Good*	*Good*	*Average*	*Poor*	*N/A*
Holds User's Interest	***					
Ease of Learning				***		
Level of Challenge	***1					
Level of Recreation		***				
Documentation				***2		
Graphics Quality			***			
Graphics Variety						***
General Evaluation		***				

[1]The level of challenge offered depends to a great extent on the quality of the playing competition. This is *not* a "player against the computer" game. The better the opposing player(s), the better the challenge offered by the game. We rate challenge as excellent nevertheless for the inherent challenging nature of the game itself—the need for creative thinking and strategy in order to score the greatest possible points with a given set of letter tiles.

[2]The game provides sufficient assistance with its built-in help to get players started. Nevertheless, players must have available a copy of the board game's rules, else the game will not be enjoyed to its full potential. There is no assistance whatever in the brief help screen as to how the game is played; it is presumed that players are already familiar with the Scrabble board game.

The Trivia Machine™

Trivia quiz games have enjoyed enormous popularity in recent years. Trivial Pursuit in its various editions has been a best-selling board game

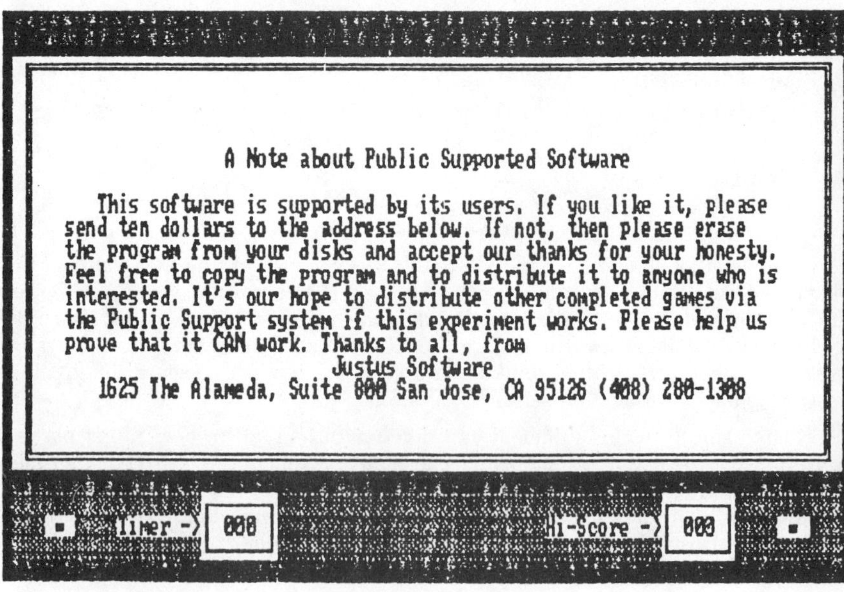

Top: **Figure 7.38: Opening screen and copyright notice for The Trivia Machine.**
Bottom: **Figure 7.39: Important notice about user-supported software included in The Trivia Machine are equally applicable to other shareware offerings.**

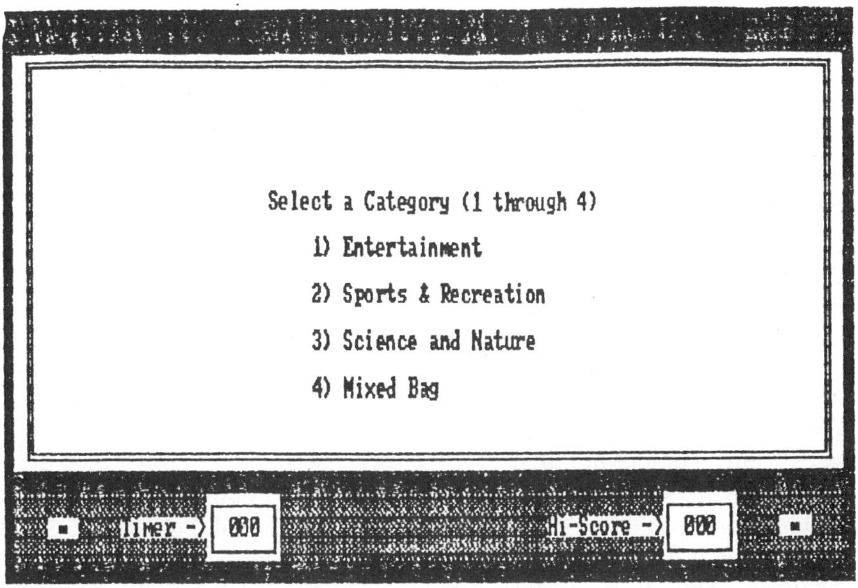

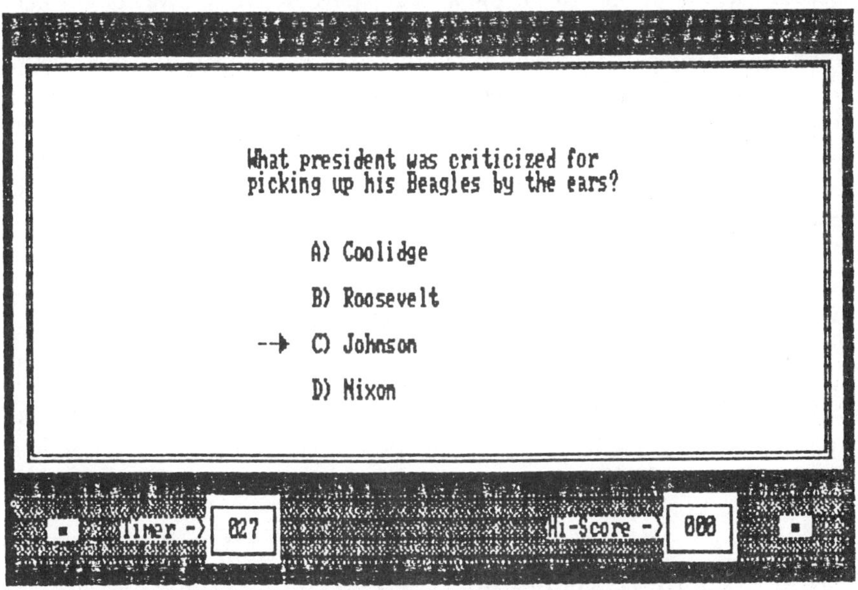

Top: Figure 7.40: Category selection screen for The Trivia Machine. *Bottom:* Figure 7.41: Sample question from The Trivia Machine. The game scores players not just on the accuracy of their responses, but on the speediness of their answers as well. Some credit is given for second-choice answers if the first answer is wrong—but the player's response must be quick to earn such credit.

and many imitations have sprung up, both in competing board games and in computer software. The Trivia Machine, while a trivia quiz game, is not an imitation or a copy of Trivial Pursuit, but a unique game in its own right.

The Trivia Machine is a one-person game which offers a variety of difficulty levels and questions which are quite challenging. There are four categories of questions from which to choose: Entertainment, Sports and Recreation, Science and Nature and Mixed Bag. The questions in any of the selected areas are by no means easy; those who like to play trivia games as a means of massaging their egos are in for a surprise with this one. Not only are the questions more difficult than one might expect, but they must be answered within a set time limit which varies in relation to the difficulty level chosen (the higher the level, the shorter the time period allowed for a valid answer). If one selects a wrong answer, it is still possible to get some credit by quickly selecting an alternate choice; hence, the game stresses—and rewards—quick thinking.

Unlike many trivia games in which questions are, indeed, trivial, The Trivia Machine offers an excellent selection of meaningful questions. That is perhaps the main reason we selected this particular game over others like it for inclusion in this text; playing the game is not simply an empty pastime but can be a rewarding learning experience for players of any age. As to playing ages, it should be noted that although precocious teens will both enjoy the game and do well in it, the intended audience is perhaps the average adult (or the serious trivia buff). Playing this game can be a humbling experience for most players, which is arguably another important benefit in and of itself. Scores improve as a player gets used to the game's fast pace, and a player's intellectual ability is certainly not injured in the process.

Program: The Trivia Machine © 1984
Author: Bob Perez
Company: Justus Software
Address: 1625 The Alameda, Suite 800, San Jose, CA 95126
Category: Board Game
Graphics Display: Color Graphics Adapter or Hercules-compatible monochrome display.
Registration Fee: $10

General Evaluation: The Trivia Machine

	Excellent	*Very Good*	*Good*	*Average*	*Poor*	*N/A*
Holds User's Interest		***				
Ease of Learning			***			

General Evaluation: The Trivia Machine (cont.)

	Excellent	*Very Good*	*Good*	*Average*	*Poor*	*N/A*
Level of Challenge	***					
Level of Recreation		***				
Documentation				***		
Graphics Quality						***
Graphics Variety						***
General Evaluation		***				

Appendix A

Sources of Public Domain and Shareware Software

For users with a modem and telecommunications software, the world of public domain and shareware may truly be sampled free of charge. There are myriad bulletin boards in just about every community that allow users to log-on and download such "free" software without charge. There are a great many published sources of national and local bulletin boards which can be found in nearly any public library. But the very nature of privately maintained, not-for-profit bulletin boards makes many such listings unreliable; these come in and out of existence on a daily basis. One of the best, up-to-date sources of current bulletin boards is published monthly in *Computer Shopper,* a national publication catering to mail-order computer buyers (Ziff-Davis Publishing Company, One Park Avenue, New York, NY 10016). Since these listings are updated regularly, they tend to be quite current.

Getting free software via non-profit bulletin boards is the least expensive means of procuring such software as long as a local board is used. Downloading software via modem is *not* a quick process. Finding your way around a given bulletin board takes time, and so does downloading software into your system; depending on your modem's speed, downloading files will take several minutes each, and easily 15 minutes for an average size program if you are using an old 300 baud modem. For this reason, downloading programs from a distant bulletin board is usually not feasible; the telephone long distance charges can soon become substantial.

The same holds true for downloading programs from for-profit, commercial bulletin boards such as *The Source, Compuserve* and *Genie.* Commercial boards allow users to download free software. but at their regular hourly connect rate, which ranges from about $6 to $12 per hour. Unless you know exactly what you want, browsing through the considerable titles these boards offer and then indiscriminately downloading software can become quite expensive. Finally, public domain and shareware programs are available from an ever-growing number of shareware distribution companies. A veritable industry has sprung up in the past several years to take advantage of growing public awareness of the existence of public domain and shareware software. The best of these companies provide a valuable service to the public and to the shareware authors whose work they distribute. The low fees they charge for copies of such software ensures that it can get before the greatest possible number of people who can then register copies of the programs they like and use. As with any other field, there are a fair number of unscrupulous operators who charge high fees for such software or provide mislabeled, incomplete software on low-quality disks.

Most public domain and shareware distribution services are above-board, however, charging reasonable fees for the programs they offer and providing reasonably prompt service. A buyer should certainly beware of operators who overcharge for disks (anything over $5 per disk is usually too much—especially when a minimum of $3 or so is typically charged per order for shipping and handling). Most shareware authors specify a maximum rate that can be charged for distributing evaluation copies of their software; generally, the maximum rate ranges between $6 and $10 per disk. Fortunately, competition between shareware and public domain distributors has brought disk prices down to a very reasonable level. Some companies are distributing disks for under $2 each as of this writing. The best approach is to order one or two disks from a company to see what service is provided and the quality of the disks offered. Check the classified section of most any computer magazine to find suppliers of public domain and shareware; they almost always advertise under "Free Software." Send for their catalogs and look carefully at the selection they offer and the real per-disk charge. (A company which advertises disks "as low as $1 each" may not be a bargain if you must buy 30 disks in order to qualify for the low per-disk price, or if it charges a minimum fee of $3 or more for shipping and handling *plus* a per-disk additional shipping charge.) Companies which charge higher than average fees may offer better quality disks and larger selections, along with batch files to make setting up and running the software easier. This is not always the case, however. Read the fine print of the ads carefully, and then order one or two disks from the most promising suppliers.

There are new suppliers advertising on a monthly basis, and old ones leaving the business as well. Check the classifieds of leading computer magazines for the latest listings. (*Computer Shopper* probably carries more advertising in this area than any other leading magazine.)

Appendix B

Getting Started: Setting Up and Running Your Public Domain and Shareware Software

One of the few disadvantages of using public domain or shareware software is that documentation files are seldom as complete as those accompanying commercial packages. Although documentation manuals for even the most expensive programs are seldom truly well written and easy to understand, at least they do make an attempt to make the setting up and running of the packages they accompany as easy as possible for the consumer. With "free" software, such an attempt is not always made. Nevertheless, there are certain conventions and practices which are frequently used; knowing these can be of invaluable assistance whenever one receives a public domain or shareware disk, or downloads files from a free or for-pay bulletin board.

As with any software package one receives, it is *always* a good idea to make a backup copy of the distribution disk before using the software. You should never use the original copy of any program; save in the case of copy-protected software where a backup copy of the program cannot be made. To copy a disk, you should use the DOS DISKCOPY command (see your MS/DOS or PC/DOS operating system manual for specific instructions on copying disks). Once a working copy of the software is made, the original disk should be stored in a safe place and the backup copy used to run the program.

Once a working copy of the disk has been made, you must find out how to run the program. Depending on the source of the software, the steps needed to prepare the software for use can be quite varied. The first thing to do is to do a directory search of the disk containing the programs. This will give you important information on the files the disk contains. Files to look for are README, README.DOC, README.TXT, README.1ST or some other closely related name. These text files provide important information to assist you in setting up the program and running it. You should type out such files either on the screen, read import them into your favorite word processor or type them out to a printer, if you have one available. If you don't know how to type out text files to your screen or printer, consult your DOS manual on using the TYPE command and on REDIRECTING OUTPUT to a printer.

After the README files have been read, look for any document files which may be available. Common names for document files are DOCUMENT.TXT, DOCUMENT.DOC, DOCUMENT.DCT, but other names are also possible. Look for files with a three-digit extension (the part of the file after the period separator) of DOC, DCT or TXT; these are almost always text files, and usually part of the program's documentation. You can also type out these files onto the screen or to a printer. For example: to type out a file called README.DOC on drive B to a printer, you would type at the A (system prompt, driveA) the following command: TYPE B:README.DOC PRN [RETURN]. This command would type the text file README.DOC and redirect the output to a printer. To see the content of such a file on the monitor's screen, simply type TYPE B:README.DOC followed by a carriage return [RETURN]. In the latter case, you can temporarily stop text from scrolling by pressing down the [CTRL] and the letter C at the same time [CTRL-C]; striking any key after that would resume the screen's scrolling. Once all documents and README files are printed out or read on the screen, the user will have the information he needs to use the program at hand.

Not all programs have document files included with them. The most common examples of programs which do not contain documentation or README files are games and some of the smaller utilities. In these cases, one must simply do a directory of the disk and find out what program files are in it. Any files which end in COM or EXE are executable program files; you need only type out the filename (the extension is not necessary) and the program it represents will be automatically loaded and run. (We have not reviewed programs written in BASIC which require that program to be run. While many of these programs are available in the public domain, and some in the shareware area as well, they are generally slower and less powerful than the compiled programs we have selected for review. If you get any BASIC programs, you will need a BASIC interpreter such as BASIC.COM or BASICA.COM (IBM PC/DOS for true IBM PCs] or GWBASIC.EXE for all IBM's and work-alikes. Consult your BASIC manual for further instructions on loading and running programs written in interpreted BASIC).

In the following example (page 213), we have two executable files: DND.EXE and MAROONED.EXE. To run the adventure game DND, you need only type DND [RETURN], and MAROONED [RETURN] to run the adventure game Marooned Again. There is also an important README file in the directory and a MAROONED.DOC document file, both of which should be printed and read before the game is loaded and run.

Volume in drive B has no label
Directory of B:

README		1088	12-13-86	9:46p
SHVENK	BIN	8000	2-02-84	9:36p
WARREN	BIN	8000	2-02-84	9:28p
LAMORTE	LO2	10880	9-05-89	10:47p
LAMORTE	LO3	10880	9-05-89	11:23p
MAROONED	DOC	5061	5-19-87	8:43a
DND	EXE	124346	2-22-87	12:08p
MAROONED	EXE	45741	5-19-87	8:44a
HELP	BAT	128	10-09-89	10:00p
31 File(s)			809984 bytes free	

Programs which do not come with README or other document files generally have on-line help which is accessed through the [F1] key. Instructions to this effect are usually available upon booting up of the program.

If the software was downloaded from a bulletin board, it is almost definitely in archival format—a method to squeeze one or more related files into a single smaller file to save time, communication costs and disk space when transmitting data over telephone lines. To find out what format the software is in, you must do a directory of the disk in which the software is found. Simply type DIR and the drive designator for the drive holding the software disk (e.g., to do a directory of a disk in drive B, type DIR B: [RETURN] at the system prompt). This will give you a listing of every file on the disk. (Consult your MS/DOS or PC/DOS manual if you need further instructions.) If a file is in archival format, you will see the name of the file followed by a file extension of ARC; for example: PROGRAM.ARC would be an archival file. If the files on the disk are in this format, you must unarchive them. Instructions for doing so are almost always found in accompanying README files, as is the program needed to unarchive the files.

Another source of assistance comes in many disks through batch files. Batch files are essentially mini program files which are executed automatically to automate the performance of certain functions. Where these are available, the README files will discuss their use. In the above sample directory, you can see a batch file as the last directory entry (HELP.BAT). By typing the filename (in this case HELP), additional preprogrammed options or instructions will be available. You should also always look for such files in any public domain or shareware disks you purchase.

Finally, many distributors of public domain and shareware give additional information on setting up and running the programs they distribute. Some go as far as to provide useful simple menus through batch files to assist new users in getting their programs up and running. This is one of the major advantages of getting software from a good distributor; much of the guesswork of getting programs up and running is taken away by the use of additional help files or automated batch files.

Running public domain and shareware programs can take a little getting used to, but it is a skill quickly acquired. Sometimes exploring the intricacies of a software package which may not be fully documented can be part of the challenge and fun. Most every package reviewed in this text is fully documented and easy to use; some otherwise excellent programs were not included because of unacceptable documentation which would have made it difficult to learn or use. Game packages generally do not offer much documentation, but they do offer various help screens and messages to help a user set up a program and use it with a minimum of preparation.

Each of these programs reviewed herein is well worth the small investment in time they may require of a user to be properly set up and used.

Index